D0174352

WASHINGTON COUNTY COOPERATIVE
LIBRARY SERVICES

Pedaling Revolution

Pedaling Revolution

How Cyclists are Changing American Cities

by

Jeff Mapes

OREGON STATE UNIVERSITY PRESS

CORVALLIS

WEST SLOPE LIBRARY
36   SW 78   Ave.
Po   nd OR   225
(92-6416

The paper in this book meets the guidelines for permanence
and durability of the Committee on Production Guidelines for
Book Longevity of the Council on Library Resources and the
minimum requirements of the American National Standard for
Permanence of Paper for Printed Library Materials Z39.48-1984.

Library of Congress Cataloging-in-Publication Data
Mapes, Jeff.
  Pedaling revolution : how cyclists are changing American cities /
by Jeff Mapes.
      p. cm.
  Includes bibliographical references and index.
  ISBN 978-0-87071-419-1 (alk. paper)
  1. Cycling--United States. 2. Cycling--United States--Safety
measures. 3. City and town life--United States. 4. Urban
transportation--United States 5. Urbanization--United States.
6. Cycling--Europe. 7. Cycling--Europe--Safety measures. 8.
Urban transportation--Europe. 9. Urbanization--Europe. I. Title.
  GV1045.M36 2009
  796.6--dc22

                              2008042772

© 2009 Jeff Mapes
All rights reserved. First published in 2009 by Oregon State
University Press. Second printing 2009
Printed in the United States of America

Oregon State University Press
121 The Valley Library
Corvallis OR 97331-4501
541-737-3166 • fax 541-737-3170
http://oregonstate.edu/dept/press

for Karen

Contents

Introduction

From New York's Williamsburg Bridge to San Francisco's Market Street, rush-hour traffic jams—those iconic emblems of American life—teem with millions of cars, trucks, and buses. At first glance, only the increasing miles of congestion and the stylized curves of the cars distinguish twenty-first-century gridlock from decades past. But now, bobbing lightly in the exhaust-filled urban streams is a new addition: the bicyclists. By the hundreds of thousands, these unlikely transportation revolutionaries are forgoing the safety of a steel cage with airbags and anti-lock disc brakes for a wispy two-wheeled exoskeleton as they make their way to work, school, and store.

There are, of course, the ever-present bike messengers, fueled by pure adrenaline and their own private code of survival. But stand on the new bicycle and pedestrian ramp over the Williamsburg Bridge and you'll also see well-dressed men and women, riding upright on shiny bikes outfitted as carefully as an executive's BMW. Tattooed young hipsters rush by, handling their battered bikes with nonchalant ease. Young women glide by on beach cruisers. Grim-faced riders in spandex and aerodynamic helmets speed by on expensive road bikes that seem more air than metal. Only their document-packed saddlebags hint at a day of serious desk work.

For the first time since the car became the dominant form of American transportation after World War II, there is now a grass-roots movement to seize at least a part of the street back from motorists. A growing number of Americans, mounted on their bicycles like some new kind of urban cowboy, are mixing it up with swift, two-ton motor vehicles as they create a new society on the streets. They're finding physical fitness, low-cost transportation, environmental purity—and, still all too often, Wild West risks of sudden death or injury.

These new pioneers are beginning to change the look and feel of many cities, suburbs and small towns. In the last decade, thousands of miles of bike lanes have been placed on streets around the country, giving cyclists an exclusive piece of the valuable asphalt real estate. As gas prices rise, traffic congestion worsens, and global climate change becomes an acknowledged menace, a growing number of cities have launched programs to shift a measurable percentage of travel to cycling. Take Chicago, for example. When it comes to transportation, the Windy City is known as the nation's railroad crossroads. But it has adopted a blueprint calling for 5 percent of trips under five miles to be made by bike. In the concrete canyons of lower Manhattan, New York City is literally pioneering a new kind of street, one designed to allow cyclists to peacefully pedal while largely separated from cars and trucks. And in my hometown of Portland, Oregon, local officials have built a bike network that in the span of a little over a decade has helped turn about one in twenty commute trips into a bike ride.

In these cities and elsewhere, motorists are learning to share the streets with a very different kind of traveler, one who often perplexes and angers them. Listen to talk radio and you can hear the backlash as callers vent about bicyclists who blow through stoplights or who ride in the center of the street and slow drivers behind them. Bicyclists express their own anger at inattentive drivers and a car culture more concerned with speed and aggressiveness than safety. And that sense of fury helps fuel a bicycle-rights movement that is growing in visibility. Bicycling, once largely seen as a simple pleasure from childhood, has become a political act.

The burgeoning bicycle culture is a rich tapestry. It ranges from the anarchic riders of Critical Mass to the well-heeled Lance Armstrong look-alikes on bikes expensive enough to rival the cost of a low-end car. For the young "creative class" that cities are fighting to attract, bicycles are a cheap, hip way to get around town. That's why Louisville—not exactly a beacon of the counterculture—has made a determined effort to become friendly to bicycling. The city's mayor sees it as a good way to attract those young people who will power the economy decades from now. On the other end of the age spectrum, bikes are a low-impact way for AARP-age adults to exercise after their joints can no longer take the pounding of jogging. In fact, the two baby boomers who competed for the presidency in 2004, George W. Bush and John Kerry, are both avid cyclists who would cart their bikes along on campaign trips. Four years later, Democrat Barack Obama became the first mainstream presidential candidate to promote cycling as a transportation tool and to actively solicit the support of cyclists in his campaign.

Like most Americans, I didn't think seriously about the bicycle for most of my life, even though I've loved to cycle since I was a kid in the 1960s, riding my Schwinn Sting Ray around the hills of Oakland, California. As a teen, I graduated to a ten-speed, which I often rode the six miles to high school. But, like most teen-age males, I hankered for my driver's license and a car. And for years after that, as I chased a career in journalism and started a family, I never thought about bicycling much. It just wasn't something my peer group had much to do with, and like many reporters, I spent a lot of time in a car. But in the mid-1990s I bought a new hybrid bike, which was more comfortable for city riding than my old ten-speed. I would occasionally pedal the three miles to work on sunny days. At the time, the city of Portland, where I live, had embarked on an ambitious program to build a network of bike lanes, trails, and low-traffic "bicycle boulevards" that would crisscross the city. These improvements helped turn me into a daily bike commuter. The treacherous exit—for cyclists anyway—off the west end of the Broadway Bridge turned calm after the city reconfigured the lanes and added a new signal light phase that allowed riders to take the left exit off the bridge while right-turning motorists had to wait. And a new, well-lit pedestrian and bike path along the east side of the Willamette River helped give me the confidence to begin riding during the dark months of the year.

My own perspective shifted as I became comfortable maneuvering next to cars and trucks and my physical fitness began to improve. I joked about wearing a sign stating, "Ask me how I lost weight while commuting to work." The political reporter in me—I've been one for three decades—began to wonder, what spurred the city to make these improvements? Is the same thing happening in other cities? Can Americans really be seduced out of their cars in large numbers, at least for short trips?

My search for answers led me across the country, as well as to the Netherlands, the Mecca of American bike advocates. As I discuss in later chapters, there is no American Amsterdam ... yet. But I did find that cyclists have become part of a much larger movement to reduce the dominant role of automobiles in American cities. Imagine fewer parking lots and more public plazas. Think of urban neighborhoods that have the walkable ambience of an old European city, not wide streets and strip malls. Or maybe just the kind of street that is safe enough for kids to once again play in.

Sometimes it is tempting to think of these urban cycling advocates as the crazy Jihadists of the sustainability movement, given the physical risks and cultural opprobrium cyclists often encounter. But the truth is that cycling has attracted a much broader— and often more sophisticated—demographic than many might think. Take Mark Gorton, who has minted a New York fortune at the intersection of finance and high tech. Gorton's empire includes a hedge fund that uses sophisticated computers to make lightning-fast trades as well as a controversial internet file-sharing company under attack from the music industry. But he is also an avid cyclist who has become one of New York's chief patrons of the "livable streets" movement. It all started years ago, he explained, when he just wanted to ride his bicycle a couple of miles to work at the Credit Suisse Bank in midtown Manhattan.

"It was one of those things that I was aware of when I was riding there that if I did it long enough, I was going to get into a pretty bad crash—it was just inevitable," he explained. "When you almost get killed a few times you start to realize, this is stupid. Here I am doing something that is more environmentally friendly, healthier, it's the sort of behavior that the city should be trying to encourage, and yet it has designed the system so that it's really hostile to bicyclists."

When animated, Gorton barely pauses for breath. A wiry, dark-haired man on the cusp of forty, he's adopted the Silicon Valley look: immaculate blue jeans and a black t-shirt with his company logo, Lime Inc., tastefully affixed on the left breast. We sat on the outdoor roof patio of his penthouse offices in lower Manhattan. With twelve stories separating us from the street, the traffic sounds were gently muted. "I'm like, this is just wrong and this is just screwed up," he said. "And then the more I started thinking about it, I started realizing that it didn't have to be that way. That it wasn't that the world was inevitably hostile to bicycles. And I think that once you start opening your eyes to these things you realize it's not just about bicycles, it's about everything ... I would be walking down the street and I would think, 'What a nice little street, I really like this,' and I started realizing that the times that I felt that way, there was very little or no traffic. And all of a sudden, I'm like, wow, the world is much better without traffic."

Gorton leaned forward in his wrought-iron chair. It was almost lunchtime and some of his employees were drifting out into the spring sunshine. One sat near us, listening to his boss with bemusement. "After thinking about it," Gorton added, "I realized you probably could reduce the amount of traffic in New York by 80 percent and not have any negative economic impact at all—and probably only positive economic impacts. And once that gets in your head, I couldn't be content with the world anymore."

Gorton began plowing his money into the notion that he could change the realities of the New York streets. He became the largest donor to Transportation Alternatives, the city's chief bicycle and pedestrian lobby. He started his own nonprofit, with the idea of giving neighborhood activists software tools they could use to develop plans for such amenities as public plazas and low-traffic streets. And perhaps most prominently, he financed a new internet site, Streetsblog, which became a rallying point for cyclists, urban planners, mass transit geeks, and everybody else who had come to question why so much space should be turned over to cars in a city so compact that most residents don't even own one. From checking the internet addresses, Gorton's bloggers found out that city bureaucrats, particularly in the Department of Transportation, were also loyal readers—if only to see how streetsblog was beating up on them each day. Like a modern-day William Randoph Hearst, he had found his megaphone.

Streetsblog came at a propitious time and maybe even had some impact. Within a year of its launch, the city government under Mayor Michael Bloomberg abruptly turned from celebrating New York's auto-choked streets as a sign of economic vitality into warning that the city could not accommodate population growth without reducing the role of the private automobile. Following the lead of London, Bloomberg pushed to enact a congestion charge on all motor vehicles entering most of Manhattan. He also brought in a new transportation commissioner, Janette Sadik-Kahn, who adopted the livable streets agenda with a vengeance—she made a point of cycling to work her second day on the job—and stocked the agency with many of the same reformers featured prominently on Streetsblog. And the city moved ahead with an aggressive plan to create more than two hundred miles of bikeways over a three-year period.

In many ways Gorton is an archetype—a privileged, well-educated white guy who wasn't used to being treated shabbily until he tried to ride a bicycle on the street. And that turned him into an activist. But he is also a dramatic example of how bicyclists are beginning to win a place at the table of the transportation industrial complex—that interlocking network of industry, politicians, planners, and builders who control the billions of dollars spent on roads, bridges, and rail. As rudimentary as the bicycle may seem to Americans more accustomed to using automobiles for even the shortest of trips, the simple two-wheeler is attracting new attention because of a confluence of factors largely driven by that very reliance on the auto.

The bike offers a non-polluting, non-congesting, physically active form of transportation in a country, and in a world, that increasingly seems to need such options. The heightened global competition for the world's oil supplies has ended the era of cheap fuel that made our automobile dependency possible. Our increasingly sedentary lifestyle raises the specter of an obesity epidemic that could shorten the life span of the next generation. And we're outstripping our ability to maintain and expand our network of roads and bridges.

At first blush, it may seem odd to talk about the humble bicycle in the same breath as electric cars or biofuels or hydrogen-powered fuel cells that are presented as the ultimate solution to our energy and environmental woes. In fact, though, bicycling can accomplish more than most people think.

Paul Higgins was a postdoctoral scientist at the University of California at Berkeley when he dined at a restaurant one night with his parents, both of whom are physicians. His mother sighed when the waiter brought huge platters of food. "Think of all the resources that are wasted in this food on this plate," he remembered her saying, "and it's just going to make us fat." Higgins, who was studying climate change at the time, turned it around in his mind. He asked himself, What if we saw that food as the original biofuel? How far could we go on it? Higgins calculated the energy savings if every adult walked or cycled for a half hour or an hour a day and then reduced their driving by the distance they covered walking or biking. The savings were the most dramatic for cyclists, of course, because they can easily travel about three times as fast as a walker. If everyone cycled for an hour and reduced their driving by an equivalent distance, the U.S. would cut its gasoline consumption by 38 percent, Higgins found. Greenhouse gas emissions would be reduced by about 12 percent, which is greater than the reductions called for in the Kyoto treaty (which the U.S. saw as too onerous and never signed). To add to the bargain, the average person would lose about thirteen pounds a year.

Higgins, who later became a senior policy fellow at the American Meteorological Society in Washington, was quick to acknowledge this scenario won't become reality. Many people can't reduce their driving by cycling for an hour every day. They may not be physically capable of riding or they drive such long distances that they can't substitute cycling for any trip. But what's important about Higgins' calculations is that it gives you a sense of how the bicycle, coupled with relatively minor changes in habits, could actually produce serious reductions in oil consumption and greenhouse gas emissions.

It is true that tougher emission and mileage standards for cars have the potential for far bigger reductions than would likely be gained by the increased use of bicycles. Even the most bike-centric countries in the developed world—such as the Netherlands—rely much more heavily for mobility on the automobile. However, because the bicycle in all of its simplicity does so many things at least a little well, it could become an important part of a twenty-first-century transportation system. Since 40 percent of U.S. trips are two miles or less, a bike can often substitute for the car (which now accounts for two-thirds of those under-two-mile trips), saving not only gas but also the space it takes to move and park a car. And bicycling makes an elegant link to mass transit, which lacks door-to-door service. Or think of the health side of the equation. I could probably get a better and more complete workout if I went to a gym for an hour every day. However, like most Americans, I can't or won't take the time to do that. But I can spend roughly an hour "accidentally" exercising on my ride to and from work and not take any more time than it would to fight rush-hour traffic (after a move my commute has now grown to about four and a half miles each way). The cold efficiency expert in my soul loves that.

Moreover, cities like Portland have shown that they can boost bike ridership out of what amounts to spare crumbs in the overall transportation budget. Surveys show that nearly 5 percent of Portlanders are bicycling to work. That's not a bad deal given that the city has been spending less than 1.5 percent of its transportation money on bikeways. It's also a good deal for me personally: I've financed a fleet of bikes in my garage, plus an assortment of raingear and other bike paraphernalia, out of savings in bus fare and parking (I used to mostly take the bus but often drove as well). Perhaps more importantly, bicycling is a good deal for society. One study found savings in energy, pollution, and other costs of as much as 22 cents for each mile in which a bike could be substituted for a car, and that study was done before gas prices spiked above four dollars a gallon. If 10 percent of Americans biked instead of drove just ten miles per week, that's a savings of more than $3.4 billion a year. That's more than the entire federal energy research budget. The bike may not be a wonder drug for what ails America, although it is amusing to think how it would be promoted if the pharmaceutical industry could patent it. But the bike can play a serious role in America's transportation network—if society will take this simple contraption seriously.

In recent years, several European countries have made major steps to promote bicycling for short urban trips. Paris now has twenty thousand short-term rental bikes on the street and they have quickly proven to be a popular alternative for short trips. Amsterdam and Copenhagen have come to rely more heavily on bikes than cars. London and Stockholm charge motorists to enter their central city areas and have seen major increases in cycling as a result. A new bike chic is spreading on the continent. Still, Americans are often loath to follow European trends, as anyone familiar with our very different health-care system can tell you. And our sheer size makes us vastly different when it comes to transportation.

Our communities tend to be more sprawling and our commutes longer. Europe is also dotted with ancient cities too cramped to accommodate rampant auto use, unless you want to sacrifice the very attributes that make them so vital and lively. Most Americans live in the suburbs, often in housing developments connected to each other only by busy arterials. It may be pleasant to bike or stroll in the immediate neighborhood, but it can be hard to cycle anywhere useful without braving intense and swift-moving traffic. In much of the country, bikes have been marginalized for so many years that motorists never learned to be around them, which in turn made cycling more dangerous and further discouraged their use for even short trips.

I may like to see my bike as my exoskeleton, a device that efficiently magnifies my power and makes me stronger even when I'm not tethered to it. But the truth—as one *Wall Street Journal* commentator once wrote—is that cars have become our real exoskeleton. We rely on them not only to take us almost everywhere we want to go, but for protection from the elements, for status, and even for sensory pleasure (it is for good reason that car ads tout blinding acceleration, prowess in the wilderness, and the rush of racing down empty, twisting roads; the vehicle marketers know what makes us feel good). For almost all of us, the car is the exemplar, our magic personal flying machine, keyed to our own music. If it fails to deliver on perfection, the fault lies elsewhere: with the reckless idiot who gets in a wreck and ties up traffic, the government's failure to build enough roads, and other peoples' insistence on jamming up the parking lot you're trying to use. The harder we work to afford them—and the average working-class family now spends slightly more on transportation than on housing—the more we demand of them.

We've been lectured about our near-total reliance on the car ever since the Saudi princes and the rest of OPEC tried to cut off our oil in the early 1970s, but for years we shrugged it off as little more than a bump in the road. Four-dollars-a-gallon gasoline is finally starting to change that. But it's hard to change decades of relying almost exclusively on the automobile. Our cars solve so many other problems: you can plop homes—and ever-bigger ones, too— farther out in the countryside where the land is cheaper. Businesses can move into tilt-up concrete buildings with little regard to the proximity of their workforce, just as long as there is also room for a big parking lot. The middle class can buy out of urban poverty; whatever frightens you can be kept at a distance. Between 1990 and 2001, the number of miles we drove grew more than twice as fast as the population. In that same time, the average motorist went from spending forty-nine minutes a day in their auto to more than an hour. The long-distance commute was no longer remarkable. In one suburban county near Atlanta, the average commuter now travels more than thirty-one miles just to get to work. America's cars may have lost the gaudy tail fins and ornamental chrome of the fifties, but they morphed into an extension of the household, a place where there is just as much eating, media consumption, and heart-to-heart conversation as in the family room off the kitchen. The hard edges, sketchy brakes, and no-seat-belt cars of the tail-fin era also gave way to a sophisticated steel cage that somehow usually keeps people alive when they ram into other objects with g forces equal to a rocket launch. More than forty thousand people in America die every year in motor vehicle crashes, but the decline in fatalities per mile driven—from more than 5 deaths per 100 million miles in the pre-Ralph Nader 1960s to about 1.5 per 100 million miles by the turn of the twenty-first century—has been steep enough to provide such a sense of safety and security that we're constantly thinking of new ways to do other things, like talk on the phone, while we're driving.

And into this highly engineered world that would be as weird and futuristic to our great-grandparents as interstellar travel is to us come an increasingly assertive breed of cyclists riding human-powered machines that our great-grandparents could identify in an instant. We barely tolerate the frail senior poking along in his car. To deal with a cyclist, without all of the customary protection, traveling at such different speeds—you whiz past them when traffic is light; they zip by you when you're in gridlock—well, it's as unsettling as seeing a naked guy run out on the gridiron and line up at quarterback.

While we may celebrate individuality in most aspects of American life, most motorists expect strict conformity on the road. On a trip to Washington, D.C., I ran into a prominent anti-poverty expert who for years has fought politicians who demagogue about welfare queens and people too lazy to work. But when we got to talking about bicycling, he quickly complained about a cyclist who had recently pedaled ahead of him but wouldn't move out of his way. "He was delaying me," my poverty expert fumed, his voice rising into a whine. I sighed. The truth is that my acquaintance didn't think about whether the cyclist would risk being hit by a car door if he moved to close to the curb, or whether the street was too narrow to pass safely. All he knew was that this asphalt queen was in his way.

It is true that I see bad behavior on the part of cyclists every day. Part of it is a lack of education and training. And part of it is simple human nature: many cyclists will take shortcuts if it seems like they can, just like drivers tend to exceed the speed limit because it feels safe and they know they are highly unlikely to get a ticket. I'll get into this topic more in a later chapter. The other big charge that gets flung at cyclists needs to be dealt with up front: which is that, unlike motorists, cyclists don't help pay for the roads. That thought is deeply ingrained in the American psyche and is routinely used to argue that cyclists do not have—or should not have—any right to use the roads. Once I was waiting at a stoplight in downtown Portland on a weekday morning watching a drunk stagger in the crosswalk in front of me. He turned, stared at me as he teetered, and said, "Goddamn it, you don't even pay any taxes."

It is true that cyclists don't pay gas taxes (except when they are driving, as most cyclists do at one time or another). But they do pay property taxes, which nationally account for 25 percent of spending on local roads, which is what cyclists most heavily use. These streets have always been seen as public space, free to whomever wanted to use them. Motorists may want to turn them into a kind of gated community, but that is contrary to our traditions and to our law.

More importantly, very little is said about the huge subsidies received by motorists that far outweigh any freebies received by cyclists. The largest is free—or cheap—parking. Cars take up a lot of space and it is expensive to provide the room to park them (parking garages can cost upwards of $10,000 a space). When I ride my bike to the grocery store, I don't take a space in the parking lot. But the cost of providing that acre of parking at my local store is reflected in the prices of everything I buy there. That may sound trivial, but it isn't. One study estimated that drivers received as much as $220 billion in 1991 in parking subsidies—more than was spent on roads that year. UCLA Professor Donald Shoup[1] calculates that all of the country's parking spaces take up an area roughly equivalent to the size of Connecticut. And I won't even go into such subsidies as the military costs of keeping our oil supplies flowing in the Middle East.

---

1. Shoup is another influential figure in transportation who has been affected by his years as a cyclist. He argues that cities should base parking fees on demand so that there are always a few open spots. This will reduce cruising for open spaces—which studies suggest accounts for a major amount of traffic in dense urban areas—and encourage drivers to seek other alternatives. Several cities, including New York, are beginning to put his ideas into practice. "I think that most decision makers ... look at the world from behind the wheel of a car," he told me. "And they easily understand that parking is a necessity because if you have a car you need a place to park wherever you want to go. But they think by necessity, that means free places to park ... Whereas if you're a bicyclist you tend to say, 'Well, why shouldn't they pay? They're using it. Why should I pay for their parking?'"

For all of the ire directed at urban cyclists, most people do have a fondness for bikes themselves. Almost everyone has at least tried to learn how to ride a bike at some point in his or her life. The sporting goods manufacturers, who do a big survey every year, say that some thirty-six million Americans cycle at least once a year. But not since the Great Depression or the gas rationing of World War II have most people expected to do much of a utilitarian nature with their bike, at least as adults. For that reason, it's easy to infantilize cyclists, to think that they simply need to grow up. Politicians find that bicycling is an easy target if they need a scapegoat. After the Minneapolis freeway bridge collapse in 2007, Transportation Secretary Mary Peters complained that too much transportation money was being spent on things like transportation museums and bike paths, although the latter was a tiny fraction of federal transportation spending. No politician, I've observed, wants to be accused of telling his or her constituents they have to get out of their car and onto a bicycle.

However, just as it seems we're reaching the zenith of a mechanized, electronic age where every movement is power-assisted—think how ancient hand-crank car windows now seem—you can see the beginnings of a cultural shift. Cycling advocates have been the sparkplug for a broad coalition pushing government at all levels to adopt "complete street" policies that require the public right of way to accommodate all users, whether motorists, walkers, transit users, or bikers. Cyclists also started a movement now gaining nationwide acceptance to encourage children to walk and bike to school. Cyclists have joined with health professionals, who have failed for decades to persuade most adult Americans to exercise, to help figure out how to spur people to incorporate walking and cycling in their daily lives. Cyclists are also prominent in the so-called "smart growth" movement, which encourages density and a mixture of residential and commercial uses over suburban sprawl. And, of course, all too many cyclists (myself included, I confess) are aggravatingly cheerful about high gas prices and all too ready to offer a two-wheeled solution.

All of this comes as our central cities, which once threatened to become ghost towns as jobs moved to the suburbs, began to reinvent themselves as arts and entertainment centers catering to knowledge workers and creative young college graduates looking for interesting places to live. The 2007-2008 jump in gas prices led many Americans to reconsider where they resided. When the housing market, fueled by subprime mortgages, collapsed, the biggest price declines were in the outer suburbs.

It was becoming clear that while we were all in a hurry to get somewhere in our car, the places we wanted to linger are places kind of like … quaint European downtowns, where you could sip espresso in a café or stroll down a pedestrian-only street and peer leisurely into shop windows. There is, in the planning literature, a lot of talk about walkable communities. American culture is finally catching up to what Jane Jacobs wrote in her landmark book, *The Death and Life of Great American Cities*, more than four decades ago: communities thrive when they offer a variegated mixture of housing and retail, and when people are encouraged to stroll and interact with their neighbors.

In the last decade, new studies have suggested that people who live in the cities are thinner than suburbanites, in part because they walk more instead of being constantly delivered from front door to front door by car. And as we age as a society, we seem to be rediscovering the pleasure of a nice amble. The trail-building movement in America is booming, chiefly on old right-of-ways abandoned by the railroads. And it is increasingly regarded as malpractice now to build a subdivision without sidewalks, unlike in the old days when many developers and homeowners alike thought that sidewalks ruined their rural ambience. (It should also be noted that it was cheaper for the developer to eschew the sidewalks. The problem is that as traffic became more intense the effect was to force many people into their cars even if they just wanted to walk the dog). The "New Urbanism" movement that has sought to create denser communities with a mixture of commercial and residential uses has also made it easier for people in those communities to walk someplace useful or at least interesting. One curious thing about humans, we like having a destination, even if we're just out for a stroll.

But there's a big gap between the speed of cars and of humans on foot. And that's where the bike comes in. A cyclist traveling at an easy pace can cover a mile in about six minutes, which is three or four times the speed of a walker. Ten miles an hour may not seem like much, but it's competitive with a car for short distances, particularly when the congestion is thick and the parking difficult. In other words, do you really need more than a ton of steel to move your rear end two miles?

Elevating the role of the bicycle gets us into some much tougher issues. How do we integrate two very dissimilar vehicles into the road system? Do we follow the precepts of John Forester, an iconoclastic engineer who has gained a following by insisting that cyclists simply operate as much as possible like motor vehicles, with all the same rights and responsibilities? Or, do we join in with the bicycle planning professionals who are busily building a wide variety of special facilities for bicycles (which I will in general refer to as bikeways)? Does it only involve some paint on the road to provide some bike lanes, or to get serious do we need to move toward what they've done in the Netherlands and create what amounts to almost a second road system, physically separated from the first one?

Whatever we do with the roads, it's clear that bicyclists have an impact on the streetscape. For example, one favorite tool to provide room for bikes is to put streets on a "road diet." That involves reducing the width of the travel lanes—or maybe even eliminating some of them—to make room for striped bicycle-only lanes. This can both serve cyclists and increase overall safety because narrower lanes tend to slow motorists.

The more that cyclists use that bike lane, the more life on the street changes. Most mornings I ride for about a mile in a bike lane along Southwest Broadway, which runs through the heart of Portland's downtown. In the years after the bike lane was striped, I increasingly saw a new form of behavior by motorists: when they plan to make a right turn off Broadway, they stop, look over their right shoulder and make sure it's clear of cyclists before going. That doesn't happen all of the time. It's still all-too common to see near-misses between right-turning motorists and cyclists going straight ahead in the bike lane (and that conflict is one of the issues with bike lanes). Still, Southwest Broadway is not what it used to be, whether you're on a bike or not. Here is the really odd part: there is probably more traffic conflict on Broadway now than when the cops were coping with the cruisers who once dominated the street at night. But that conflict may not be all a bad thing. With a more complicated traffic flow, everyone is forced to be more alert and careful. It is a bit like being in a supermarket parking lot. You are more cautious and watchful because you know there are pedestrians all around, and cars and bicycles are coming from all directions. One planner I know even refers to it as "good chaos."

If bikes, in sufficient numbers, can have a traffic-calming effect on their own, cyclists themselves are also safer just by being more numerous, according to a study by California engineer Peter Jacobsen. He argues that this is also true for pedestrians, and it certainly seems to be borne out by casual observation. On the popular Burke-Gilman Trail in Seattle, for instance, I was intrigued to watch how most motorists automatically stopped as they approached an intersection with the trail, even if no bicyclist or walker was readily visible. They've no doubt been trained by thousands of near-misses over the years. In the university town of Davis, California, where about one out of seven trips is by bike, I watched a driver waiting to make a left turn in front of me shake his head in disgust when I didn't automatically assert my right of way and quickly ride through the intersection.

So cycling advocates face a dilemma. Safety is probably the biggest barrier that discourages people who would otherwise be more willing to cycle. And clearly cycling is more dangerous in this country than in European countries that have done more to encourage cycling and gain safety in numbers. One study, for example, calculates that the fatality rate for America cyclists is at least three times greater than in the Netherlands, even though virtually no Dutch cyclist wears a helmet. Bicyclists find themselves in the position of not being able to promise new riders that they will be as safe on two wheels as they would be in their cars. But I have no doubt that safety improves with each new rider. So one could argue there's an almost cult-like desire by bicyclists to gain converts. As I said, cyclists are assuming a certain amount of risk (although I think it can be mitigated by following some common-sense riding practices) in the name of the greening of the city. They are naturally allied with environmentalists, the New Urbanists, the public health professionals, and people who like to walk. But cyclists have a place at the table in large part because they are rabid enough to join organizations and agitate politically. They don't begin to rival the National Rifle Association when it comes to single-issue lobbying, but there's a lot of that same fierce insistence in the rightness of their cause.

Of course, I doubt many people ride to save the environment or for other abstract reasons, although it may add an extra motivation. It's hard to imagine people riding if they don't simply love it. Those of us who do love it think about enjoying the outdoors, moving at a speed that fends off boredom but gives you time to scrutinize interesting sights, and that sets your body working just hard enough to release those pleasure-inducing endorphins. As one of my fellow bike commuters likes to tell skeptics, "It's like being able to golf to work."

I see two sides to the future of cycling in this country. One is that many people are turning to bicycling in search of a different, freer lifestyle. As I said, they're like urban pioneers, setting off with a minimum of provisions to explore the frontier, even if that frontier is a city landscape most people are only dimly aware of through a car windshield. The other side is a piece of geopolitical reality. After walking, the bicycle is the world's most common means of locomotion, thanks in large part to the five hundred million bicycles in China. But now that millions of Chinese—and Indians and Malaysians and people in so many other developing countries—are abandoning their bicycles for autos, we're finding more competition for the fuel it takes to support our car-centric lifestyle. As I write this mid-2008, gasoline has reached four dollars per gallon and, for the first time in decades, Americans are actually driving less. They are snapping up compact cars, particularly hybrids, and letting SUVs molder on dealers' lots. Transit use has jumped and I constantly hear and see stories about people dusting off the bikes in their garages to use for short trips.

As journalist Thomas Friedman notes, the world is getting flatter, meaning that peoples' lifestyles and incomes are becoming more similar no matter where they are on the globe. In China, car ownership is growing by 20 percent a year—and it wouldn't surprise me if the reverse happens in America and bicycle use begins to grow rapidly as we adjust to ever-rising fuel prices. Beijing and New York streets could well look more alike, both jammed with cars but also with hordes of bicyclists.

Right now, I understand this is a prospect many Americans don't relish. Many see bicycling as too dangerous, too sweaty, unreliable in bad weather, rough on clothes, and a bane to carefully coiffed hair. People live on steep hills, are too far away from work and stores, have to drop their kid off at school, need to carry too much, have to get to daycare after work, use their car for work, enjoy driving anyway because it's easy, and—let's not forget this, even though it usually goes unstated—we drive because our cars are so wrapped up in our personal identity. Most of us buy as much car as we can afford, and maybe even a little more, in part because it sends a message about our status to the rest of the world. Who isn't a little more muscular or beautiful or stylish behind the wheel of that curvaceous new vehicle?

I'll take the real muscles I get from riding my bike, not to mention the freedom from counting calories, the improved stamina, and the promise of a longer sex life. A little sweat isn't that big of a deal if you shower regularly and the truth is that every day, there are millions of car trips that can be easily substituted by the bike. To a degree, I think most people understand that. Several surveys have shown a sizable percentage of the population is willing to consider using a bicycle for some transportation purposes, if the circumstances are right. I think most people still retain fond memories of cycling, and I don't think it would be the hardest thing that Madison Avenue has ever had to sell. Ironically, the bigger problem is that the advertising industry isn't really selling cycling to Americans because it's just too economical. Cycling was about a $6 billion industry in 2007, roughly equivalent to the hosiery business. Automakers spend more than that just on advertising.

I was in San Francisco a while ago, on one of those achingly beautiful sunny days in early fall when the California light is so crisp that it brings out a boldness in colors that you normally miss. As I rode past Fisherman's Wharf, I saw several tourists wobbling along a bayside path in rental bikes, just beginning to knock the rust off long-unused cycling skills. But they all had big grins on their faces. Maybe they will realize that cycling is a simple pleasure they don't have to reserve for a vacation in exotic San Francisco. And that someday they may be able to feel that same glee taking a simple ride through their own town.

1

How Cyclists Created a Political Movement

In the early 1970s, the American bicycle industry was caught flatfooted by a mysterious phenomenon: sales were suddenly skyrocketing. The famous Schwinn Bicycle Company, surprised as anyone by the surge, was forced to ration its dealers. Retailers scrambled to import European bikes. An industry once focused on children's bikes retooled to meet the new demand from adults for lightweight ten-speeds. Theories abounded as sales climbed from 6.9 million bikes in 1970 to 15.2 million in 1973. Some pointed to the new environmentalism spawned by Earth Day, others to the physical fitness craze (remember when jogging was invented in the 1970s?). Or maybe it was the new bike technology that allowed riders to cover distances they never could have imagined on the one-speed, balloon-tire bikes of their childhood.

The *National Geographic* chewed through these theories in a May 1973 article ("Bicycles are Back—and Booming!") that captured the craze with the same zeal it usually brings to studying the folkways of a lost Amazon tribe. "[L]ike millions of other Americans," explained writer Noel Grove, "I have mounted again the toy of my youth, and found it an exhilarating new transportation tool."

In an America that was becoming accustomed to revolutionary change—think of women's liberation, racial equality, the anti-war movement, gay rights, and R-rated movies—it was easy to think that bikes just might spark a transportation counterculture.

Bicycle advocacy groups formed in several cities and government agencies turned their attention to such issues as bike safety and the construction of bike paths. "We were all dreamers," recalled Dan Burden, one of the early bike advocates. "We assumed that at some time maybe 10 percent of all Americans would ride their bikes to work, to shop, to school, you know, things like that." Burden chuckled. "Those would have been big dreams because the percentage was puny compared to that."

Burden, too, was chronicled in that same issue of *National Geographic*. Or, more accurately, he did the chronicling, in an accompanying article he wrote that described the first leg of an epic bike journey from Alaska to the southern tip of the hemisphere that he planned to take with his wife and another couple. Burden had to drop out in Mexico because of sickness, but in 1976 he organized a mass ride across America—the "Bike-centennial"—that cemented his place in the national bike scene. He was asked to take the reins of a new group, the Bicycle Federation of America, which would seek to make the bike an everyday presence in the U.S. Burden went on to become one of the first state bike and pedestrian coordinators in the country, in Florida. And, three decades later, he is once again traveling the country, this time mostly by plane, teaching communities how to tame auto traffic and promote walking and bicycling. A tall, gregarious man with a grandfatherly walrus mustache, Burden tends to stride out into streets of fast-moving traffic with the bravado of a wildlife wrangler wading into crocodile-infested waters. He explains that he just wants to get a better feel for what he can recommend to slow down cars. "The human body is not designed to move faster than fifteen miles per hour. Our sight, our ability to interpret things, to process things is bicycling speed," Burden said. "Anything higher is against human evolution. And I'm convinced that as people end up spending more of their lives at a human speed, they're going to be happier. That happiness cannot be attained at higher speeds."

Burden was not alone in seeing his life change during the bike boom. The surging interest in bicycles created a movement that saw the bike as a cornerstone of not just a different transportation system, but of the resistance to the kind of sprawling, auto-oriented development that was remaking America. This movement would wax and wane depending on factors ranging from the price of oil to crime rates in the inner city. But it would never entirely disappear, and it would eventually gather enough force to help rewrite federal transportation policy and to become embedded in the power structure of many cities. And eventually, not long after the turn of the century, amid a new spike in gas prices as well as problems unimagined in the 1970s—such as global climate change and rising obesity—the promise and hopes of the bike boom once again flowered.

The seventies boom, at least as measured by sales, disappeared almost as suddenly as it started. By 1975, sales had dropped back to 7.2 million—less than half of what they had been at the peak—and bike shops were closing throughout the country. "The dealers were saying, 'Stop, we can't take it anymore,'" said Jay Townley, a former Schwinn executive. "For the next few years, the mindset of bike industry was that it would come back. Well, it didn't." I went to visit Townley at his home, nestled in the Wisconsin Dells, a resort area a couple of hours drive north of Madison. Now in his sixties, he's still involved with the industry, both as a consultant and as an entrepreneur who sells a body-scanning system to help properly fit bikes to their riders. "In the beginning we thought there was a sudden interest in the bicycle as an alternative form of transportation," he said, but the answer proved more complicated than that. He rummaged through the files in his basement office and brought a thick black binder up to his kitchen table. It turned out to be a 1978 Schwinn strategic plan that tried to make sense of an industry that the company's executives simply found puzzling. Yes, he said, part of the boom could be attributable to the rising interest in physical fitness as American life became more sedentary. And the Arab oil embargo in the fall in 1973 certainly encouraged some people to ride bikes instead of sitting in gas lines. But Townley didn't buy the argument that environmentalism had much to do with it. Cyclists may *like* the fact that they are environmentally benign, but he argued that those concerns don't drive people to get on their bikes if they aren't otherwise predisposed to do so. More persuasive to Townley were the sales data from his old strategic plan, which showed that in the late sixties and early seventies teenagers were increasingly moving up to ten-speed bikes.

He pointed to the relevant passage in the old Schwinn plan: "This dramatic increase in 'adult' style 26- and 27-inch wheel multi-speed bicycles is attributable in large part to youth riders in the thirteen- to seventeen-year-old segment of the population, graduating from the hi-rise bicycle to the sophisticated derailleur-equipped lightweight bicycle." In short, the bike boom was a manifestation of the baby boom. These teens and young adults may have found themselves stranded in suburbs without transportation (many suburbanites in those days only had one car, which Dad—and it was usually Dad then—drove off to work). Or they were looking for cheap transportation on college campuses, or they just saw it as a great weekend form of recreation. Whatever the case, "we saturated that market," said Townley. And once that happened, it was the end of the boom. As I drove away, I thought how much sense his theory makes. Perhaps because I'm a boomer myself, I tend to subscribe to the school of history that argues that American culture has fundamentally changed as my oversized demographic moves through the different stages of life (and if nothing else, my thinking certainly mirrors the narcissism of the boomers). I think it helps explain the rebelliousness of the 1960s and early seventies, the conservatism of the 1980s when boomers were preoccupied with young families, and the mixture of angst and prosperity that marked the 1990s when we moved into our middle-aged years.

As it happened, I bought two very cool Gitane ten-speeds during the boom years (the second because the first was stolen), both of which seemed so lightning quick next to the heavier Schwinn road bikes to which we were accustomed.

In one sense, the bike boom was a sign that given the right conditions—and in this case it was a lot of young people entering the years when bicycling is a particularly attractive alternative—cycling is always ready to thrive, like a plant that will flourish if given half an ecological niche. But the bike boom was also the last act of the robust children's bike culture that we had in the 1950s and 1960s, when it was common to bike to school and parents thought nothing of telling us to ride down to the grocery store for a half-gallon of milk. I have spent many an hour in the last few years talking with fellow boomers who remember fondly how a bike was their ticket to independence and freedom. We were, it seems, the last generation of children who headed out into the neighborhood with no more guidance than to be home by dinner. And that also spelled trouble for the bicycle, for what if there was not another generation that learned to adore the bike as a child?

As it happens, the bike boom was perfectly in keeping with the history of the bike in America. Ever since inventors began their quest for a human-powered machine in earnest in the early 1800s, they have made striking advances while never quite fulfilling their own high hopes. In short, bicycling has had more ups and downs than the stock market. At the same time, the bicycle for more than a century has remained one of the most common items in America, something that most people have savored at least at some point in their lives.

David Herlihy, whose 2004 book, *Bicycle,* exhaustively chronicled the early evolution of the bike, told how proponents saw it as a kind of poor man's horse that would provide a personal mobility that the masses had never seen. In 1817, Karl von Drais unveiled a two-wheeled carriage straddled by a rider using his feet, almost like a modern child astride a plastic toy car that she propels with her feet. The draisine, which more commonly came to be known as the velocipede, was a strikingly simple machine with surprising abilities. At a normal stride, a rider on a velocipede was about twice as fast as a walker. And at a running pace, riders could get up to twelve miles an hour, as fast as a horse. And on a good downhill, of course, using a velocipede was effortless. But this new conveyance was met with intense criticism by many people who saw it as a menace and succeeded in banning it from many public ways. In New Haven, the one American city where velocipedes were found in great numbers, one newspaper complained of the "wild and sundry riders," which makes me think that some things are truly enduring when it comes to how many people view riders of two-wheeled vehicles.

Herlihy suggests that the public opprobrium toward the velocipede hindered the development of the bicycle, which after all should not have been that great of a technological leap. But it was not until 1867 that Parisian Pierre Michaux[1] marketed a machine that had pedals attached to the front hub of a velocipede. The concept quickly caught fire, with the *New York Times* writing that the new vehicle promised independence, "great economy of time as well as money," and "immense development of muscle and lung." It was yet another timeless description, this one to be repeated by generations of proponents.

The bicycle became popular on both sides of the Atlantic, but the new vehicle was more for the elite than the masses. The high wheeler, with an oversize front wheel that provided the greatest

---

1. Michaux has frequently been credited for inventing the bicycle. But Herlihy explains that it was based on a design by Pierre Lallement, who had built his own prototype in 1863.

movement for each stroke of the pedal, was both expensive and difficult to ride. Cycling became a sport of well-to-do young men. Practicality was not the high wheeler's strongest suit. Perched on top of these contraptions, a rider may have been well positioned to light oil streetlamps, but that was about it for utility. For the most part, bicycling was a recreation, although racing and endurance contests quickly made it a popular spectator sport as well.

Albert Pope, the first American manufacturer of bicycles, was both the Henry Ford and the P.T. Barnum of the cycling movement. A shrewd businessman, he helped form the League of American Wheelmen in 1880 to promote the bicycle, as well as to fight off those who wanted to ban it from the roads. And, knowing the advantages of the paved road to cyclists, Pope also was a leader of the Good Roads movement (besides the steel rails of the trains or the decks of boats, Americans at that time largely traveled upon a sea of mud in wet weather and rutted, bone-shaking hardpan when it was dry). Eventually, he financed the nation's first road-engineering courses at MIT and built his own stretch of macadam near Boston to show off the wonders of smooth asphalt.

After some initial hesitation, Pope also produced the first American version of the next great technological advance: the safety bicycle. Using a chain and gears to drive the rear wheel, the safety bicycle no longer needed the dangerous oversized front wheel. The bicycle as we know it today came into being, sparking a true bike boom in the 1890s. Prices fell so much that the bike was affordable for the average person (albeit often only with financing, however) and it became a more practical machine, and one more socially acceptable, and appealing, for women to ride. By 1896, more than four million bicycles were in American homes, at a time when the total population had not yet topped seventy-five million. Manhattan's broad boulevards were filled with cyclists at all hours. The bike became a common commuting tool; as late as 1906, for instance, Minneapolis found that cyclists made up a fifth of its downtown traffic. Police bicycle patrols became popular, and many postal carriers and other deliverymen took up the bicycle. The military dallied with the bike, although it never went beyond limited use in the U.S. (However, several decades later the North Vietnamese extensively used bicycles on the Ho Chi Minh Trail moving men and supplies in their fight against the American military).

The bicycle also became an important part of the history of the emancipation of women. The bicycle gave women a freedom of movement that few had known. Even the restrictive clothing of the day—long, flowing dresses that clearly didn't work on a bike—began to wilt before the new device. "Dress reform talked of for a generation or two," said one 1896 commentator quoted by Herlihy, "has suddenly become a reality." Susan B. Anthony declared that the bicycle "has done more to emancipate women than anything else in the world." Belva Ann Lockwood, the presidential candidate of the Equal Rights Party in 1884 and 1888, used an adult-sized tricycle to travel about the nation's capital and proclaimed after she was photographed riding: "There is a principle behind that picture. A tricycle means independence for women, and it also means health." (Although, as always seems to be the case with the bike, critics were quick with their own ill-informed worries. Marguerite Lindley, a professor of physical culture in New York, warned in 1896 that bicycling hindered "feminine symmetry and poise" and was a "disturber of internal organs.")

Cyclists also won several important legal victories that cemented their right to the road. As Bob Mionske's book, *Cycling and the Law*, explains, the New York Legislature in 1887 gave cyclists all of the same rights and responsibilities as carriages. It was a concept that became widely codified, with almost all states defining cyclists as vehicles with the same right to the road as autos.

The bike became established through much of the world in the years around the turn of the twentieth century. In Europe, the bike became an accepted means of transportation and achieved an enduring place in adult society. But in the U.S., the bicycle seemed to literally pave the road for the motorcar. Pope himself began to make cars in 1897 and Ford—who himself preferred to cycle in his later years—turned the auto industry into a powerhouse that transformed the country's economy. Bicycle sales tanked in the late 1890s and within a few years, the bicycle receded into the background. The League of American Wheelmen withered and the good roads movement was taken over by the automobile lobby. Hiram Maxim, who worked with Pope on his first automobiles, described the bicycle not as an end in itself, but as the consciousness raiser that led to the car:

The reason why we did not build mechanical road vehicles before this, in my opinion, was because the bicycle had not yet come in numbers and had not directed men's minds to the possibilities of independent, long-distance travel over ordinary highway. We thought the railroad was good enough. The bicycle created a new demand which it was beyond the ability of the railroad to supply. Then it came about that the bicycle could not satisfy the demand which it created. A mechanically propelled vehicle was wanted instead of a foot propelled one and we now know that the automobile was the answer.

Throughout the first half of the twentieth century, the bicycle enjoyed periodic revivals and it always maintained a certain fan base. Woodrow Wilson took a cycling tour of Bermuda before assuming the presidency in 1913 (and then attracted headlines after he took office when his automobile collided with a bike). In the 1930s, cycling became a fad among Hollywood stars, although not because of the same economic privation that led millions of adults to take up riding during the Great Depression. By now the bike was also well established as an essential tool of childhood. Bike touring became popular and was spurred by the development of hostels. In fact, well into the 1970s, American Youth Hostels served as a kind of de facto lobby for cyclists. During World War II, Americans were encouraged to cycle when gas was rationed and the domestic auto industry was shuttered. But when the war ended, Americans went on a car-buying binge and the modern suburbs were created. Public transit went into a long decline and the world's largest public works project—the interstate freeway system—dominated the attention of transportation engineers.

Still, the bicycle was too appealing and too useful of a machine to disappear even under the assault of roads that were increasingly dominated by the automotive monoculture. Children routinely biked to school, the park, and the closest food store. I have one photo from the 1950s of a school in Los Angeles with children around dozens of bikes parked outside. I don't know what's more striking to me now, the idea of all those kids riding bikes in the city at the heart of America's car culture, or that they looked so well groomed with their shiny shoes, slacks, and dresses.

Grownups were not so often seen on a bicycle. Burden joked that growing up in Columbus, Ohio, "I knew all three adult cyclists." But there was an active club racing and touring scene around the country, and when given the chance, the bike could flourish. In Davis, California, Emil Mrak, chancellor of a new branch of the University of California, banned cars from most of the sprawling campus and encouraged students to get around on their bicycles. By 1966, bicycling was so well established in the small university-and-farm town that a pro-cycling majority was elected to the city council and Davis set about building the country's first comprehensive network of bikeways.

There was also a nascent bike trail movement in America, sparked in part by Paul Dudley White, the famous heart surgeon who treated President Eisenhower after his 1955 heart attack. White spoke approvingly of the cardiovascular benefits of cycling, although he didn't think much of cycling with auto traffic. In the 1960s, a bike path named for him was constructed along both sides of the Charles River in the Boston area.

The bike boom of the 1970s helped drive a more assertive advocacy, one that had a critique of the automobile-dominated culture mixed in with it. I met one of the early grassroots advocates, John Dowlin, on a cold but sunny Sunday morning one March in Philadelphia. A surprise late-season storm had dumped more than a foot of snow on the city the day before and I waited for him outside a popular brunch spot in the Spruce Hill neighborhood. As I looked down the street, I could see Dowlin, burly, white-bearded, and grinning puckishly, slowly pedal through the slush toward me. He removed his lock from the plastic crate on the back of his bike, which he explained rode better than it looked, with its battered appearance serving as a theft deterrent. Dowlin is something of an historian of the movement, dating his activism to a 1970 bike ride led by New York Mayor John Lindsay down Fifth Avenue to promote cycling. In 1972, he was one of the founders of the Philadelphia Bike Coalition and for several years ran a clipping service that distributed articles about cycling.

"I really felt the bicycle could be for the world's cities what the spinning wheel was for Gandhi," he said as we sat inside and warmed ourselves with coffee. Just as Gandhi saw India producing its own cloth as a way to free itself from British domination, the bicycle could free urban centers from an over-reliance on cars. And just as peace activists now are quick to tie the war in Iraq to the world's thirst for oil, Dowlin recalled how activists of his day also linked the Vietnam War and American oil interests in Southeast Asia. He gave me one 1973 flier from the Philadelphia Bicycle Coalition that shows major oil company concessions in the region along with a picture of a bike and the slogan: "No American soldiers were killed to fuel this vehicle."

Dowlin and his compatriots also had a lighter touch. After seeing Ford's advertising slogan, "When Ford has a better idea, we put it on wheels," Dowlin and his friends sent a bike frame to the car company (which, according to Dowlin, promptly sent it back). Dowlin also collected testimonials from prominent public figures about the value of the bicycle. For example, the elder George Bush, while serving as American ambassador to China in 1975 wrote Dowlin:

The more I think about the U.S. domestic transportation problems from this vantage point of halfway around the world, the more I see an increased role for the bicycle in American life. Obviously, some terrains make it more difficult, obviously some climates make it more difficult; but I am convinced after riding bikes an enormous amount here in China, that it is a sensible, economical, clean form of transportation and makes enormous good sense.

Grassroots advocates began winning victories in the seventies. In Washington, D.C., the city began closing Rock Creek Park to cars on weekends to create a prime recreational opportunity for cyclists. In Oregon, the state legislature passed a path-breaking bill requiring that at least 1 percent of the highway fund be used to accommodate bicyclists and pedestrians on new road projects.

In 1977, Washington, D.C., attorney Tedson Meyers gathered a small group together at the Golden Temple restaurant on Connecticut Avenue to talk about replicating local successes at the national level. A former D.C. city councilor, Meyers admired the local bike group, the Washington Area Bicycle Alliance, and wanted to set up a national organization that would help seed groups like this around the country. He also saw the national group as a clearinghouse for safety and planning information. "I suggested we call ourselves the 'Influence Pedalers,'" recalled Meyers decades later. "We wanted above all to train advocates in small communities." Perhaps most importantly, Meyers had two young but well-placed federal officials in on the planning with him—Bill Wilkinson at the Department of Transportation and Katie Moran from the National Highway Traffic Safety Administration. Both had become key proponents of cycling inside the government, and they helped funnel federal grants to Meyers' newly created organization, the Bicycle Federation of America.

Burden took over the leadership of the Bike Fed and began working to stitch together bike advocates from around the country. But he left after only a year and a half to go back to school and Moran eventually took over the federation in 1980 and ran it for about six years. Wilkinson then assumed command and headed the group, which was eventually renamed the National Center for Bicycling and Walking, until his retirement in mid-2008. Unlike the League of American Wheelmen, a membership group that was primarily about recreational riding and would dip into and out of advocacy, the Bike Fed became the national gathering spot for bike advocacy. Starting in 1980, it sponsored the biennial Pro-Bike conference, which brought together local bike advocates, government safety experts, bikeway planners, and anyone else with a big interest in the subject.

Moreover, Wilkinson and his group became part of the coalition that rewrote federal transportation law, was midwife to the 1990s creation of a national network of local bike groups, and helped the Robert Wood Johnson Foundation get involved in promoting bikeways as a form of community health. Wilkinson is "the Godfather of bicycling," explained Charlie Gandy, a former Texas state legislator who later worked for Wilkinson's group. Talkative and opinionated, Wilkinson evolved into an all-purpose critic of transportation and land-use planning in America. Growing up in Princeton, "I had the run of the community from nine years on," Wilkinson said one night over a long dinner in an Italian restaurant near his Bethesda, Maryland, office. "I could go anyplace. The only admonition was, be home for dinner. My dream is to make our neighborhoods places that work like that again."

Wilkinson was not without his detractors, who have been known to claim that his group's initials actually stand for the National Center for Bill Wilkinson—which is, at least in part, a reflection of the suspicion directed at anybody who actually manages to make a living as a bike advocate. But the biggest critic of Wilkinson and other bike advocates who set out to change transportation in

America was himself one of the most important figures in American cycling in the last three decades: John Forester.

The shorthand version of the Forester story is that he codified rules for riding on the road—starting with the premise that "cyclists fare best when they act and are treated as the drivers of vehicles"— that became the basis for cycling education in this country. Sensible riders ignore his precepts at their peril.[2] Beyond that, Forester was also a powerful voice, particularly in the 1970s, in defending the rights of cyclists to the public roads. To the extent that cyclists were able to stop legislation that sought to shunt them off to paths, Forester deserves immense credit.

But the Forester story is about so much more. Shakespearean in his feuds and his intense passions, Forester refused to abide by a central tenet of the mainstream bike movement: that there ought to be special accommodations to encourage cycling. Forester fought bike lanes, European-style cycletracks, and just about any form of traffic calming. In fact, he didn't think cycling would ever become a mass form of transportation in America, and that was fine with him. He fumed at the "anti-motorists" who had taken over the bike movement and—living in California suburbia himself—he saw nothing wrong with sprawl and an auto-dependent lifestyle. In later years, he became a featured speaker for the American Dream Coalition, a conservative pro-automobile group that argues that what the country needs most is another major highway-building program.

I spent a spring day in 2007 with Forester at his modest ranch house in the San Diego suburb of Lemon Grove. Forester, seventy-seven, bearded and with a full head of gray hair, met me late in the

---

2. This is not a how-to book, but I can't resist passing on the internet link to a video by Dan Gutierrez and Brian DeSousa of Dual Chase Productions, who deftly show the basics of vehicular cycling in just a little over four minutes. Go to http://www.youtube.com/watch?v=rU4nKKq02BU.

John Forester, a fierce advocate of bicyclists' rights to the road and an equally fierce opponent of much of the modern bike advocacy movement, stands in his bike room at home in Lemon Grove, Calif.
(Photo by Jeff Mapes)

morning still dressed in his bathrobe, focused as he had been on an engine problem involving one of his radio-controlled model airplanes. There was an eccentric bachelor's atmosphere to the house. The living room was largely used as a workshop for his airplanes, and a wide variety of books spilled out of his shelves. He devoted a spare bedroom to his bikes, eight of them, along with several parts bins. In his own bedroom, bookcases separated his bed from a cramped office. In a clipped British accent, a remnant of his childhood in England, Forester spoke with a novelist's eye for detail, appropriate given that he is the son of writer C. S. Forester (perhaps best remembered today for his Horatio Hornblower series). Forester was ten when his family moved to the States, and he grew up bicycling in the hills of Berkeley and devouring British cycling journals. He became an accomplished club racer and worked in a variety of engineering jobs, including the aerospace industry.

Forester first became a bicycle activist in 1971 when he was ticketed one day in Palo Alto for riding in the street instead of following a new city rule to use the sidewalk on one section of road. "I knew from my reading of the British racing journals that the British faced the same thing in 1937, fought it off and won," he explained. Forester did the same, explaining that he got Palo Alto to repeal the ordinance requiring him to ride on the side path. That launched him into his own brand of advocacy. In his view, road officials had a simple plan for coping with the rising number of cyclists as the bike boom of the seventies took off: force them off the road and onto paths. Never mind that in cities like Palo Alto and Davis it was cyclists who were pushing for a network of paths, bike lanes, and other bikeways. Forester said they only succeeded because motorists wanted to keep cyclists out of their way.

Soon Forester had talked his way onto a California committee studying bikeway standards. He fought the Consumer Products Safety Commission over its proposed safety standards for bikes, saying the standards were largely useless and even potentially dangerous. And he began developing his own cycling education curriculum after concluding that nothing existed to promote vehicular cycling. "It turned out I could not even find a proper description of how to fix a flat tire," he said. "I realized I'd have to write the whole damned thing." As is often the case with Forester, there was a bit of hyperbole in there. You could, he finally acknowledged when I pressed him about it, find perfectly adequate repair books.

However, Forester's style was often to go for the jugular. Even many of his ideological allies cringed at his harsh attacks on foes. Paul Schimek, a transportation planner in Boston and former bike coordinator for the city, said he agreed with 90 percent of what Forester had to say. But "he's shrill and nasty, and that wasn't ever a selling point," Schimek said. Forester verbally bludgeoned opponents, suggesting they were corrupt or dishonest. Wilkinson liked to quip that Forester would be more effective if he simply passed his treatises under the door and avoided public contact. But Forester did have many strong allies. John Finley Scott, a sociology professor at the University of California at Davis, played an important role in persuading the state legislature to preserve the vehicular rights of cyclists. And like Forester, Scott was quick to attack critics of motoring and was not afraid to tilt against the prevailing fashions of academia.

Forester had an undeniable impact. He certainly was in common cause with other advocates in arguing that bicyclists had a right to the road, no matter what kind of other paths might be present. And he established an educational program—effective cycling—that was adopted by the League of American Wheelmen. The league still uses a slimmed-down version of the program that Forester, at odds with the league's current leadership, regards as insufficient. Forester popularized his style of riding in a thick book, *Effective Cycling*, which inspired thousands of the most ardent cyclists. One of them was John Allen, an electrical engineer from Waltham, Massachusetts, who said he quickly transformed his style of cycling after reading Forester's book. "Not only did it work, but it gave me a tremendous feeling of empowerment," said Allen, recalling how he became comfortable riding in almost any kind of traffic. Allen eventually wrote his own cycling guide, which followed Forester's commandments. It was abridged into a forty-six-page pamphlet called *Bicycling Street Smarts* that may be the most widely circulated bicycling education guide in America.

Forester also played a role in the 1970s in discouraging many localities from building bikeways, whether they were bike lanes or separated paths. He particularly attacked protected bikeways running next to roads, and the influential traffic engineering guidelines from the American Association of State Highway and Transportation Officials still recommend against these types of facilities. And he savaged the bike industry for supporting bikeway proponents and what Forester saw as misguided safety regulators. The industry, of course, wanted to encourage more people to become cyclists. Forester wanted to see only properly trained riders on the streets.

Forester battled over control of the California Association of Bicycle Organizations and became president of the League of American Wheelmen in 1980. However he was ousted three years later in a power struggle over the organization's direction. As usual, the fight revolved around whether the wheelmen would stick strictly to the precepts of vehicular cycling or would support bikeways and other facilities aimed at encouraging more bicycling. "John was very much of an elitist," said Katie Moran, the second director of the Bike Federation, arguing that he seemed to only care about a small corps of strong and well-trained cyclists. "His focus was, don't make it bad for those of us who know how to do it," she said. "He was constantly at loggerheads with the industry, which wanted to get everybody to bike." Indeed, Forester could see no common ground with his opponents. "The anti-motorists I have dealt with in my life, they are religious frankly about anti-motoring and they will do anything to carry on their cause," he told me. "Nasty people!"

The changing political and economic realities of the 1980s soon became more important than any internecine warfare among bicycling advocates. During the Carter administration, from 1977-81, it was an article of faith that oil shortages would only grow worse. Predictions of gas rising to three or four dollars a gallon were not uncommon, and apocalyptic predictions were in vogue. CIA Director Stansfield Turner warned in 1980 that a "vicious" struggle for oil could soon break out between the U.S. and the Soviet Union. Congress and the Carter administration focused on such grand schemes as gasifying coal, extracting oil from shale in the Rockies, and building vast tracts of solar panels in the desert.

There was also openness to the bicycle. First Lady Rosalynn Carter bicycled on a visit to a solar-powered home in Davis. In Congress, Sen. Paul Tsongas, D-Mass., pushed through legislation requiring a study of the transportation potential of bicycles that committed the federal government to encouraging bicycling as a form of energy conservation. On Earth Day 1980, Tsongas and Transportation Secretary Neil Goldschmidt led bicyclists on a well-publicized ride from Lafayette Park across the street from the White House to Congress to formally deliver the report. It concluded that, with the right incentives, the number of cycling commuters could rise from 470,000 to at least 1.5 million, saving seventy-seven thousand barrels of oil a day (albeit a pittance compared to the roughly seventeen million barrels a day Americans then consumed).

Things quickly changed after Ronald Reagan took the presidency in 1981. In his first week in office, Reagan lifted the remaining price controls on oil and also began to dismantle many of the Carter-era energy programs. In the Reagan creed, the marketplace would solve the problem. Bike advocates soon found themselves frozen out at the federal level. Moran said the Bike Federation was working on several safety contracts with the federal government that were soon canceled by the new administration. "I had friends in government during that time who said it wasn't good politics to be seen with me," she said, explaining that the Reaganites saw the bicycling programs as an "over-involvement of government in unimportant and trivial matters."

In his later years in the presidency, Reagan liked to cite his quick action to remove price controls as the big reason for the long dip in oil prices that stretched through the 1980s. That may have been a factor, but energy analyst Daniel Yergin, in his magisterial history of the oil industry, explains that the major reason was a big slump in demand for oil just as production had ramped up in response to high oil prices in the 1970s. In part, this decline was caused by an economic downturn in the developed countries due to rampant inflation. In addition, coal, nuclear power, and liquefied national gas took a larger share of the energy market, particularly for electrical generation. As a result, cheap oil returned. Drivers started seeing bargains at the gas pump, and they responded. The thrifty sedans that had symbolized consumer response to gas lines of the 1970s gave way to the hulking SUVs that came to dominate American highways. When the housing industry took off again in the late 1980s and 1990s, the phrase "drive until you qualify" became a standard for the real estate industry as buyers searched further out into the suburbs for homes they could afford.

Several local bike advocacy groups shriveled or even became moribund in the 1980s. The trend toward kids being driven to school accelerated and, as Moran put it, the bicycle "lost its panache as an energy conservation thing." The bike industry, preoccupied by a growing shift to overseas production and the long slide of Schwinn, gave little financial support to advocacy efforts.

Still, there were some positive signs for cycling. Bicycle racing was a popular sport at the 1984 Olympics in Los Angeles and two years later, Greg LeMond became the first American to win the Tour de France, both of which brought more visibility and interest to recreational cycling. The railroad industry continued to consolidate and abandoned tracks throughout the nation. That helped open up even more opportunities for biking and walking trails, which turned out to be exceedingly popular in community after community. In 1986, the Rails-to-Trails Conservancy was created to help broker these conversions, and it quickly became an important lobbying force in the national bicycling community.

As would happen so many times in bike history, technological change also played an important role. Beginning in the 1970s, a group of Marin County cyclists had developed the mountain bike, which eventually took the industry by storm. In one of those small-world coincidences that seem endemic to the bike scene, one of the Marin pioneers, Gary Fisher, received a $10,000 loan to help produce bikes from John Finley Scott, Forester's friend. Scott had himself built an early version of the mountain bike in 1953 that he called the "woodsie." (Sadly, Scott disappeared in June of 2006; a handyman who had worked for Scott was convicted of his murder.) Just as most SUVs never went off the paved road, most mountain bikes sold probably never touched the dirt. But they offered would-be cyclists a more stable, upright ride than the lightweight ten-speeds with drop handlebars and skinny seats. "The mountain bike saved the bike industry's butt," said Jerry Norquist, an industry veteran who worked at Trek Bicycles for many years and now runs Cycle Oregon, which sponsors an annual bike tour of the state. Indeed, mountain bikes proved an excellent vehicle for short urban trips. The mountain bike spawned the hybrid, which with its slimmer tires and larger frame also became popular with commuters. "Click" shifters were also developed, making it easier for riders to change gears.

In the same decade, Congress passed the last major funding for the interstate highway system, which had been the focus of federal surface transportation policy for so many years. As the 1980s ended, Congress began gearing up to write another authorization bill guiding the nation's transportation spending. For good reason, this legislation, which typically came along every four or five years, was often colloquially known as the "highway bill," since this was where the vast bulk of money from federal gas tax revenues went. It was generally an insider game, dominated by road-related industry and the state departments of transportation through their powerful trade group, the American Association of State Highway and Transportation Officials. But the end of the interstate era also provided an opportunity for change, and the bill that eventually passed Congress in 1991 would indeed prove to be different. A rump group of transit advocates, mayors, historic preservationists, environmentalists, cyclists, and everyone else who had ever despaired over the nation's transportation priorities, decided to hijack the bill. They formed their own group, the Surface Transportation Policy Project (STPP), and began to strategize. "We called it the losers' coalition," explained one of the founders, David Burwell, who then headed the Rails-to-Trails Conservancy. "The highway lobby had no idea what was going on."

The new coalition went to work on Sen. Daniel Patrick Moynihan, a New York Democrat who chaired the Senate Environment and Public Works subcommittee dealing with transportation. Moynihan, according to several sources at the time, was not sure how deeply involved he wanted to get in the issue. But one of his former top aides, Bob Peck, worked for the American Institute of Architects, an STPP member. And Peck dredged up an article the senator—a former academic famous for his social commentary on a wide variety of subjects—had written in 1960 titled "New Roads and Urban Chaos." Moynihan had correctly predicted that the states would fall over themselves to crank out questionable highway projects when the feds were paying 90 percent of the bill. And he fretted about the impact of crisscrossing cities with new freeways without really understanding their impact. "For good or ill, the location of the interstate arterials would, more than any other factor, determine how this growth would take place," the young Moynihan had written. "Yet no planning provisions of any kind were included [in the interstate legislation]. In the absence of any other provisions, the 'planning' would be done by highway engineers." Moynihan went on to approvingly quote John T. Howard, a planning professor at M.I.T., who argued that just as war is too important to be left to the generals, so highways are too important to be left to highway engineers.

Peck and other members of the coalition persuaded Moynihan that he had an opportunity to correct the wrongs that he had so presciently predicted. And so the senator, with the help of a young aide, Roy Kienitz, fresh from a landmark fight over reauthorization of the Clean Air Act, plunged into the issue. With the help of STPP, Moynihan drafted a bill that shifted much of the control over highway funds from the states to metropolitan planning organizations. The bill also provided much more flexibility in how this money could be spent and set aside pots of money to fund bicycle and pedestrian projects. Moynihan rushed the bill through committee before the highway lobby knew that they faced a serious threat. "I did not think they would go as far as they did," said Thomas J. Donahue, president of the American Trucking Associations in April of 1991. "I don't think anybody did." Moynihan didn't get everything he wanted by the time the bill finally passed Congress several months later. But he was coming from a position of strength. With the interstate program passing into history, the road builders needed to demonstrate there was still a need for a strong national presence in transportation. And the new bill broadened the coalition that supported this continued federal role.

The Intermodal Surface Transportation Efficiency Act, universally known as ISTEA, as in "ice tea," transformed the landscape for bicycling advocates. The new law gave metropolitan areas a big role in transportation planning and allowed localities and states more flexibility to shift money among different modes of transportation. In addition, two new programs were created—Transportation Enhancements, and Congestion Mitigation and Air Quality Improvement (CMAQ)—that were aimed in part at funding bicycle and pedestrian projects. The bill also included $180 million over six years specifically for trail projects. All told, funding for bike and pedestrian projects (quite frequently, the two modes benefit from the same projects) climbed from $23 million in 1992 to a high of $427 million in 2004. In the overall scheme of things, it was still a relatively small share—less than 2 percent—of the federal highway fund. But advocates could suddenly compete for real money and start thinking seriously about building bikeway networks. Years later, Ben Gomberg, Chicago's bike coordinator, spoke reverently when he listed all of the bike projects he's funded with congestion mitigation money. "There are two favorite words on my list," he quipped. "One is my wife's name, and the other is CMAQ."

ISTEA also required each of the states to designate a bicycle and pedestrian coordinator responsible for "promoting and facilitating the increased use of nonmotorized modes of transportation, including developing facilities for the use of pedestrians and bicyclists and public education, promotional, and safety programs for using such facilities." In short, the bill sought to create cycling and walking advocates within the state departments of transportation, which were often regarded as enemy territory by members of the "losers' coalition." The legislation also gave a boost to local bike advocacy groups and it also began to wake up the bike industry. "ISTEA was a windfall for our industry, and it happened with very little industry support," said Ray Keener, a longtime bicycle industry consultant from Boulder, Colorado. "In fact, that happened almost more in spite of our industry than because of it." After the law passed, however, he added, "We did feel we needed to get in there and make a pitch for that money." In 1993, Keener became the point man in an effort by the bike industry to run its own trade show and squeeze out a private company that operated the country's main bike show, known as Interbike. In part, the bicycle manufacturers wanted to capture Interbike's healthy profit margin. But Keener said the industry also saw the trade show as a way to raise money for advocacy. Unfortunately for the manufacturers, Interbike was hard to dislodge and the bike industry gave up after running a competing show for two years.

Despite such setbacks, the machinery of a real and enduring bike lobby began to emerge in the 1990s. ISTEA provided some of the lubrication, but so did the emerging interest from the health community in integrating physical activity with transportation. Also, the continued expansion of the suburbs and the explosive growth of traffic contributed—as do all trends—to a counter-reaction. Grassroots efforts to calm traffic and protect the bucolic feel of small towns swallowed up by the suburbs led to more interest in alternatives to a car-centric lifestyle. Central cities, which had been on the decline for so many years, began to see a revival as many people in two book-end generations—college-educated twenty-somethings and empty nesters—saw dense urban living as a more exciting and convenient alternative to suburban subdivisions. As urbanist Christopher Leinberger has written, you knew something was up when suburban sit-coms like *The Brady Bunch* were replaced by shows like *Seinfeld* and *Friends*, which celebrated city living. This trend was championed by the "smart growth" movement, which succeeded in persuading several cities to begin new urban rail lines and to change zoning rules to allow mixed-use developments. Cyclists now found they had allies among the planners, developers, and urban boosters who saw walking and biking as another attraction of urban life.

In 1994, the Federal Highway Administration released the National Biking and Walking Study that called for doubling the share of trips taken on foot or by pedal, the first time the federal government had committed itself to a specific mode share for these activities. The baseline was the 1990 Nationwide Personal Transportation Survey, which showed that 7.2 percent of trips were by foot and 0.7 percent by bike. The report called for states and localities to be more aggressive in building bikeways and sought aggressive promotion and safety programs. While biking and walking grew over the nineties, motor vehicle travel grew much more rapidly and the study's goals were not met. But the report did signal the beginning of a more fertile period of research into bike safety and infrastructure issues. Bicycle and pedestrian planners, advocates, and researchers got a toehold in the transportation industrial complex. And the bike community was starting to come together. That became evident in 1997 as the interest groups began gearing up for the reauthorization of ISTEA. The transportation reformers knew they had their work cut out since the highway lobby made it clear they wanted to strip out the programs that had benefited bikes—a notion that had some attraction to the new Republican majority in Congress that was suspicious of so many federal programs. All of this led to what is celebrated in bike advocacy circles as the $100,000 pledge. That amount of money would be pocket change for most of corporate America. But when John Burke, the chairman of Trek Bicycles, said he'd put up a hundred grand for a lobbying effort to protect the ISTEA enhancements, it thrilled the crowd gathered at an advocacy dinner at the 1997 Interbike show in Las Vegas. His only caveat: the rest of the bike industry had to match it. Charlie Gandy, who worked with Wilkinson, was the one to make the dinner pitch encouraging the industry to kick in. And he said a group of dealers huddled and came up with another $25,000.

Other bike manufacturers followed. By the end of the dinner, they had the match, and much more was soon on the way. "That's where we turned," said Gandy, from a motley collection of advocates into something resembling a lobby force. Several groups formed with the industry to create Bikes Belong and make their voices heard in D.C.

The industry's emerging clout was also cheered on by an avid cyclist who was emerging as the best friend that the bike movement ever had in Congress, Rep. Jim Oberstar. A Democrat from the Iron Range of Minnesota, Oberstar was an old-fashioned New Deal Democrat who believed in public works. Through the years, his office wall became increasingly thick with plaques from grateful transportation lobbies, whether the barge operators or the airline industries. But Oberstar had a deep emotional connection to bikes. When his first wife, Jo, was diagnosed with breast cancer in the 1980s, the two took up bicycling together. She needed the exercise and riding was an activity gentle enough for her. As her disease worsened, Oberstar increasingly rode alone. "It became this kind of therapy when his wife was dying," explained Bill Richards, his longtime chief of staff. After her death in 1991, he continued to cycle and was vociferously outspoken about its benefits, sometimes in unexpected places.

I saw that for myself in 2007 when Oberstar spoke to hundreds of local government officials gathered for the annual National League of Cities convention in Washington. The emcee introduced Oberstar as an avid cyclist who bikes twenty-five hundred miles a year. "Now, how's that for eco-friendly transportation?" said the presenter in a jocular tone. The seventy-two-year-old Oberstar stepped in front of the crowd and announced, "Are you ready to convert from the hydrocarbon economy to the carbohydrate economy?" That got a big laugh, which sounded to me like most people thought it was a joke. In his speech, Oberstar mostly championed the virtues of rail transit. But afterwards, he met in a back room with several officials from small Minnesota towns and began lecturing them

Rep. Jim Oberstar, D-Minnesota, shows off his road bike while out for a ride. Oberstar, who became chairman of the House Transportation Committee after Democrats gained control of Congress in 2006, was widely regarded as cycling's most important supporter on Capitol Hill.

(Photo courtesy of Bikes Belong)

about how the city of Muenster, Germany, has a mode share of almost 50 percent for bikes. "The mayor rides to work every day on his bike," he said. "So we can do it." I followed Oberstar out, curious if he really believes American cities can start resembling a town like Muenster. "It's just a matter of political will," he insisted. "It's entirely doable and at minimal cost." The key, he insisted, was getting people to change their habits. "We are asking Americans to reconsider their love affair with their car." And, noting that I was from Portland, he added that the rest of the country needs to look at the kind of policies that have nurtured cycling in my home city: a cap on downtown parking and an urban growth boundary that has limited suburban sprawl. "They said no more parking, and then since you made that decision you also said you had to have a new Starbucks on every corner," he said with a laugh. And with that, he hopped behind the wheel of his Plymouth PT Cruiser, his staffers piled in next to him, and off they went.

Oberstar helped protect the bike and pedestrian programs in what became TEA-21, the Transportation Efficiency Act of 1998. Another big factor was a clever bit of political jujitsu by the transportation reformers. They went to Rep. Bud Shuster, R-Pa., chairman of the House Transportation Committee, who, like Oberstar, cherished his ability to fill the pork barrel with local projects. Shuster was in a fight with House Speaker Newt Gingrich, R-Ga., and other Republican leadership figures, who wanted to strictly limit the committee's spending authority. The transportation reformers, including Kienitz, the former Moynihan aide who now worked for the Surface Transportation Policy Project, told Shuster they would support him in his fight. In turn Shuster said he would protect the enhancement programs. As it happened, Shuster lost his battle with the leadership. But Shuster, despite being a proud ally of the highway lobby, stuck with his bargain and protected his new bicycling friends.

Gandy, who worked with Wilkinson at the bike fed, also played a role in bringing together the disparate local bike groups. He had been traveling the country training local bike activists, and decided to hold a retreat for twenty-five key local advocates at famed trial lawyer Gerry Spence's Thunderhead Ranch in Wyoming. Many of the attendees found it an eye-opener to see how similar their battles were in city after city. They decided to meet again in 1997, and that year they formed the Thunderhead Alliance. In part, said Gandy, the hope was that this new alliance—with its own grassroots membership—would prove a counterweight to the venerable League of American Wheelmen, which had been renamed the League of American Bicyclists in 1994. The league still veered between the mission of growing the number of cyclists in the country and that of serving the interests of their core membership: avid, fit, well-trained cyclists who didn't need any more encouragement to ride.

"The league wasn't doing a very good job even at the federal level, let alone at the state and local level," said Gandy, "yet they were clearing that turf, so we had to muscle in in some way." John Kaehny, another Thunderhead founder who at the time headed New York City's Transportation Alternatives, said many of the local bike advocates also thought too much of the federal bike and pedestrian money was going to recreationally oriented trails, and that they wanted to counter the influence of the Rails-to-Trails Conservancy.

Thunderhead had its own series of false starts before it settled into a core mission of helping to nurture local bike groups around the country, under the leadership of Sue Knaup, a former bike shop owner from Prescott, Arizona. But Gandy believed the alliance played a role in helping spur the League of American Bicyclists to become more advocacy oriented. In 1998, the league moved from Baltimore to Washington in hopes of becoming more of a lobbying force. It also started an annual bike summit that attracted advocates from around the country and became an important unifying voice. Andy Clarke, who became the league's director in 2004, represented a clear break with the Foresterites. While he had the requisite cycling chops himself—he typically made his twenty-four-mile round-trip commute to work by bike—Clarke also was a firm believer in the idea that bicycles could transform society. The son of an English minister, he worked for the European Cycling Federation before moving to America in the 1980s where, after a stint with the league, he worked for the Bike Federation of America, the Association of Pedestrian and Bicycle Professionals, and on a contract basis with the Federal Highway Administration. In the latter role he wrote some key studies supporting bikeway development. "I'm not interested in it being a tiny, elitist, marginal activity," said Clarke, recalling how astounded he was that many league cyclists didn't like the big rides for the disease charities "because all these unwashed cyclists were taking to the streets."

Forester was irked enough about the league's new direction to run again for a seat on the board in 2005 and to devote a page of his Web site to an attack on Clarke. "Clarke has opposed lawful, competent cycling throughout his career as the nation's most prominent bikeway promoter," wrote Forester, adding that "Clarke's aim was to reduce motoring by taking advantage of the public belief that bikeways make cycling safe for those without traffic-cycling skills." Forester lost that election, a clear sign that bike advocacy had largely moved past him. (It should, however, be noted that John Allen, who is close to Forester in philosophy, did win a seat on the board. However, Allen is also more of a diplomat and willing to consider the views of bikeway proponents, albeit skeptically.)

After the reauthorization of ISTEA in 1998, the bike industry turned Bikes Belong into an industry-dominated advocacy group. But it joined in creating an umbrella organization, America Bikes, which represented the other bike groups. The new unity in the bike community became vivid in 2003 when a conservative Oklahoma congressman, Republican Ernest Istook, decided to launch another assault on the transportation enhancements program. The chairman of the House appropriations subcommittee on transportation, Istook zeroed out the program in the annual funding bill from his panel. With road congestion rising, he said, "highway funding is the main priority." At first, the bike partisans were unsure what to do. Oberstar, according to several accounts, cautioned that it might be best to let Istook's bill advance unimpeded to the Senate, where perhaps the enhancements could be restored. If the cyclists fought and lost, it would be a huge blow to the movement, he said.

Martha Roskowski, who headed America Bikes at the time, said friendly Democrats told her they needed to find a Republican willing to take Istook on, which was not easy since members were wary about angering a leader of the powerful appropriations committee. But Marianne Fowler, a veteran lobbyist for the Rails-to-Trails Conservancy, managed to persuade Rep. Tom Petri, R-Wisc., a longtime bike supporter, to lead the fight to restore the enhancements. Then Fowler and Roskowski went to Yosemite National Park, where Oberstar was at a conference, and persuaded him that cycling advocates should fight the bill on the House floor. The two women said they realized that Istook had made a key error by bringing the bill out of committee shortly before the August recess. "He played right into our strengths," said Roskowski, which was their grassroots support. Trails, in particular, have become popular in many communities and anyone who gets involved in the arduous process of developing one becomes fervent on the subject. As a result, it was easy to make sure that representatives would be constantly badgered about Istook's bill while they were home for the recess. In the end, the vote wasn't even close. The House voted 327-90 against Istook, although Fowler said many Republicans switched their votes and abandoned the Oklahoma congressman after it was clear he would lose. In short, the members realized what was popular in their districts. "We didn't know it at the time, but that changed everything for us in Washington," said Roskowski. The cyclists were now a legitimate force, one that any legislator would have to take into account before challenging their flow of federal money. The bike lobby could then turn its sights to the next big transportation bill, in 2005, while playing offense.

As ranking Democrat on the House Transportation Committee, Oberstar was now well positioned to push the cycling agenda. And he put his muscle into it. In addition to preserving the current programs, Oberstar shepherded through a new $600 million program called Safe Routes to School that seeks to get more kids walking and biking to school (more on this program in Chapter 9). And he won funding for a $100 million program to secure $25 million apiece for four communities to see if they could increase the mode share for bicycling. All told, on top of the current programs, Tim Blumenthal, the executive director of Bikes Belong, said the bill could produce as much as $4.5 billion for bike-related projects over five years, nearly twice what cyclists had been getting before.

As it happened, both of the new programs carried the fingerprints of an unlikely power broker: Deb Hubsmith, a cycling advocate from Marin County who less than a decade before had been trying to make a difference by riding a solar-powered bicycle to presentations she gave at local schools. Hubsmith, who ran the Marin County Bicycle Coalition for several years, first met Oberstar in 2000 at the Sea Otter Classic, an annual bike festival in Monterey, through two Marinites prominent in the bike industry: Patrick

Seidler, the owner of a bike component business, and Joe Breeze, another mountain bike pioneer who now focuses on selling a line of commuter bikes. Hubsmith, diminutive and seemingly blessed with inexhaustible storehouses of energy, said Oberstar was excited to meet Breeze. But he clearly was also taken with Hubsmith, who was promoting a safe-routes-to-school program she had picked up in England. Oberstar, after hearing a presentation by health officials about the rising obesity crisis, was thinking along the same lines.

Marin County was chosen for a pilot safe-routes program later that year, and Hubsmith became a regular visitor to Congress. In the 2005 transportation bill, Marin County was chosen as one of the four communities that would each receive $25 million to boost bicycling. The selection process, not surprisingly, was highly political. Minneapolis, one of the chosen communities, of course, is in Oberstar's state. Columbia, Missouri, was chosen because Sen. Kit Bond, R-Mo., chaired the Senate appropriations subcommittee on transportation. And Wisconsin's Petri, who had been so important in the 2003 fight, wound up with a pilot program in his district, in Sheboygan County.

President Bush signed the bill despite grumbling from some conservatives that it was a piece of political pork laden with congressional earmarks (it was that very bill that also contained $400 million for the infamous "Bridge to Nowhere" in Alaska). Bush did seem favorably disposed to the bike provisions. He had become an avid mountain biker in 2003 after, like so many baby boomers, having to quit running because of chronic knee problems. Trek's Burke, who became chairman of the President's Council on Physical Fitness, had helped introduce Bush to the sport and given him one of the company's top-of-the-line bikes. Shortly after Bush signed the bill, he took a small group of reporters on a seventeen-mile mountain bike ride around his Crawford ranch. Steve Madden, the editor of *Bicycling* magazine, asked Bush if his ardor for biking affected his decision to approve the bill. "Absolutely," replied Bush, adding that many people didn't ride for fear of getting hit by a car.

"The more accessible [streets and paths] are for bikes, the more likely it is people will use them. But it's got to start at the local level." Bush met with a small group of industry leaders during both the 2006 and 2007 bike summits, but when I asked Burke about whether the meetings produced much of value, he waved the question away. "I think he has a lot of issues to deal with and I think he sees a lot of those issues as local issues," Burke said, echoing what Madden reported.

Still, the 2006 elections, which were a slap in the face to Bush, wound up giving bicyclists a major political victory. Democrats took over both houses of Congress and Oberstar became the transportation chairman. Rep. Peter DeFazio, a Democrat from the Eugene area of Oregon who calls himself the only former bike mechanic to serve in Congress, took over the subcommittee that would write the next version of the transportation bill, due in 2009. Hubsmith, who had taken over leadership of a new advocacy group, the Safe Routes to School National Partnership, was lobbying for two to three billion dollars for the safe routes program. Rails-to-Trails started shopping a plan around the country to give forty communities—not just four—$50 million each to increase bicycling. If you do the math, that's another $2 billion.

Just as importantly, bicycling advocates were becoming establishment figures in many of the country's cities. Cyclists are hard to count and they are not tracked as closely as motorists. The major commuting surveys conducted by the Census Bureau showed no national uptick in the percentage of people bicycling to work (although there were increases in the number). Instead, a utilitarian bicycling culture flourished in many large urban areas and in several college towns. Measurable ridership increases were seen in about a dozen good-sized cities, most notably Portland, Minneapolis, San Francisco, Seattle, Chicago, and New York, and many more cities were actively establishing bikeway programs of one kind or another.

Louisville Mayor Jerry Abramson was treated as a conquering hero at the National Bike Summit in 2007 when he told about trying to jump-start an urban bicycling culture in a city far outside of the lefty-enviro-healthy-living circles that were quicker to embrace urban cycling. After seeing so many bicyclists on a trip through Colorado, Abramson explained how he returned home and called a bicycling summit to figure out what to do. Within a couple of years, the city had striped thirty miles of bike lanes, raised donations to complete a one-hundred-mile loop trail around the city, and worked to build bike and pedestrian links on bridges across the river from Indiana. Abramson said he was also pushing through a "complete streets" policy requiring the city to accommodate cyclists, pedestrians, and transit riders when building or reconfiguring roads. "We're not Portland or Boulder yet," he said. But he added, "Give us another three or four years and you're going to see one of the fastest-growing, most engaged bicycling cities in America." Later, Abramson told me that when he first became the mayor in 1985, his major focus had been on making sure the city's taxes and infrastructure were attractive to business. Now, he said, "What I find myself selling more often than anything else is the great quality of life of Louisville." And part of that is figuring out what will attract the educated people who will drive the economy in future decades, he said.

Abramson's talk seemed to particularly inspire Burke, who has a similar Midwestern business practicality about him. "If we can win in Louisville, we can win just about anywhere," Burke said in his own speech at the summit. "We've spent a lot of time working with people to convince them bicycling is important and sometimes you're just pulling teeth. But there gets to be a point where there is a tipping point and today was a tipping point for me listening to the guy from Louisville. Because you know how Memphis is going to get it? Somebody from Memphis is going to go to Louisville and they are going to see what's going on in Louisville and they're going to say, we've gotta do what they're doing in Louisville."

2

Learning from Amsterdam

Roger Geller's eyes danced with pleasure as he intently watched the street scene along the Amstel River on an unseasonably warm and sunny day in Amsterdam in late fall. An elderly couple leisurely pedaled in unison along a lane of cobblestones and casually turned left onto a busy bridge that leads over the river. Another couple, with a toddler nestled on a small seat in front of the handlebars on the dad's bike, rattled by and slowed for just a moment at the intersection before forging onward. Moments later, a young woman rode over the bridge, carefully balancing a wrapped package of food flat in one hand. An eye-catching red Ferrari convertible rumbled down the lane. The couple inside happily chatted as they meandered along, not going much faster than the bikes around them. A tram whooshed over the bridge as cyclists streamed around the vehicle. "Look how close everybody comes and nobody seems to mind," said Geller as we sat at an outdoor café table. "It's a complicated dance and everybody knows the steps."

It is also for people like Geller, Portland's bicycle coordinator, almost a religious affirmation. Back home, even in a relatively bike-friendly city like Portland, it's hard to stay true to your vision. The vast majority climbs into their cars for almost every trip and they can't imagine it ever being any different. After a while, if you're a bike advocate, it wears you down. But in the Netherlands, you can restore your faith. No Western country—with the possible exception of Denmark—has a cycling culture so rich, so nurtured by government, and so seemingly enduring. Fly to Schiphol Airport, jump on a train to central Amsterdam (and, if you're so inclined, tune out the busy freeway you parallel for a few miles), and you will be in the middle of a city of 750,000, where on any given day, half the population is out on a bike. The effect is roughly akin to an American communist traveling to Cuba and finding that, in truth, Fidel won free and fair elections, there are no political prisoners, and socialism allows the Cuban people to live in well-fed, beautiful harmony.

Ever since I started hanging around bike folks, I had wanted to experience Dutch cycling. I lost count of the number of bike advocates who told me about their life-changing trip to Amsterdam or other bike-legendary cities in Holland like Delft or Groningen. So I jumped at the chance to spend a week in the Netherlands with a group of bike advocates and city officials from Portland. I arrived in Amsterdam early on a Sunday morning, emerging from Central Station to see one lone bicyclist on an otherwise deserted street—a fellow wearing leather chaps but no pants. Just a working stiff from the red-light district heading home, I guessed. I dumped my luggage at my hotel, where I was also able to rent one of the small fleet of bikes they kept on hand for guests. I rode around by myself for a while, trying to gain a sense of how to navigate the separated bikeways that snake along next to roads, through parks, and sometimes down the middle of a sidewalk.

Later, I met Geller and we set off on a tour of the city, guided by a map from a Web page set up to show off Amsterdam's bikeways. As the streets began to fill with more traffic, we realized that one of our toughest challenges was being assertive about taking the right of way. You will hardly find a stop sign in Amsterdam—indeed in the whole country—and we learned to watch the "shark's teeth" found at almost every intersection. If the teeth of the white painted triangles are pointed at you, yield to oncoming traffic. If they're in the opposite direction, you have the right of way, and you're expected to take it. That's where the dance comes in. Falter because you don't trust the other cyclists and drivers and everyone gets annoyed, at least mildly so (Amsterdammers are accustomed to clueless tourists).

If you're the kind of cyclist used to riding in American cities, it doesn't take long for Amsterdam's bike magic to wash over you. Here, you feel like part of the majority, not the oddball. Like most everyone else, we rode heavy, one-speed bikes that discouraged us from setting a torrid pace. And in fact, we didn't feel much need to rush. We didn't worry about sprinting past potentially dangerous traffic situations because there usually weren't any. When you are sharing a street with cars (generally on low-speed neighborhood streets) you are not wondering when to take the lane or when to stay to the side; that's simple in Amsterdam. If you are in front of a car, you can just stay in front. Motorists know they have to poke along behind you until they're given the lane.

Todd Boulanger, a Vancouver, Washington, transportation planner and longtime bike advocate, has been traveling regularly to Holland for years and keeps getting drawn back. "The first time I was in Netherlands, I was just there on a stopover," he said. "But it felt like coming home ... You almost have to retrain yourself there. You don't wear a helmet, you can just relax. And then I came back home and felt tense again." He feeds his mental addiction by compulsively bringing home Dutch bikes of all sorts, a half-dozen of which he has stashed in various nooks of his apartment building. But that's another story.

Geller and I rode through Amstelpark and stopped at a T-shaped intersection to check our bearings. In the U.S., this kind of intersection wouldn't cause most drivers more than a moment's thought. A road from the park dead-ended at a boulevard where cars in both directions had the right of way. Here it was more complicated because an off-street bicycle path came through the park and intersected with another path that paralleled the boulevard. An American traffic engineer would see plenty of potential for conflict. I watched an older couple in a station wagon prepare to take a right off the boulevard to drive through the park. They halted just before the intersection as the woman in the passenger's seat craned her neck to make sure no one was coming down the bike path to the right of the car. As it turned out, they had to wait at least thirty seconds while all of the cycle traffic cleared. I watched closely, struck by how not even a hint of irritation came across their faces. They clearly recognized it as just part of the dance.

We rode along toward a bike and pedestrian bridge and watched a man on a bike with a large wooden box on the front slowly pedal up and over the span. Three young kids were seated in the box, staring out like little potentates. "There's the answer," cried Geller, "to the women who say, 'How am I going to get around?' You *can* do it." Well, that would be an interesting sell to your minivan-driving mom back in the states. Would stay-at-home parents of little kids learn to appreciate combining their exercise with a pollution-free trip to the store if they had a bike that could handle their groceries and their progeny?

American observers often dismiss the importance of the Dutch experience with bicycling by pointing out that the Netherlands is a virtually flat, densely populated country tailor-made for the bicycle. To some extent that's true. But the Dutch aren't all crammed into Manhattan-style apartment towers either. Amsterdam is a largely low-slung city and the rest of the country leaves an impression of well-ordered cities and small towns dotted among plentiful farms and forested areas. There are long distances to drive, and the Dutch seem as avid about their cars as people anywhere in the world. After I left Geller on that Sunday, for instance, I found myself, lost as usual, on a bridge heading out of the city in the late afternoon. In the other direction was a mile-long backup of weekend motorists returning to Amsterdam. Roughly three-quarters of the (non-airplane) distance traveled by the Dutch is by car. Between 1993 and 2005, motor vehicle miles climbed by 13 percent while overall bike mileage went up by 5 percent, according to the government's official statistics.

That alone is enough to persuade skeptics who think it shows the futility of trying to replace the car with the bike. But that isn't what the Dutch have tried to do. Instead, their goal is to provide a healthy, non-polluting alternative for short trips, particularly in their jewel-like cities, which they want to protect from the ravages of huge volumes of motor vehicle traffic. They have been able to maintain a high level of cycling—27 percent of all trips are by bike, comprising about 7 percent of total miles traveled—because they reoriented their traffic system over the last three decades to preserve the primacy of the bicycle in cities and residential neighborhoods. Essentially, they've turned over many of their short urban trips to the bike.

The most vulnerable road users—cyclists and pedestrians—are treated as the exalted kings of the Dutch road hierarchy. Pedestrian advocates often grimly remark that the only legalized form of homicide in the U.S. occurs when a walker gets mowed over by a motorist. Not in the Netherlands. At one point, Dutch law presumed motorists to be at fault in a collision with a cyclist or pedestrian unless proved otherwise. That's no longer the case, but that attitude has widely been adopted in society, several officials told me. One Dutch cop I met on the streets of Amsterdam bluntly told me it was easy to assign blame in auto-bike crashes. "It's always the car's fault," he said. In a sense, Dutch drivers are treated like hunters. They are the ones with the dangerous weapon and they are assumed to be at fault if they shoot another person in the woods, even if it's a clueless hiker who has wandered off the trails and is not wearing bright clothing.

Our group from Portland talked about this with Roelof Wittink, a phlegmatic Dutchman in his fifties who has been involved with bike issues since he was a young researcher at the country's major traffic safety institute. Now he runs the Utrecht-based Interface for Cycling Expertise, which consults on cycling projects in cities around the world. One of ICE's most notable projects involved working with the city of Bogota in Columbia to build a major system of bikeways. Bogota's former mayor, Enrique Penalosa, now spends much of his time in New York City and has become a major figure in the international livable cities movement.

"We are still trying to figure out how to bring cars down" to a more reasonable level, said Wittink as he walked with the Portlanders from the train station to his office in the old-town section of Utrecht, about an hour south of Amsterdam. "There are still fights going on." We crossed over a highway aimed at the heart of downtown that displaced part of a canal and was meant to ring the city. But opponents had stopped the road before it was completed, Wittink explained. Residents did not want to sacrifice the canal-laced character of their old town. Now they're fighting over whether to abolish parking next to a remaining stretch of canal to improve the pedestrian ambience. For years after World War II, Wittink said, Dutch planners thought that accommodating the car would be the sole future of the traffic system. As car ownership rapidly grew in the 1950s, Amsterdam officials even considered a plan to fill in up to fifteen of their own world-famous canals to accommodate auto traffic. Dutch journalist Geert Mak quotes a city official from Rotterdam, the Dutch industrial city razed by German bombers in World War II, as once remarking, "We in Rotterdam know from experience that traffic demands space. I once said during a lecture that Rotterdam had the 'privilege' to have been bombed."

However, many Dutch weren't interested in paving over the cities the Nazis did spare. And they were less wedded to the car for urban transportation because cycling runs so deep in Holland's culture. To this day, a favorite Dutch gibe at the Germans is "give me back my bike," a reference to how the Nazi occupiers took their bikes for the steel and rubber during World War II. "A very bad action," one Wehrmacht commander noted in a report, "the worst one can do to a Dutchman, is take away his bike. He is—so to say—born with it." By the early seventies, protests about car-centric policies had become a regular feature in Amsterdam, Utrecht, and other cities. Traffic deaths were escalating, the historic centers of Dutch cities were threatened, and the environmental movement was gaining enthusiastic adherents. The 1972 Club of Rome report, arguing that economic growth could not continue because of its drain on natural resources, was particularly influential in the Netherlands. Then there was the 1973 Arab oil embargo, initially aimed at two countries that had supported Israel: the United States and the Netherlands. The Dutch quickly imposed car-free Sundays to save on suddenly scarce oil. Wittink, then a college student, remembers the sight of people bicycling on empty freeways.

Bicycling on the empty macadam may have been fun, but the Arab oil embargo scared people, Wittink said in a later conversation with me. "All of a sudden you get a different perspective. We were afraid that we could not use the car in a boundless way, but maybe you have to use it a little more selectively ... We had to take control of the future, and maybe that was the most important thing." With a series of policy documents and demonstration projects—and the prodding of the newly formed Dutch Bicyclists Union—the national government reoriented its philosophy. Transit, bicycling, and walking would be encouraged for short trips, particularly in urban areas. Local streets would be designed for the safety of the most vulnerable users, not to carry the maximum number of cars. On busier streets, the Dutch developed a sophisticated network of cycletracks, which are dedicated bikeways separated from motor-vehicle traffic (more about them later in this chapter and in Chapter 7 when I discuss safety issues).

Land-use planning encouraged businesses and housing near train stations and there were attempts, albeit often unsuccessful, to spur people to live near their jobs. Even on the highways, the government pushed to preserve the space for the movement of freight—a crucial sector of the Dutch economy—over lone commuters in their cars.

Officials admit they've only been partially successful at that. Motor vehicle mileage continues to climb and traffic congestion is a huge issue in the Randstad, the western region of the country that includes most of the population.

However, just on the basis of traffic safety, the Dutch experiment has been a marked success. It has the lowest per-capita vehicle death rate in Europe, with the exception of the island nation of Malta. At just under five deaths per hundred thousand people, it is about a third of the U.S. rate. Since, 1987, the Netherlands has cut total traffic fatalities roughly in half, to 791 in 2007. In comparison, the U.S.—despite widespread adoption of airbags, broader seatbelt use, and tougher drunk-driving laws—had a decline of just over 6 percent. If we had the Dutch record, we would be saving some twenty-five thousand Americans a year from gruesome, violent deaths. Of course, American safety officials like to focus on our deaths per vehicle mile driven, and on that basis the U.S. did have big improvements, until the last few years at least. But the Dutch are also safer than the U.S. even on a per-mile basis. And they have also done a better job at reducing traffic injuries. "The data say, everywhere that cycling is promoted, you contribute to road safety," said Wittink. "It is not the case that when you promote cycling that you get more road fatalities. In fact it is the other way around and it has to do with the fact that you have more cyclists on the road, so you force another kind of interaction between car drivers and cyclists. You need a critical mass of cyclists before car drivers realize that they have to share the road." In the final analysis, he said, "You change your traffic system in a way that it makes the system safer, not only for cyclists but for pedestrians and for car drivers. It has to do with speed limitation, which you need anyway in inner cities."

Ah, speed. Like in the U.S., "speed kills" is a hoary slogan in the Netherlands. But there they really seem to mean it. With the Portland group, I visited a special police speed-enforcement team near Utrecht that bristled with enough high-tech gear to merit a CSI spin-off. We sat in a high-speed chase car filled with electronic equipment that can instantly read a vehicle's license plate and tell the police whether it's stolen or has not undergone the required safety checks. Photo radar is widespread and on one highway entering into Amsterdam, electronic devices record when a car enters a certain point on the road and then calculates its average speed when it leaves the section. In urban areas, 30-kilometer-per-hour zones—about 19 mph—have become commonplace as part of the government's "sustainable safety" program. I've seen people drive in parking lots faster than that in the States. I've probably done it myself. Fred Wegman, who directs Holland's Institute for Road Safety Research, said that Dutch authorities have strong public support for decreasing speeds. "There's a strong political and social interest to save vulnerable road users, to protect vulnerable road users, to protect children, to protect elderly people" who are bicycling and walking, he said.

For all that, Amsterdam traffic can look quite chaotic on the busiest streets if you're not someone like Geller who studies this stuff for a living and can appreciate the dance steps. I often saw cyclists running red lights, riding the wrong direction on one-way streets, and weaving through thickets of pedestrians with abandon. And did I mention that no one is wearing a bike helmet? In the inner city, ringed by a spider's web of canals and narrow streets, tourists are often hazy on the difference between a bikeway and a sidewalk (and sometimes there isn't a sidewalk at all). The city's legendary mix of legal prostitution and drug emporiums—called, humorously enough, "coffeehouses," as if everyone is just waiting for Starbucks to enter this line of business—attracts a young, hard-drinking crowd from all over the world, and they roam the tourist areas with a certain abandon. Some older Dutch people from more sedate towns (where cyclists wait obediently at red lights) say they won't ride in Amsterdam.

To get a sense of how Amsterdam makes the chaos work, I went to visit Jack Wolters, the city's top traffic-safety officer. I arrived early at the Department of Infrastructure, Traffic and Transport, hard by

Young cyclists in Utrecht pedal home together after school. School buses are rare in the Netherlands, where most secondary students bicycle to school. (Photo by Jeff Mapes)

the Nieuwe Vaart canal. So I sat and watched the variegated stream of traffic on the boulevard in front of the nearby central train station. Suddenly, I saw a woman riding with an arm on the shoulder of her youngster, cycling next to her. A common sight, except they were riding against traffic and a van was headed toward the two. It got even more complicated as a motor scooter roared around the van and squeezed by the bikes. But everyone managed to miss each other. Okay, I thought, this meeting should be interesting.

Wolters, a bearish man with an un-Dutch-like fondness for Hawaiian shirts, shrugged off the bad behavior I saw on the streets outside. "When the speeds are low, the consequences are not severe" if there is a crash, he said. And then he launched into his set lecture—which he has now given literally to visitors from around the world—about how Amsterdam has cut its traffic deaths from a high of about one hundred ten a year to somewhere around twenty now. Just as in the rest of the country, the city has sought to move cyclists to cycletracks separated from motorists on arterials where speeds are high. At the same time, officials have been working to create 30 kph zones through most of the local streets in the city. They don't just toss up new signs, either. They engineer the roads to produce lower speeds, by narrowing streets or making drivers cross over sidewalk-high bumps to enter these streets. The zones grew out of the Dutch experiments in the 1970s with "woonerfs"— or shared streets—where cars, cyclists, walkers, and even children would all use residential street space. I saw these shared street spaces in Groningen. To my eye, they had a similarity to the parking lots of working-class apartment complexes, where playing children, chatting neighbors, and carefully moving cars shared the parking lot. The idea of different road users negotiating over the use of space has spread to some Dutch towns, where officials are experimenting with removing all of the traffic signals.[1] "Then the car driver doesn't know what is happening," chuckled Wolters, explaining that it forces drivers to be more careful.

Wolters was surprisingly adamant in dismissing the notion that the police should target cyclists or pedestrians who violate traffic laws (with the exception of the requirement that cyclists have lights at night; the police do regard that as important and well worth enforcing). "The target of the police is not to control cyclists and pedestrians," he said. "It is to control the most dangerous part, motorcar drivers."

He betrayed a peculiarly Dutch kind of pragmatism—the same kind, it occurred to me, that led them to allow the drug

---

1. Dutch engineer and traffic planner Hans Monderman pioneered the concept of removing traffic controls to force drivers to negotiate their way along the road. "The many rules strip us of the most important thing: the ability to be considerate," Monderman, who died in 2008, told the German magazine *Der Spiegel* in 2006. "We're losing our capacity for socially responsible behavior." The concept, which some call "naked streets," has spread to several towns in Europe.

and prostitution trades. It's not because the Dutch are particularly libertine. Instead, many joke about the rather staid, albeit tolerant, Dutch lifestyle. But they think it makes more sense to regulate these vices than to fight the black market. Similarly, the Dutch don't see much sense in going after cyclists and walkers when the only people they are putting at risk are themselves. "It's their choice," shrugged Wolters. Once again, the statistics seem to bear him out. Amsterdam has been averaging about six or seven cycling deaths a year, a remarkably low number considering the large number of cyclists on the street every day and the fact that the city hosts a large number of risk-taking young people, from college students to sin-seeking tourists.

One influential 2003 study, by researchers John Pucher and Lewis Dijkstra, found American cyclists were at least three times as likely to get killed as Dutch cyclists, while American pedestrians faced at least six times the danger of dying.[2] Unlike in America, where far more men cycle than women, in the Netherlands woman average more trips by bike than men. And the average Dutch man or woman over the age of sixty-five makes a bike trip almost every other day. If you needed evidence for the "safety in numbers" theory, you can find it in Holland. Caspar Chorus, a transportation researcher at Eindhoven University, said Dutch drivers—who usually have small cars with stick shifts—can have a lead foot at times. But he said they also have a keen respect for cyclists, and that makes all the difference. "I think it is because all their children are on their bikes," he said. "People know it is dangerous to just go

---

2. One unusual way to look at Holland's safety for bicyclists is that a relatively high proportion of cycling fatalities are among the elderly, who are more at risk of being injured if they fall or are in a collision. In 2005, 23 percent of those who died cycling were sixty-five or older. In the U.S. about 10 percent of cycling fatalities were in that age group, almost certainly because they make up a smaller percentage of on-road cyclists than in the Netherlands, where it is common to see elderly bicyclists in traffic.

into their streets and not watch out for cyclists. People have this image that they have to look out for their children because they are vulnerable." This attitude is reinforced by the educational system, which begins to teach children at a young age how to safely cycle on city streets. And watching out for cyclists and pedestrians is an important part of a driver's training as well. By the time children are in what would be the equivalent of our middle school, they are mostly riding to school. As a result, school buses are also a rare sight in the Netherlands.

With all the support for cycling, it was enough to make me wonder what it was like to drive in Amsterdam. So I dragooned Micon Schorsij, a thirty-eight-year-old Amsterdam resident I met through a friend from Portland, to give me a rush-hour tour of the city in his dark green Citroën sedan. Micon, who has a friendly, open face framed by short black curls, lives with his wife and two young children in a condominium apartment in a newly renovated area west of the central city. The old warehouse district is now crammed with stylish new housing, similar in feel to many of the emerging residential areas in reviving city centers around the U.S. As we walked to his car, he explained that he didn't want to pay the extra $39,000 it would cost for a parking space in the garage under his building. So he forks out $78 every six months for a permit that allows him to hunt for a space on the street in his neighborhood. "I think what we're looking for is a little trouble," he said impishly as he unlocked his car. Clearly, he didn't think that would be hard.

"A lot of times I think, 'Why do I have a car?'" he added as we eased out onto the road. "I use it to visit friends and family, to go on trips. That's about it." He rides his bike to his work as a project manager for an internet company. The two-mile commute takes him about fifteen minutes. He and his wife also do their grocery shopping by bike, ferry their kids around by bike, and let their car sit most days of the week. In fact, he said he was thinking about selling his aging Citroën and signing up with a car-sharing company. Everything about owning a car is expensive, from taxes to insurance. Micon didn't get his driver's license until he was thirty, and only after shelling out the equivalent of more than two thousand dollars for the lengthy series of lessons required of all would-be drivers.

By now, we've negotiated several "shark's teeth" intersections—Micon has to think a moment before realizing that he has indeed occasionally seen a stop sign—and are turning onto the Marnixstraat. This arterial is part of a ring road that encircles the central city, and it is also a major thoroughfare for bikes and for the tram. Wolters had showed me some slides of conflict zones along this very route that weren't easy to fix. Micon calmly turned onto the street, as a cyclist zipped by in front of him. "Now I have to take care of bicycles, cars, and trams," he said. "But usually you go slowly and it works out." He shrugged. "There's no place to drive fast here." Nevertheless, even though it is around 6:30 p.m., we moved along without much delay. Either Amsterdam's rush hour ends early or it's not very fearsome. Micon tends to think the latter. "If you've ever been in London or New York, this is nothing, of course," he said. After a while, we turned toward the heart of downtown. We cruised down a narrow street, lined by bollards on either side to prevent parking, as cyclists came from both directions (it's what's known as a "contra-flow" street, one-way for cars, two-way for bikes) and pedestrians rushed around the edges. I felt like I was in a tank lumbering through a street fair. "On this street, they do not care," said Micon with a laugh. "There are so many bikes, they do not care about the cars." Micon said he's become a more cautious cyclist as he's gotten older and started a family. We watched a woman on a pink bike weave dangerously in and out of traffic. "Sometimes I just think, 'Do these people want to die?' Even when I'm not in a car, I see some people on a bike or a pedestrian, I don't know … ," he said, searching for the right words. "They trust in God probably," he concluded.

Maybe I was just diverted by the conversation, but it seemed like we were out in front of Central Station, the heart of Amsterdam, in a surprisingly short amount of time. I told Micon he actually could drive his car to work almost as quickly as he could travel by bike. Of course, that's unrealistic, he pointed out. Parking is prohibitively expensive—at least $26 a day, he said. City officials are pretty clear that they don't like cars in the central city. Ria Hilhorst, Amsterdam's bike coordinator, said local officials would like to adopt something like London's congestion fee on cars entering the central city. However, the national government won't let the city do that. Miriam van Bree, a lobbyist for the Dutch Cyclists' Union, said political leaders don't want to alienate constituents who do bring their cars into the city. Even in Holland, government officials are wary about getting on the wrong side of motorists.

We drove next to the Prinsengracht Canal, past the tourists waiting to get into the Anne Frank House. Micon finally found some trouble when he turned up an even narrower side street. Suddenly he found himself radiator-to-radiator with a black Audi. Micon noted the German license plate on the car, prompting him to explain how easy it is to miss the one-way-only signs. The German motorist carefully backed up as Micon explained how he's sometimes found himself on streets where only trams and taxis are allowed, with no obvious way out. Clearly, driving in Amsterdam takes some thinking.

We drove by a gas station where fuel was selling for twice what it was in the U.S.—and American drivers are complaining about the cost, I told Micon. "It's almost for free," he exclaimed of U.S. prices. After a quick spin on an antiseptic highway that rings the city, we eventually made our way back to Micon's neighborhood, where he was pleased to find a convenient parking spot. We walked to a nearby pub and sat at an outside table on a narrow street where cars aren't allowed at all. It was hard to believe we were in a major city. The dominant sound was the chatter from inside the pub, mixed with the rattle of cyclists riding over the cobblestones.

Occasionally I could hear the whine of a motorcycle on a nearby street but it occurred to me that Amsterdam had to be the quietest big city I'd ever visited. As he sipped his beer and answered my questions, Micon betrayed no particular dismay at the difficulty of moving around Amsterdam by car. "Using a bicycle for me is not a disadvantage," he said. "It is just normal." At the same time, unlike every American bike commuter I've ever met, he didn't wax eloquent about the virtues of his bicycle or the joy of his ride to work. "It's just a tool," he said with a shrug.

The typical Dutch bike does seem to have the practicality of an everyday appliance. Most have fully enclosed chain guards that protect pant legs and help keep the chain from rusting when the bike is left out in the rain. Sturdy racks on the rear of the bikes can hold the weight of another person, and it's hard to think of a cuter sight than a couple on a date, the woman perched sidesaddle on the rack with her arm around her beau's waist. Skirt guards over the rear wheels keep long coats or dresses from getting caught in the spokes. Tires are usually wide enough to avoid getting stuck in train tracks and coaster brakes are common so you can steer the bike while holding, say, an umbrella in the other hand. The idea is that riders can hop on their bike and go, garbed in whatever they happen to be wearing. That is why almost nobody wears a helmet. It would just make riding that much more inconvenient, and bicycling seems plenty safe as it is. My Portland group was quite impressed when we arrived at one government building just as a city councilman rode in on his bike, wearing an immaculate gray suit, white shirt, and stiffly knotted tie. And no helmet hair, either. And here is another piece of Dutch pragmatism: they also like the bicycle because it is cheap, for riders and for the taxpayer. Hilhorst, Amsterdam's bike coordinator, said the city spends about $26 million a year on bike projects, which would be a windfall for bikes in most American cities. But in Amsterdam, it's only about 5 percent of the transportation budget while supporting the 40 percent of all non-walking trips that are by bike.

A cyclist in Amsterdam uses a typical Dutch cycletrack,
which physically separates riders from motor vehicles.
Cycletracks are commonly used on higher speed roads.
(Photo by Jeff Mapes)

Unfortunately, in Amsterdam at least, parking the bike can offset some of the time savings. While the city did invest in a multi-story bicycle-parking garage with room for twenty-five hundred bikes next to Central Station, it's not always easy to find a secure parking spot in the city. And it will need to be secure, since about 10 percent of the city's bikes are stolen every year, according to Hilhorst. That's a big reason why so many Amsterdammers ride such battered bikes, which they protect with heavy chain-link locks. Hilhorst said the city has been pushing the police to make combating theft a higher priority. In several other Dutch cities I visited, the bike fleet seemed a little spiffier, and people often got away with using a simple—and fast—key-operated lock that prevents the rear wheel from turning.

As I said, for many Amsterdammers the bike seems to be barely worth talking about. That was a common reaction I got when I spent an afternoon talking with average cyclists who spoke English. Near the Van Gogh Museum, I chatted with Martine Nijstad, twenty-five, who lived in Amsterdam but was studying business at a university in Rotterdam. "It's just too crowded, so you're better off with a bicycle in the city," she said. "I just ride it to get where I'm going. We don't have beautiful bikes like you do in the U.S." She was looking forward to establishing herself in business and buying a nice car. Her face lit up at that prospect. Still, she added, she'd continue to bike in the city. "We're very impatient people," she said, "we're always on the run. It takes too long by car." I heard variations on that all day long, although some people did talk about the environmental and health benefits of bicycling. One college student told me that her father was fat because he drove everywhere, even the half-mile to the grocery store. I thought how rarely I had ever heard average people in America make that connection. Several people said they didn't like to ride in the rain, of which there is plenty in this country by the North Sea. But they also said it was just generally best to get on with it. "Sometimes I take the tram when it is raining, but then I have to wait and I just think, 'I could have biked it by now,'" said Jetske Witte, a nurse. One day, while riding with my Portland group in Groningen, we were caught in a rainstorm. At a stoplight, I noticed that we were the only people wearing gloves. The Dutch, indeed, were just getting on with what was probably a short ride. In fact, the average bike trip in the Netherlands is only fifteen minutes, according to the government statisticians.

When the system works right, bicycling can be so workaday that it still amazes me, fixated as I am by the demands of girding myself to play bicycle road warrior on the streets of America. One drizzly Sunday afternoon in Amsterdam, my wife Karen and I sat under an awning at a café, sipped espresso, and watched the traffic on a narrow one-way street on the north side of the Princen Gracht canal. It was an ordinary Amsterdam street, one that was marked as neither a major route for cars or for bikes. In a half hour, I counted twenty-six cars, twenty-six bikes, and one scooter. The bicyclists looked so utterly ordinary. Here's who they were:

A thirty-ish woman holding an umbrella, on a classic black bike.

A man in his twenties in a blue raincoat on a black bike.

A man in his fifties, in a leather jacket, on a battered black bike.

A man in his late twenties wearing a baseball cap on a white folding bike.

Another man of roughly same age on an old black bike, jeans jacket, riding the wrong way.

A man in his sixties, red jacket, black bike.

A fifty-ish man in a suit coat on a red bike. Next to him, a woman on a red bike.

Three young people, tourists probably, on bright red rental bikes.

A woman, maybe her thirties, with white slacks, black top, on a nice black bike with white fenders.

A young woman with striking blonde hair on a white bike.

Two men on a bike, one perched on the rack. Driver is balding, younger man on back.

A woman with a daughter on the back of her bike. She turns the wrong way onto the road. Pedals off out of sight.

A young man bicycling while dressed in black, carrying a folded umbrella, even though the drizzle is turning into rain.

A woman, looking to be in her forties, with blonde hair, brown pants, darker brown jacket. You'd peg her for a mini-van driver in the U.S. She's on a black bike.

A six- or seven-year-old boy in blue jeans and denim jacket rides by. A man on a bike rides next to him, also wearing a denim jacket.

A clean-cut, late-twenties man in a corduroy jacket, on a battered old bike. Black, of course.

A couple in their thirties on one old black bike; she's riding sidesaddle on the back. They look comfortably married. They're going the wrong way as they chat companionably in Dutch.

A cyclist in blue raingear, hood tightly buttoned up around his head.
A women on a black bike with a large wicker basket, maybe in her
  thirties, a little girl, under ten, riding next to her.
A twenties blonde woman talking on her cell phone while riding.
A fifty-ish woman in a black trench coat, on a basic black bike.
A man with toddler on rear seat of black bike.

Not a single person looked like they wore anything special to bicycle. It is true that early on a weekend morning, you will see packs of lycra–clad and helmeted riders on lightweight road bikes heading out to the countryside. And even during rush hour, you'll see the occasional rider in full cycle-racing regalia eschewing the cycletracks to speed along the main road with cars. You can also find celebrants of the traditional Dutch bicycling culture. I shared an espresso with Wessel van den Bosch, an animated artist/bike builder who runs the Frame Fiets Gallery in a quiet neighborhood of stylish shops and graceful stone apartment buildings. Wessel originally included bicycles built by others in his gallery only as a counterpoint to the art on the walls. But the idea of re–imagining the classic Dutch bike in bright colors and elegant curves captured his imagination, so he learned how to build bikes. He also insisted that his creations be practical. He built one for a masseur who needed to be able to carry his table to clients. Another customer delivers specialty foods. But one buyer, from Phoenix, simply hung the bike on his wall as art. "It's like sailing with a ship, that's what riding a bike is like for me," Wessel said. "When you drive, you are tense here," he added, pointing to his chest. "And when you ride, you are relaxed here," he said, pointing to his stomach.

The Dutch cycling model has been adopted most enthusiastically in Copenhagen, which is now seen by many bike advocates as the world's most innovative bicycle city. While cycling has always been popular in Denmark, the growth curve for cycling has been striking as the city installed bikeways and made driving in the city less convenient.[3] In the early 1970s, according to a city report, motorists outnumbered cyclists during morning peak hours by about three to one. By 2003, the lines diverged and cyclists now outnumber motorists. (It should also be noted that transit has also grown in popularity.) Cycling has also been an integral part of Copenhagen's drive—if you'll pardon the pun—to create lively outdoor spaces that have transformed the feel of the city. Legendary planner Jan Gehl, who in 2007 became a consultant for New York City, is often regarded as the father of Copenhagen's livable city movement. When Copenhagen began creating pedestrian streets and public plazas in the 1960s, "there was a furious public debate," Gehl said in a documentary, *Contested Streets*, produced for Transportation Alternatives in New York. "[People said] it would never work in Denmark. 'We are Danes, we are not Italians, we will not come out, we will not walk. We have no tradition for urban life or whatever and all the businesses will go broke.'" Instead, he said, shopkeepers thrived as residents flocked to appealing outdoor spaces. Gradually, with no master plan, the city expanded the number of public spaces and built a dense network of cycletracks while taking space from the automobile. One of the city's recent innovations is the "green wave" along one popular cycle route. Traffic lights are now timed so that cyclists can travel about 12 miles an hour without stopping during the inbound and outbound commutes. Roughly a third of the city's trips are by bike and people seem to be plenty happy about it. In fact, researchers from the University of Leicester have proclaimed Denmark as the world's happiest country. So much for the melancholy Danes. A story by ABC News cited Denmark's prosperity, economic equality, and dense social networks as major reasons for the country's high marks. But the pleasures of riding a

---

3. It should be noted, also, that taxes on the purchase of a car in Denmark outweigh the cost of the car itself, so there is a significant disincentive to driving.

bike also seem to have an impact. As the story concluded, "[P]erhaps the bicycle is the best symbol of Danish happiness. Danes can all afford cars, but they choose bikes—simple, economical, nonpolluting machines that show no status and help keep people fit."

The humble bicycle is also beginning to attract broader attention in Europe outside of the Netherlands, Denmark, and Germany (which ranks third on the continent in the mode share for bikes). Obesity is a growing concern and it is not lost on observers that those three countries have among the lowest obesity rates in Europe. The Dutch rate of 10 percent is about a third of that in the U.S. The Dutch also have lower rates of heart disease and the elderly report higher levels of physical wellbeing. Concern about global climate change has also grown rapidly after the turn of the century, and the European Union has committed itself to tougher reductions in auto emissions than the U.S. That's one big reason that European transport guidelines explicitly encourage non-motorized travel in cities. But it's not the only one. "Cycling is a relatively low-cost way to improve transportation in urban areas," said Mary Crass, an official with the European Conference of Ministers of Transport. "The investment is not nearly as expensive as the most minimal public transit improvement." The ministers' support for cycling is not binding on national governments, but the European Commission is also studying green transport policies that could carry teeth. What there does seem to be, Crass said, is strong agreement among transport officials that they want to reduce auto travel in urban areas—a position long ago arrived at in the Netherlands and Denmark. In fact, curbing the auto beast in the inner city has become a major political issue, with London at ground zero. The city's cage-rattling mayor, Ken Livingstone, in 2003 imposed a stiff congestion fee on all vehicles entering the central city. The charge cut traffic in the central city by about 16 percent while raising millions of dollars for additional public transit. The city also stepped up its efforts to encourage bicycling, with ridership climbing by 49 percent between 2002 and 2006. And, just as in many American cities, bicycle commuters are now becoming a common sight on London streets, where few were seen before. In 2008, Livingstone unveiled a $1 billion plan to boost cycling that would include the development of twelve bicycle superhighways that would crisscross the city. "We want nothing short of a cycling transformation in London," announced Livingstone, who said he was aiming for a quadrupling of the number of cyclists by 2025. However, Livingstone was defeated when he stood for re-election later in 2008 by Conservative Party candidate Boris Johnson. While Johnson criticized some of Livingstone's proposals for toughening the congestion charges, he supported the basic program. And Johnson was an avid cyclist himself who regularly rode to his pre-mayoral job as a member of Parliament. Cycling has also caught the eye of Britain's Conservative Party leader, David Cameron, who has been trying to rebrand his party with a more moderate, environmentally friendly image. As part of that image, he also often cycled to Parliament, although the British press was quick to pounce when it emerged that, on at least a couple of occasions, a driver had followed him with a thick stack of his work papers.

However, it is in Paris where the most stunning change in the role of the bicycle has occurred. Mayor Bertrand Delanoe has also been waging an aggressive campaign to restrict car travel in the central city for years. He riled many suburban commuters by shutting down a highway along the Seine during the summers. Now the city trucks in sand to create an artificial beach along the river. Cyclists and rollerbladers use what road surface is left for car-free travel and recreation. Delanoe made his biggest splash in bicycle circles in the summer of 2007 when he introduced the world's largest bike-sharing program. The city flooded Paris with ten thousand bikes paid for by advertising giant JCDecaux, which in turn received free billboard space from the city. For a small annual fee, Parisians use a plastic card to release the bikes from their high-tech docking stations. To encourage their use for short trips, the first half hour is free. Known as *Velib'*—short for *velo libre*, or free bike—the program was an immediate hit and the city expanded to more than twenty thousand bikes at some 1,450 stations. The sight of Parisians taking to the streets on the sturdy gray bikes (reportedly somewhat clunky but outfitted with a useful basket, fenders, and chain guards) generated worldwide publicity and inspired rival London to study setting up its own program. Several American cities are also looking at the idea, with Washington, D.C., the first to start a small pilot program with one hundred twenty bikes. In Paris, while *Velib'* has been a success, not everything has worked as Delanoe intended. As driving in the city becomes more inconvenient, there has been a huge increase in motorcycles, which many Parisians regard as more obnoxious and dangerous than autos, according to a report in the *Times* of London.

The Dutch have had their struggles as well. Immigrants from outside Europe, who make up a growing part of the population, are less likely to cycle. Many two-income families are spurred to drive because their workplaces, home, and their children's school are widely separated. Chorus, the Eindhoven transportation researcher, said he's struck by how many colleagues wistfully tell him they would like to cycle to work, but cannot because of the spread-out nature of their daily life. Dutch officials in many cities are also working hard to continue to make it safe for children to bike and walk to school—and to make their parents feel it is safe for them to do so. Van Bree, the cyclists' union lobbyist, criticized the national government for refusing to allow Amsterdam to implement a London-style congestion charge. "Cars on the main roads are fine with me," she said. "The problem with the car is in the central city." However, I suspect that Micon Schorsij, my friendly driver, speaks for a lot of his countrymen when he said, "People use a bike, but if they have a choice they use the convenience of the car." In a follow-up email several months later, Micon told me he had sold his aging Citroën. But he wound up buying a newer one. Despite all of its costs, he still wanted his own car.

Still, the Dutch success with cycling has had an undeniable impact in the U.S. Bike advocates have been able to point to the safety successes in the Netherlands to counter John Forester and his followers, who argue that any kind of special bike facilities are dangerous. Forester remains convinced that the heavy bike ridership in cities like Amsterdam is more a function of the large population of young people and Holland's deep cycling culture than of any special bike facilities. But it is clear his view has lost ground, as bike lanes, trails, and traffic-calmed streets become more common in the U.S. What are not common in the U.S. are the separated cycletracks routinely built in the Netherlands. Even many of the biggest fans of Dutch bicycling question whether they would work well in the U.S. without wholesale changes in our streets, traffic laws, and driving culture (a simple first step of banning right turn on red, which is not allowed in the Netherlands, would be a tough sell by itself).

When Atlanta Mayor Shirley Franklin was quoted in a Danish newspaper praising the separated bikeways she saw in Copenhagen during a 2006 visit, it touched off a furious exchange of posts on the List-serv of the Association of Pedestrian and Bicycle Professionals. Several planners and bike advocates—including the head of Atlanta's major bicycle group—argued that such facilities would be misguided in the U.S., as well as too expensive for overburdened local transportation budgets. And some cited studies suggesting they were more dangerous in European cities too, although others argued that wasn't the case for properly designed cycletracks. As I read the studies and arguments, they seemed to me to almost take on a religious tone. And one thing I noticed: the people most enthusiastic about Netherlands-style cycletracks were those who had spent the most time there.[4]

---

4. Forester, in contrast, said that, besides a childhood train journey through Holland before World War II, he has never been in the country. "However," he told me in an e-mail, "I have several cycling associates

Anne Lusk, a visiting scientist at the Harvard School of Public Health, who frequently raises the blood pressure of many bike planners with her adamant pro-separated-bike-path views, made this argument:

In the 1970s, on[-]road bicyclists, primarily white males, lobbied for and were successful at getting bicycle facilities on the road on which "they" could ride. In the 1970s in Europe, the white males lobbied for and achieved getting bicycle facilities on which "everyone" could ride. It would appear as if the U.S. population of males did not care about children and seniors? [sic] I know they did because they have children and parents. Did they care for their children and parents by providing busing to school, driving children to school, or providing driving opportunities for seniors and mass transit? Did they listen when the children and seniors said they didn't want to bicycle in the road, even when taught?

Mighk Wilson, the bicycle and pedestrian coordinator for Orlando, has frequently tangled with Lusk on-line, arguing that such things as high car and gas taxes and parking restrictions have more to do with high rates of cycling than do cycletracks (which he also thinks lead to more crashes). "I agree that if you have an increased number of cyclists you reduce the risk per individual, but I wonder where the increase in cyclists came from," he wrote. "If they were new trips and we can be fairly certain the cycletracks were responsible for the increase, then it seems like a reasonable trade-off. But if the increases were due to other policies (say, reduced auto parking supply) or social factors, then the increase in crashes is troubling. Even more troubling would be if the increase in bicycle trips on the cycletrack streets was due to cyclists shifting from other streets without cycletracks. If that is the case, continued cycletrack construction would be quite unethical."

---

who have cycled there, and they inform me that they didn't like cycling there for reasons which I see as eminently reasonable and conforming to my feelings about the few imitations implemented here."

Still, cycletracks are gaining a foothold in the U.S. As I discuss in a later chapter, New York City is conducting an important experiment with an American-style cycletrack that could influence cities around the country. And by 2008, Portland was looking at installing a cycletrack on a street that the city was planning to completely rebuild in any case. Geller said the city was unlikely to quickly build a large network of cycletracks, both for cost and logistical reasons. But it's only the latest example of how the city has looked to European bike treatments as Geller and his predecessor, Mia Birk built Portland's bike network. In a nod to the special coloration of Dutch bikeways, they created blue bike lanes in problematical intersections to quickly warn motorists they might be crossing a cyclist's path. Portland's network of directional signs and pavement markings to guide cyclists was inspired by Amsterdam's signage. In recent years, Geller and other Portland bike advocates have pushed hard to create bike boulevards—which are designed to discourage through auto traffic while providing direct routes for cyclists—that would run near major arterials.

While Portland is still working on this, it's a lot further along than most cities. Adam Fukushima, who runs the San Luis Obispo County Bicycle Coalition, became a bike advocate after a fellowship in Groningen, where more than 38 percent of all trips are by bike, the highest in the Netherlands. But he doesn't make a big deal about that. "When I talk to city staff, I never mention Holland," he explained. "We're not Holland. I just talk about Portland. It's more immediate to people. If I talked about Holland, people would say we're not Holland, we're not Europe." So, in other words, he launders Netherlands thinking through Portland.

Geller often talks about wanting to replicate Amsterdam's feel in Portland. He looks like a Dutch rider, favoring dark street clothes and dress shoes. He uses an unobtrusive pants clip to protect his nice slacks. He finally broke down and bought a pair of neoprene booties to cover his shoes in the rain, deciding he preferred that to having to change his shoes at work. He rides with ease, too, explaining that he's happy to take a "no sweat pace" in a bike lane. He had also wanted to stop wearing his helmet, which didn't sit well with his family. But after a few years, as Portland's ridership continued to climb by double-digit percentages, he was more likely to be seen riding around town sporting a beret or a straw hat instead of a helmet. Portland may not be Amsterdam yet, but he could feel it starting to get there.

3

Creating the New Urban Bike Culture

As I knocked around the urban bike world, Phil Sano—or Rev. Phil, as everyone called him, because of his mail-order divinity degree—became a Zelig-like figure to me. I showed up at a mini-bike chariot race, and there he was, never giving up no matter how often he'd get whacked off his chariot by a foam-covered lance. I would see him hanging with the bike messengers, competing to stop in the shortest distance using only a stick as a brake. And I was reading about him in the newspaper after he attracted the ire of an off-duty Portland cop at the World Naked Bike Ride and was charged with four misdemeanors, which the D.A. dropped a year later after it became clear that the trial could prove embarrassing to the police.

So I guess I shouldn't have been surprised when, across the continent, I ran into him at the New York City headquarters of Time's Up!, the confrontational bike group embroiled in a War of the Roses-length epic struggle with the city over Manhattan's Critical Mass ride. Phil, pushing thirty, tall, balding, and with an ever-changing repertoire of facial hair, was on one of his periodic forays out of Portland in search of bikey culture (the "y" being important, to distinguish it from people who merely recreated on bikes; these are people who bring their lives, passion, and art to bicycling). He had something complicated going on with a bicycle gang in Richmond, Virginia, of all places, and he decided to stop in New York City for a bracing immersion in the city's bike scene.

It was almost 9 p.m. on one of the first nice days of spring, fully dark out but warm enough so that people would linger in the night air as they prowled the bars and restaurants near the ramshackle Houston Street storefront that housed Time's Up. Phil and I were both heading back to Brooklyn, so we rode together, moving down Bowery in search of the Williamsburg Bridge. Phil, as always, rode fearlessly, even though he had only a glancing idea of where he was going. He pushed through small gaps in traffic and didn't hesitate to grab the middle of the lane on Delancey Street as we looked for the ramp to the bikeway across the bridge. Finally, we saw three guys on swift road bikes head up the middle of Delancey and veer off onto a ramp on the road's median. We hustled our way across another lane of fast-moving traffic and flew up the ramp, exhilarated by the clear path in front of us. As we climbed, Phil bemusedly noted that he was surprised I was keeping up with him given the cheap mountain bike I was riding; he was polite enough not to mention the good twenty years I had on him. The path took us in a kind of steel cage above the traffic rumbling below, and as we reached the apex, Phil told me to look over my left shoulder.

The lights of Manhattan's skyline twinkled back at us as we stopped to take in the view. We were at skyscraper height ourselves, over the inky black East River, and I suddenly felt as powerful and as entitled as the billionaires staring out at the river from their penthouses. They may have their floor-to-ceiling windows and trophy lives, but have they enjoyed the simple freedom of wending through the streets of the most exciting city in the world, feeling the strength in their legs—and then literally climbing above it all? "This is pretty cool," said Phil with a self-satisfied grin. And then I realized, this is what the new urban bike movement is about, creating a new feeling of empowerment and independence. It is also painting a new image of urban hip that is slowly replacing that old picture in America of adult cyclists as either hapless losers or

Phil Sano, known around Portland bike circles as Rev. Phil because of his mail-order diploma, is a mainstay of the local bicycle counterculture. (Photo by Jonathan Maus/ BikePortland.org)

elite but niche athletes in garish spandex. And that's what makes people like Rev. Phil important. They are the preachers and artists of a bicycling community and lifestyle that is just starting to ripple out to the wider American culture—like the young black rappers who emerged from the inner city a quarter century ago to be embraced by young, white suburbanites.

As is always the case at the cutting edge of culture, many of these cyclists have segmented themselves into tight-knit groups designed to flaunt their exclusivity—like the Black Label bike club, which started in Minneapolis, spread to New York and several other cities, and is into mutant "tall bikes," jousting, and of course, partying. But much of this bike culture is open to anyone who wants to participate, like the well-publicized weekly "zoobombs" in Portland that begin with a party in the hills above the city's most expensive neighborhood and end with riders careening down twisting residential streets on tiny children's bikes. Some of it is much more establishment, of course. New York City's annual Five Boro Bike Tour attracts more than thirty thousand riders, making it the country's largest. Portland's annual Providence Bridge Pedal is sponsored by a hospital chain and attracts upward of twenty thousand for a ride over up to ten bridges—including two interstates—that are closed to traffic for the event. Chicago brings out a similar number for its yearly Bike the Drive along Lakeshore Drive, which is also closed to cars during the ride. And several cities are now experimenting with a Latin American export—the ciclovia. These are weekend events where organizers close off a loop of various lengths to cars and then invite residents to turn them into a gigantic rolling street party. More than that, these events invite cyclists, walkers, and even people sitting on their stoop to consider all of the space we turn over to the roads in a different way. Perhaps the best-known group rides are the decidedly unsanctioned—and not-so-mainstream—monthly Critical Mass rides that have become a fixture in cities around the world.

To observers, all of this stuff can be silly or thought provoking, entertaining, or downright exasperating. But it has an undeniable impact on participants, transforming their notion of how it is possible to use the city's streets and of how different their lives become when they transport themselves by bike. As the Rev. Phil likes to say, you can only do so much by building bike lanes and pleading with people to get out of their cars, "but if it's sexy and fun, that's going to make more people want to do it."

And as such, the new bike culture appeals to that lone rebel, an iconic part of our American DNA. There's a certain swagger you see among the young urban riders who have adopted the single-strap shoulder bags, ankle-length knickers, and single-speed fixed-wheel bikes from the bike messenger culture. I still think one of the coolest cyclists I've ever seen is a black guy I glimpsed across a crowded room at Time's Up. Clad in black spandex, he had a shaved head, a heavily muscled body and a jumble of personal electronics that casually dangled from his clothes. He looked like he came from the future, and when I sought him out to talk to him, he had already disappeared.

One of the most popular urban biking videos on YouTube features a group of New York City messengers bursting out of Central Park to fearlessly race down Manhattan's avenues, flying through red lights, weaving around pedestrians, and squeezing between buses and taxis. It is outlaw riding, totally inexcusable and dangerous—and as thrilling to watch as Steve McQueen's famous San Francisco car chase in *Bullitt*. After watching McQueen muscle his Ford Mustang around the city's streets decades ago, I felt that much cooler as I too tooled around the streets of S.F. in my own Mustang. And, once I had also experienced the feeling of cycling in Manhattan, seeing that YouTube video sent that same kind of delicious shiver of recognition through me even though I don't ride like that. Among accomplished urban bikers, dancing around two-ton vehicles on pot-holed city streets is a skill to savor, not something to fear. "You eventually become oblivious to all the traffic," said Kym Perfetto, twenty-six, a personal fitness trainer I met at Time's Up. "You learn to manage it, make it your friend." Standing next to her single-speed fixed-gear bike, tanned and without an ounce of fat, the dimunitive Perfetto is a female version of James Dean shrugging at the dangers of street racing. Actually, she added, "the faster you go, the safer it is." She laughed. "I know it sounds crazy."

And, indeed, most people are never going to ride like Perfetto, who also loves to race at the Queens Velodrome. But her style is beginning to seep into American culture, whether it is the booming sale of messenger bags—the company Timbuk2 started out catering to messengers and parlayed that into a $20 million-a-year business—or the sight of a camo-clad urban cyclist featured in a Liberty Mutual insurance ad, of all things. In one TV commercial for the Ford Escape, an adolescent girl asks her father to drop her a block from the movie theater so that she won't be seen in an

SUV because "people in that part of town are riding bikes and have hybrids and stuff." Pop calmly explains that, hey, the Escape is a hybrid too—and we're left to think that maybe the daughter will eventually migrate to the edgy part of town where she can get around by bike on her own. If the world's best marketers on Madison Avenue are stealing a little hipness from the bicycle, maybe Rev. Phil is growing less counterculture by the day.

On September 30, 2005, I was in San Francisco to participate in the thirteenth-anniversary ride of the world's first Critical Mass, a seminal event in the history of the new urban bike culture. I rode down Market Street through San Francisco's financial district and followed a woman on a bike decorated with fresh flowers into Justin Herman Plaza. It was like entering an outdoor party, one that had attracted a wide variety of cyclists, from clean-cut office workers in slacks and yellow cycling jackets to a young guy in dreadlocks wearing only sneakers and pink briefs. Someone passed around a fat joint as I watched from a small knoll, trying to count the crowd that eventually reached about two thousand. Finally, people began to mount their bikes, there was a chorus of ringing bells and we went back up Market and soon made our way onto Sutter Street. I gaped as I pedaled slowly up a canyon of skyscrapers, feeling a delicious vertigo as I eyed the concrete cliffs. In the middle of a huge pack of cyclists, shorn of any need to focus on traffic, I could appreciate the epic monumentalism of the city in a way I never had before. As we rode through intersections "corked" by riders who kept motorists from breaking up the mass, I couldn't offer any justification for breaking the traffic rules. But I couldn't deny the sheer fun of it.

As it spread around the country, Critical Mass has generated more headlines and more public attention, for good or for ill, than any other bit of urban bike culture. The ride was started by a few cyclists trying to figure out a way to energize San Francisco's emerging bike activism. In Chris Carlsson's anthology, "Critical Mass: Bicycling's Defiant Celebration," Steven Bodzin wrote about how he had thought of replicating his experience in Boston, where he and a small group of bike activists rode around the city every Tuesday morning handing out imitation tickets to motorists and award certificates to cyclists and transit riders. In San Francisco, he met Carlsson, who liked the idea but argued that the ride needed to more closely mirror the kind of society they were trying to create out on the street. They ended up individually distributing their own fliers for a "commute clot" that attracted some fifty riders, "and we had a great old time, riding in the golden evening light, ringing bells, hootin' and hollerin', confusing the world with our happiness," Bodzin related. The newly revived San Francisco Bicycle Coalition officially kept its distance from the ride, but the group's director, Dave Snyder, valued the ride as a way to attract attention to the grievances of cyclists. And he played a role in the crucial branding decision. Shortly after the first commute clots, Snyder went with some friends to see Ted White's bicycle documentary, "Return of the Scorcher," which described how Chinese cyclists would gather at intersections until they had the numbers—the critical mass— they needed to push into the traffic mainstream. Afterwards, Snyder and his friends decided this new ride should be called Critical Mass. It took off in a way that "Commute Clot" probably never could have.

Carlsson, who has come to be Critical Mass's parent figure for his consistent nurturing of the event, figures that the ride has spread to some two hundred fifty cities, towns, and suburbs around the world. While there always seem to be key leaders in the background who keep each ride going, it is officially leaderless and with few rules. Generally, the rides are held on the last Friday of the month, during the evening commute, and with no predetermined route. "My reason for being part of this," Carlsson explained one day as he sat in his Fillmore neighborhood apartment, "was that we wanted the experience of filling the street with bikes. We realized there are a lot of us on bikes already and why don't we come together rather than riding in isolation along the side of the road? You know, creeping along hoping we're not doored or run over by somebody turning right. If we're filling the streets with bikes then we are traffic, and why shouldn't we be?"

Carlsson, a writer who has derived his main income from editing the longshoreman's union newspaper, is a critic of capitalism and its intense focus on consumption instead of shared experience. And, more than anything else, that's what still seems to intrigue him about Critical Mass. "I've argued for years that it doesn't actually have an instrumental purpose," he said. "It's not trying to achieve something. In fact, it's a lived experience that's very different than anything else that is available in this society. ... It's really a place where people come together to have a lot of live experience that's not about commerce and buying and selling, and it's not about what we generally refer to as politics ... Instead, it's about being in the moment, to use something of a New Age way of thinking about it. There is some of that going on, where people just want to have this fresh, direct, engaged ride and experience."

Carlsson conceded that Critical Mass is not always an ideal society. Too often, he said, the ride has been co-opted by overly aggressive young men—who Bodzin called the "testosterone brigade"—who tend to be interested in finding the steepest hill or most confrontational route rather than in putting together a ride that can attract the widest collection of people. And, of course, to many San Franciscans, the ride is a monthly blot on the city that makes the evening rush hour more unbearable and reinforces the image that cyclists act as though they are above the law. As the ride grew in the 1990s, the conflicts with the police worsened, to the point that Mayor Willie Brown ordered a crackdown on the July 1997 ride. More than five thousand riders split into several groups that were chased by police through the streets, ending up in dozens of arrests and even worse congestion that tied up the city's traffic for hours. Eventually, city officials realized it was better to help facilitate the ride than to fight it, and by the time I rode in 2005, it had become a San Francisco institution. The only time I saw police interfere with the ride was when cyclists strayed over the center line of two-way streets to block traffic in both directions.

In fact, buried as I was in the pack of two thousand cyclists, I found it easy to tune out the logistics of the ride. I fell into an engrossing conversation with Jason Henderson, a geography professor at San Francisco State University, who had interesting ideas about how societies fight over public space. I felt for a moment like I was an Oxford don, pedaling leisurely down a country lane talking philosophy with a colleague. Occasionally, I'd hear shouted epithets from blocked motorists that Henderson shrugged off. "Just relax," Henderson advised one fuming motorist, "and turn off your engine." I found myself wondering, by shrugging off the complaints and continuing to ride, am I doing the same thing people do every day when they get behind the wheel of their car and ignore the warfare, the pollution, and the terrorists abetted by our addiction to oil? Or am I making excuses for what is, at heart, a rolling, raucous—and thoroughly extra-legal—party through the streets of San Francisco?

As we coasted downhill toward Fisherman's Wharf, it did indeed feel like a two-wheeled version of New Orleans' Mardi Gras parades. A rider holding a can of beer while he steered with one hand took a tumble when he hit a stretch of cobblestone, but he managed to twist his body as he fell so that he was able to triumphantly hold his beer aloft without spilling a drop. Applause rose from the tourists watching from the sidewalk. Even some of the trapped motorists waved and cheered us on. As we sped downhill through the Broadway Tunnel, a rider on a BMX bike stood on his pedals, pulled a beer can out of his pants, popped the tab, and showily drained it. As we moved toward Union Square, the traffic thickened and the drivers become more annoyed. I squeezed by a limo driver trying to get into his car. "I guess nobody has to work tonight," he complained, to no one in particular. By the time we reached upper Market Street, riders were beginning to peel off and the mass was breaking apart. There were some tense confrontations with motorists, including one young man in a sedan who began to inch forward into a cyclist—known as a "corker"—who was blocking the intersection. The corker stood his ground while placing his hand on the car hood. "Get your hand off my car," yelled the driver. The cyclist didn't budge and yelled back, "Sir, you moved your car out and into me. Put it in reverse!" Another motorist veered over to the opposite side of the street and burned rubber accelerating down the wrong side of Market to escape from the cyclists. A few blocks later, Henderson and I decided to stop for a beer at a tavern that catered to bikers, both motorized and not. In an open backyard, several bicycles hung from hooks on a fence. Henderson talked about how Critical Mass plays a role in making cyclists visible to the public. "In Irish terms, it's like the split between the militant Irish Republican Army and the political party Sinn Fein," he said, with the Critical Massers playing the role of the militants and the mainstream San Francisco Bicycle Coalition able to come in and offer practical solutions for what the city can do to promote bicycle transportation.

Even many bike advocates, however, don't think Critical Mass has advanced the cause of bicycling, particularly in more restrained cities. "In San Francisco, there's a long tradition of political theater and a big majority of people who are tolerant of it," said veteran national bike activist Charlie Gandy, "and that can make the tactic effective ... but I saw it backfire in a number of places." In neighboring Marin County, for instance, Critical Mass died out because it so clearly alienated car-dependent suburbanites more accustomed to earnest community meetings than noisy demonstrations. One day I was talking with Chuck Ayers, executive director of the Cascade Bicycle Club in Seattle, one of the country's strongest bike advocacy groups. When the topic turned to Critical Mass, he picked up a copy of the *Seattle Times* Sunday magazine that featured a Critical Mass ride on the cover. "Look, I support civil disobedience," said Ayers, a former community organizer. "I have been involved in actions, but we always restricted the civil disobedience to the message." He jabbed his finger at one rider who dominated the picture. "Look. Tall bike, beer, and no helmet. There is no message. This does nothing but piss people off." And even in San Francisco, the ride took a big PR hit when a suburban woman and her family in their minivan found themselves in the last stages of a Critical Mass ride in March of 2007 and wound up having their rear window shattered. In several media interviews, she claimed her vehicle was swarmed by cyclists, some of whom ran into the side of her van. Several cyclists disputed her account, saying she had endangered riders by trying to run one of them over. But as I heard the competing voices in a National Public Radio account, it was clear to me the average listener would tend to sympathize with the woman. They could visualize being in a minivan with their kids easier than they could imagine taking over busy city streets with cycles.

Nowhere has the conflict over Critical Mass been so heated as in New York. For years, the monthly ride in Manhattan attracted little police presence, and it was even for a time listed in an airline magazine as an interesting tourist activity. But one of the monthly rides came on the Friday before the start of the 2004 Republican National Convention, which took place under extreme security. The Republicans, of course, were meeting in New York largely to remind voters of President Bush's fight against terrorism in the wake of 9/11, and literally hundreds of thousands of protestors were pouring into the city to remind voters of the growing debacle in Iraq. Police documents that were later released showed that the NYPD had been keeping tabs on Time's Up, along with dozens of other activist groups, and saw the ride as a potential security threat—and I use the phrase "security threat" broadly. In my long experience covering conventions, police see demonstrators who interfere in any way with the flow of the attendees to and from the convention hall as a major problem. The Critical Mass ride before the convention swelled to about five thousand riders, with many carrying political signs. Squads of police swooped in on the riders, corralling many in plastic fencing and eventually arresting 264. Cyclist Tomas Melchor recalled how he was caught up in one of the police sweeps and held for twenty-four hours in an old vehicle-storage warehouse down at the piers. "Some people lying on the ground got rashes from the battery acid, motor oil, and other things," said Melchor, who was sixty-two at the time. "A lot of people got really dirty. I stayed on my feet." Melchor said the charges against him were eventually dismissed, as they were for most of the cyclists. But a new pattern was set. Amidst a flurry of lawsuits and counter-suits, the police continued to take a hard line against the ride, making more arrests each month and charging that riders were violating the law by failing to get a permit. By the time I showed up in March of 2006 to see what the fuss was all about, the standoff had become as institutionalized as the Arab-Israeli conflict. At the ride's start in Union Square, I saw a long row of sixteen police scooters, as well as several vans and other support vehicles. Monitors from the National Lawyers Guild, sporting green baseball caps, stood in clumps, waiting to document how the police treated anyone arrested or ticketed. Bill DiPaola, the director of Time's Up, was in constant motion, conferring with one person after another, like a football coach pacing the sidelines. Mike Pidel, a Time's Up volunteer who planned to videotape the police action, scanned the sky to see if there was police helicopter. "It doesn't look like there are any tonight," he said hopefully. "Sometimes they use spotlights from choppers to focus on people." I decided to hang back in the pack and see how things went as the riders began streaming out onto Park Avenue.

Almost instantly, the police swooped in to pick riders out of the mass as observers crowded around. Scooters and police vans seemed to be everywhere and, within a few blocks, I decided I was better off watching from the sidewalk. After a week of seeing cyclists—and motorists and pedestrians—violate every traffic law in the books on the streets of Manhattan, it was odd to watch the police suddenly writing citations for the most technical of offenses (like failing to ride as far right in the lane as practicable). Pidel suggested that I pick up the now long-gone mass by riding over to southbound Fifth Avenue. Sure enough, several dozen riders passed by on Fifth, closely followed by police scooters. I tucked in behind the police and followed the entire parade down to Washington Square Park, where the riders regrouped. Soon, we were off again, wending our way through narrow streets in Soho, where I stopped to watch the police arrest another rider, a beefy guy named Colin. Several outraged diners emerged from a restaurant to watch the scene. "Just for riding his bike," one guy yelled disgustedly at the police. As cops, riders, and bystanders milled around, one of Colin's friends asked me to watch her bike as she quietly sneaked up to Colin's bike, spirited it away, and locked it up around the corner, in hopes it wouldn't be confiscated. Then she retrieved her own bike and quickly rode off. One of the officers announced to the crowd that Colin had been arrested for blocking traffic and that he had heard that a woman had taken his bike away. "If I find her, I should arrest her too," he said. "That's interfering with a government investigation." Pidel, who had showed up to film the scene, muttered, "Blocking traffic? Cars here do that a thousand times a day."

One of the cops found the bike locked up around the corner and they brought in a chain saw to cut the lock on it. I asked one of the officers what would happen to Colin. "He'll spend the weekend in lockup," he said. Eyeing my notebook, he asked me where I was from. Oregon, I told him, and he softened a bit to talk to the out-of-town hick reporter. "They pissed off the wrong people," he said of the Critical Mass riders. It wasn't just the Republican convention, it was also the fact that the month before the convention, the riders had gone right up onto FDR Drive, the highway next to the East River. "That pissed off somebody way up in Police Plaza," he added. "That's a very dangerous thing to do." Back at Time's Up, I asked

DiPaola about riding on FDR Drive. "That could be," he said with a shrug. "They just keep altering the rules."

I returned to New York a year later, and no peace was at hand. Time's Up released documents showing the city had spent more than $1.3 million fighting Critical Mass in the two years after the Republican convention. And after a judge ruled that the city couldn't stop cyclists from riding in a group, the Police Department responded by passing new regulations prohibiting groups of more than fifty cyclists from riding together without a permit. The new rules took effect for the March 2007 ride, and the news media was out in force, and so were a long list of social activists denouncing the rules as a violation of the Constitution. "Bicycle riders have a First Amendment right of association," said Norman Siegel, the well-known civil liberties lawyer who has taken Critical Mass on as a cause. "They won that in the courts two years ago, and the bicycle riders are traffic and they have the right to be where? In the street." Despite the rhetoric, as soon as the ride began, the police once again quickly began arresting and ticketing riders. As they escorted one woman away, a crowd circled yelling, "Let her go, let her go." The police put her in a squad car and several cops stood in a circle as the crowd surged in. For a moment, it felt like things would spiral out of control. But the squad car backed down the street and the crowd melted away. I walked back to Union Square and saw DiPaola, jubilant about the heavy media coverage. We took the subway to the Time's Up office, where people trickled in with videotape, like scouts from the front lines. We watched footage of another arrest near Times Square. "It's become a game of cat and mouse, basically," said Melchor as he watched. "It draws a lot of media attention … It seems to sway the public in our favor."

But just a few weeks later, another judge turned down a lawsuit aimed at blocking the rules. U.S. District Judge Lewis Kaplan said he had to balance the cyclists' "interests in riding when and where they want and the City's interest in ensuring that all people and vehicles use its streets effectively and safely without overburdening scarce law enforcement resources." In short, the standoff continued. The rides got smaller and increasingly the province of hard-core riders, who in mid-2007 notched up the cat-and-mouse games by breaking off into small groups before meeting at another point. DiPaola and other Time's Up activists acknowledged that Critical Mass no longer gives newbie cyclists a chance to experience riding the city streets within the safety of a crowd. Police officials say they're open to the ride if participants will go through the permitting process, but activists question whether the city would indeed let thousands of cyclists gather during the evening rush hour. Ironically, a monthly Critical Mass ride is held in Brooklyn that has amicable relations with the police, who have even helped speed riders through intersections. And in Seattle and Chicago, the police have also generally forged an informal partnership with riders. I rode in one Critical Mass in Seattle where the police even purposely stayed out of sight to avoid confrontations, and the ride seemed remarkably free of bile. Maybe it was more of that laid-back Northwest attitude, but even many of the motorists waved and laughed at the cyclists.[1]

And, in fact, urban cyclists increasingly have found ways to ride in groups that don't produce police confrontations and battles over turf. I got a good sense of that in the city that really gave birth to the modern American car culture: Los Angeles. One Sunday afternoon, I wandered into the Bicycle Kitchen, a storefront cooperative just off Melrose, about four miles northwest of downtown. Outside, the largely Latino neighborhood was quiet, the sidewalks mostly empty. But inside, a half-dozen bike stands were already in use as knots of volunteers helped customers fix up their bikes. I met Jimmy Lizama, a tall, angular bike messenger who was one of the

---

1. The Seattle ride was marred, however, in July of 2008 when a motorist was beaten after he got in a confrontation with cyclists who said he had driven into a group of riders. The driver said he panicked and was not trying to hit them. The incident certainly demonstrates how the leaderless event can go awry.

co-founders of the coop. Like many cyclists, he surprised himself when he first realized that he could actually bike in L.A. He started riding when he worked at a Hollywood art gallery and decided to try the six-mile commute on bike. "By the time I got to work, I had passed three buses," he said. "I was early to work. I couldn't sleep that night; I was so excited thinking about what I could do." He quickly discovered that, off the main boulevards, there were literally hundreds of miles of wide, relatively quiet streets highly suited to bicycling, particularly in the older parts of L.A., where there was a somewhat intact street grid. With the help of friends, Lizama in 2002 decided to open a bike repair co-op in an unused kitchen in an apartment at Los Angeles Eco-Village, a two-block neighborhood on the edge of Koreatown that residents are working to make a model of sustainable living. The idea, Lizama explained, was to promote bicycling as an affordable transportation alternative by helping people get and fix up cheap bikes. The program quickly outgrew the kitchen and three years later moved into storefront on Heliotrope Drive.

Now the co-op is a center of the burgeoning urban bike scene in Los Angeles. Instead of Critical Mass, the big ride in the city is the monthly Midnight Ridazz, which at times has attracted more than thirteen hundred riders. Instead of mixing it up with rush-hour traffic, these L.A. rides don't start until well after the cocktail hour and they are more about having a good time—this being Hollywood, dressing up in a costume is also often part of it—than with getting in the face of drivers. Riders are encouraged on one Midnight Ridazz Web site to obey traffic rules and to be courteous to motorists (it's telling that the Web site also includes parking tips, since, in this sprawling metropolis, many of the participants get to the ride by driving). "Critical Mass is kind of an anarchical ride for all," cyclist Jim Bledsoe told me as he worked at the Bicycle Kitchen, "and with the Midnight Ridazz, somebody picks a theme, establishes a route, picks a destination—and a lot of times the destination is a party." In fact, the ride became so popular that the founders stepped back and let others form their own offshoots. One Web site I saw listed more than a dozen rides, ranging from mellow evening jaunts to the hard-charging Wolfpack Hustle, which celebrated its one-year anniversary with a night-time, one-hundred-mile ride around the city.

Kristen Erickson, twenty-eight, works at an architectural firm, volunteers at the Bicycle Kitchen, and is typical of the new breed of L.A. cyclist. "I used to get a lot of exercise when I worked as a carpenter. And then I got a job in an office and I was complaining about being sedentary all day," she said. "I'm talking to a friend of mine and he says, 'I've got to get you on a bike.' He's talking about the bike kitchen and I'm like, 'Bike kitchen?' It sounds like a fricking cult." But she began riding and "it became completely addictive," she said. "Since I've been riding, I know what L.A. looks like, sounds like, smells like … I definitely discovered a freedom I haven't had since I was a kid, really." Erickson also has a pickup truck that she uses for her work commute, and she doesn't bike much around her home—at least after dark—because of the fear of crime. I met some riders in L.A., like Lizama, who eschew cars, but I noticed that people who drove to the co-op were greeted with as much friendliness as those who arrived by bike. And there were a wide variety of people. Two Hispanic men walked in to look for a new tire for their worn mountain bike. They were helped by Aaron Salinger, another Bicycle Kitchen founder, who spoke to them in Spanish and got them set up on a bike stand so they could remove their old tire. "There are days when we are doing everything in Spanish, which I like," said Salinger, who teaches the language in high school. He acted as the translator for an influential 2005 article in *Bicycling*, "Invisible Riders," that chronicled the lives of the large numbers of immigrants who ride around the city because the bicycle is their only means of transportation. I have talked to many white, well-educated bike activists who read that article and expressed sorrow that they weren't able to build alliances or do more for the "invisible riders" they also saw in their cities.

As I left the Bicycle Kitchen, I ran into a guy fiddling with something on his bike outside. He's another only-in-L.A. sort, a handsome, forty-two-year-old tanned man with a stylish flattop haircut and biceps that lead you to think he's been working out at the gym. Actually, said Steve Kamajian, he's homeless, "because of addiction and all of the things I chose." He said he has been sleeping on a friend's couch and putting in big miles on his rather nice Specialized Crossroads bike. "I can beat cars to the beach from Hollywood," he said proudly. "I can get to the places, if someone says there is an opportunity somewhere—a job, food; I can get there, even if it's thirty-five, forty miles." He grinned. "I feel like it's the only thing keeping me alive sometimes."

Rev. Phil, that Portland connoisseur of bike culture, is a particular fan of L.A. "It's so exciting because it's like a new bike culture," he said, with people just discovering the joy of getting together with friends to bike around the city. He was down there for the 2005 Bike Summer, an annual month-long series of events that shifts from city to city, transmitting an urban bike culture as it goes. "It was like, 'Okay, this whole month we're just going to meet other people on bikes and go out to parties,'" he said of the mood at Bike Summer, "and the next thing is everyone is saying, 'We have to keep doing this, what do you mean it is going to end next week?'"

As I said, Phil is like a one-man tour of the counterculture bike scene. His summer of 2006 was particularly eventful. In June, he was riding with some five hundred other Portland cyclists in the annual World Naked Bike Ride, another of those events that has an international following. The ostensible reason for the ride, as he explained it, is that it "demonstrates how vulnerable we truly are when we go by bike." Besides that, he added, "It's just a lot of fun." At any rate, Phil was wearing a vest, sneakers, and nothing else when he pulled up at an intersection to block traffic so his fellow bicyclists could continue through. It was late at night in Portland's downtown nightclub district, and riders said most of the spectators seemed to appreciate the show—with a few even joining in by dropping their pants. But a woman in a Jeep continued to inch forward as he jumped off his bike and exchanged words with her. Finally, she knocked over his cycle with her car. At that point, a man jumped out of the passenger's seat and wrestled Sano to the ground, according to a police report of the incident. The passenger turned out to be an off-duty Portland police officer, Chad Stensgaard. Not surprisingly, both cop and cyclist have different accounts of the tussle, with Stensgaard saying that Sano seemed intoxicated and slurred his words, while Rev. Phil said it was the woman driving who seemed to be drunk. But after on-duty officers arrived, Sano was charged with criminal mischief, indecent exposure, disorderly conduct, and having an open alcoholic container (he had an almost empty beer can in his bottle cage, which his attorney said was left over from the day before).

As if that wasn't enough, a few months later Sano was zoobombing one Sunday night when someone tossed ice out in the road and he wiped out, sending him to the hospital with a serious compound fracture in his left leg. "Maybe kids are doing it who don't realize the consequences," he said in a video shot from his hospital bed that was posted online (where a lot of his life has been chronicled).

But just a month later I saw him with a bunch of bike messengers, hanging out in a parking lot under a freeway overpass trying to see who could stop the fastest using just a stick. The inspiration for the contest came from a local judge who ruled that state law required that fixed-gear bikes needed more in the way of brakes than the rider pedaling backwards to stop the rear wheel (accomplished fixie riders can indeed stop by such a method, but most of us are well-advised to stick with conventional braking systems). The judge said that depending on one's musculature was not a brake. "If your client had a stick she could rub against her tire, you'd have a case," the judge remarked.

Under the freeway, the riders figured out pretty quickly that a stick jammed between the rear wheel and the frame brought the bike to an abrupt halt—with the only debate then being whether the stopping point was where the bike wound up or where the rider landed, which was not always the same thing. (Actually, I preferred one of the losers, who came up with the novel idea of carrying a desiccated Christmas tree in his backpack, which he then tossed in front of him so he could run into it. Hey, it was stopping with a stick.) Phil wasn't the winner in any case, but there he was, a brace still on one leg, gamely skidding to a stop that dumped him off his bike. "It's good to, like, get people accustomed to crashing," he explained to me. "It's a great idea. The more you crash, the better you get at it, the less you are afraid of it."

Given Portland's expansive bike community, Phil was able to attract a pro-bono defense attorney and a team of investigators who turned up some embarrassing information about the driver who had hit his bike during the naked ride, at least according to an e-mail that he sent out to cyclists inviting them to the "social event of the season, legally speaking." For one reason or another, the trial was put off for six months while the two sides parried. To defray costs, the Rev. sold "Naked Justice" posters that featured a semi-nude model in the classic "blind justice" pose, only with one foot on a bike and one of her hands clutching a U-lock. Finally, in June of 2007, the district attorney's office dismissed the case, saying that the cop and his girlfriend didn't want to testify. Phil's attorney, Stu Sugarman, wrote in an e-mail to Phil that when he gave the prosecutors one of the posters they realized "they're just making a bigger folk hero out of Rev. Phil."

Sano said he found the end anti-climactic, but that didn't stop him from celebrating with another naked bike ride. And around this time, he was starting to have quite a bit of success with another artistic venture involving bikes. Phil, a devotee of open source software who worked at a computer-recycling cooperative, was also a clever writer who had experimented with bike films for several years. He stumbled on a really hot combination when he combined sex with bikes. Pretty soon he was showing his "bike porn" shorts—which have more goofy humor than explicit sex—at theaters around the country. He was making some real money and attracting the attention of Gus Van Sant, the noted film director who lives in Portland and helped him with one of the pieces. "I'm really happy making bike porn," Phil told me one day when I caught up with him at Free Geek, the computer recycling co-op. "It actually feels very cool, connecting positive, healthy bodies with sexual energy with the idea of being able to move under your own power."

What it is, really, is agit-prop art, part of what not only binds people to the urban bike community but that also gives them a different self-image. The auto industry has used sex to sell cars for decades, but it's not lost on cyclists that you're more likely to build an alluring body riding around town on a bike than tooling around in a convertible, no matter how sleek its curves. It's something that some of the mainstream bike groups are also trying to tap into. "We work hard to build the idea that biking is sexy and fun," said Andy Thornley, program director of the San Francisco Bicycle Coalition. "You know, put something hot between your legs, get a bike." The bike coalition has sponsored an annual "Love on Wheels" fund-raiser featuring a dating game-type format in a local bar. As one year's invitation helpfully explained:

For men, cycling seems to be a natural Viagra. An Italian study found that bicycling for transportation, frequently prescribed in Europe to strengthen the cardiovascular system in heart failure patients, also improved sexual performance. Dr. Romualdo Belardinelli, director of the Lancisi Heart Institute in Ancona, Italy, found that participants' blood flow and ability to use oxygen improved as a result of the simple daily exercise. Belardinelli feels the results of aerobic exercise like bicycling are comparable to those of Viagra, because both widen blood vessels. What about the perception that too much bike riding could cause impotence? Health experts agree that the tremendous cardiovascular fitness conveyed by cycling will usually outweigh any minor impacts that might occur from ordinary riding. Sexual performance becomes noticeably improved in most cases. Men can experience stronger "thrusting muscles," a heightened sex drive, reduced stress, and longer endurance-hurrah!— from cycling regularly.

Sadly, they didn't seem to make the same kind of case for women, other than noting that, "Cycling women are known to be low-maintenance, more independent, and more fun-loving than women who wear makeup to the gym."

Of course, if sex is really about power and status, it is hard for cycling to compete with the curvaceous lines of an expensive sports car. Bikes may make your body stronger, but they don't deliver your date to the valet parking of a swank restaurant with the same comfort and elegance. I was at a picnic one summer day put on by Shift, the bike culture group in Portland, talking with three or four guys as we sipped our beers. A difficult moment, one man admitted, is telling a woman he's interested in that he doesn't drive a car. Sometimes, that ends things right there. As we thought about that in silence for a bit and sipped our beers some more and waited for more picnickers—some of them women—to arrive, I marveled at how this little community is trying to upend so many cultural norms. And that made me think about Kent Peterson, who perhaps more than anyone I have met personifies the determined, individualistic cyclist who has never worried so much about being different. In many ways, I think it is people like him who kept bicycle transportation culture alive during the years that so many kids stopped riding and Americans were spending increasing amounts of time behind the wheel. He's built a no-car, bicycle-oriented lifestyle in the unforgiving surroundings of the American suburbs. Fortunately, he hasn't had to give up love to do it.

I first met Peterson early on a November morning before the sun had risen. His helmet headlight blinked steadily in the dark as I rode to his waiting spot in the old downtown of Issaquah, a suburb that has grown to drape itself over the hills and valleys at the eastern edges of the Seattle metropolitan area. Despite the early hour, Peterson, forty-seven, with a trim mustache, was alert and chatty as we began the eighteen-mile commute to his job in downtown Seattle. It quickly became clear that Peterson, a former software engineer, is a systems guy. He explained how he sheaths himself in lights and reflective clothing to be as visible as possible. His fenders are made of recycled, water-resistant campaign signs, both because they're cheap and because they provide plenty of clearance for all the leaves and pine needles on the edges of the tree-lined roads. He and his wife, Christine, didn't set out to live without a car. It happened gradually. After they had their first son twenty-one years ago, they eventually realized that, what with the savings on day care and work expenses, Christine could afford to quit her job and stay home if they ditched one of their two cars. They moved from Connecticut to Duluth, Minnesota, to run a used bookstore, which turned out not to be so remunerative. To cut expenses, they got rid of their other car and relied on their bikes. When Peterson got back into the software business, in White Plains, New York, they were happy without a car. They carefully chose a place that was within a mile of essential services. In fact, Christine walked home from the hospital after their second son was born. When they moved to Issaquah in 1993 for Peterson to take another software job, they never thought twice about abandoning their car-free lifestyle.

They moved into an apartment in the old commercial center, a still-pleasant traditional Main Street collection of businesses— although it has been eclipsed in the minds of most Issaquah residents by the shopping centers on the outskirts. They were within walking distance of schools, a grocery store, doctor, and other necessities. Their two sons grew up walking, biking, and busing around the community. "My kids did little league, they did soccer, all the normal things," Peterson said, "but when they wanted to do something, we'd say, 'Okay, how are you going to get there?'" A lot of times they could simply ride with friends in those big SUVs and minivans people bought precisely so they could haul a lot of kids around. "We always drilled into the kids, don't be a sponge. Offer to pay for gas or to bring food. Our kids grew up pretty savvy about getting around," Peterson said. Because they live in an apartment, they didn't have a house or yard to maintain. Furniture and big appliances come by delivery truck. And in a true emergency, Peterson likes to point out, you call 911.

Christine isn't much of a cyclist. She walks to her job as a personal shopper for Safeway's internet store. But for Peterson, living in the suburbs seemed to be a chance to get more mileage in. A bike racer when he was young, he spent the first half of 2005 training for the 2,500-mile Great Mountain Divide Bike Race down the spine of the Rockies, and he became the first to ride it on a single-speed bike (his time was twenty-two days, three hours, and nine minutes). And then at the end of that year, he got his dream job, as commuting program director for the Bicycle Alliance of Washington. Suddenly, his ride to work got longer—although for a guy who traversed the Continental Divide, it was not a great stretch. But Peterson was now a role model for the bicycle alliance, and the Petersons found themselves featured on the front page of the *Seattle Times* as the suburbanites who somehow managed to live without the essential tool of suburbia.

A year after my ride with Peterson, I still remember it vividly. Underneath towering Douglas firs, we rode over the lower slopes of Cougar Mountain as cars rushed by us on an old country road turned suburban byway (and I was forced to stop to clear out my fenders because they were clogged with needles, something that had never happened to me bicycling in the city). I tried to stay close to Peterson, who with all of his lights and reflectors was like a moving road sign warning drivers to move a shade to the left. We plunged down to the Bellevue Slough, reaching a path under the intersection of two elevated interstate freeways. Hundreds of feet below the roar of traffic, we rode in an odd netherworld of protected habitat punctuated by gigantic concrete freeway supports. Occasionally we passed riders headed in the opposite direction, nodding at each other like mountaineers focused on our own ascent. We climbed up a path until we were next to I-90. Then we veered off into the neighborhood streets of Mercer Island, one of the Seattle area's most exclusive communities. As we came around the west end of the island, we plunged down a trail that took us on the bike path over the I-90 floating bridge. I was separated by a barrier and a ten-foot wide breakdown lane from the freeway traffic, which was enough to shove the noise of the vehicles to the back of my mind, allowing me to appreciate the chop of the waters in Lake Washington. At the other end of the bridge, we climbed to the top of the hill and then coasted toward the city, eventually gliding through the blocks of the International District and coming to a halt at the bicycle alliance's offices, which are joined with one of the nonprofit Bikestations popping up around the country to provide secure parking for bike commuters. In its own way, the ride was as exhilarating as a morning spent on the ski slopes. As he sipped the sugary latte he buys at the end of his ride every morning, Peterson noted that he never has to worry about counting calories. When he gives talks on bike commuting, he said, "I try to get people talking about the choices that they make. There are a whole lot of things that go into quality of life. One of the spiels I give is about slowing down. We think we have to cram our lives full, 24-7, but there's something about giving yourself some extra time." I realized that nobody would think it remarkable if he went to a gym for forty-five minutes every morning and then rushed downtown in a car. Yet doing an eighteen-mile commute through suburbia on a bike is weird. Peterson said he doesn't try to argue with people. "If people say, 'I don't want to ride in the dark,' I reply, 'Don't ride in the dark. If you don't want to ride in the rain, don't ride in the rain. If you want to go one way and take the bus home, that's fine.'" Even Peterson, who admitted that he is "on the far end of the bell curve" when it comes to his love of biking, said he usually takes a break from the commute one day a week and works from home. "If we were going to move now, we'd definitely move into a neighborhood in Seattle," he said. "But we've been in Issaquah fourteen years now and we've got settled in. Sometimes the weather is just plain bad and you just say forget it and take the bus. But most of the time it just feels so good to be outside. Some days I'll find myself riding over the floating bridge on the lake and the sun is setting over Mercer Island and you just go, 'My God, we live in such a gorgeous part of the world.'"[2]

While I was in downtown Seattle, I walked a mile or so over to the offices of the Sightline Institute, an environmental think tank headed by Alan Durning. He had been getting a lot of publicity since his teen-age son totaled the family's aged Volvo in February of 2006 and the Durnings decided to try living without a car. Unlike the Petersons, they live in the city, in the old streetcar neighborhood of Ballard, which has good bus connections and a large number of businesses within walking distance. Also unlike the Petersons, the Durning family belonged to FlexCar, a car-share company since absorbed by another firm, and would rent an auto anytime they felt like it was worth the nine dollars an hour. But even his experiment was regarded as freakish. Durning's entertaining account of their adjustments—titled the "Year of Living Car-lessly" on the Sightline Web site—attracted plenty of newspaper and broadcast coverage. Fox TV even wanted to feature them on a reality show, "Trading Spouses." The Durnings turned that down, fearing that it would be edited to cast a negative light on them or the woman "swapped" from the other family. They imagined a highly car-dependent, overweight woman from the suburbs nervously biking down a city street, making both her and the idea of biking in the city look stupid. But what the attention told Durning was that the notion of

---

2. In 2008, Peterson took a new job at Bike Works, a Seattle nonprofit that helps people become bicyclists. The job switch actually increased his commute distance slightly, he said, but he didn't mind because the route is faster and the scenery is better.

a middle-class professional family living without a car was so novel that the media couldn't resist.

What intrigued me most as I read his car-less in Seattle series, was how bicycling fit into his experiment. Durning had long promoted cycling as a sensible transportation alternative. In a 1999 book published by his institute, *Seven Wonders: Everyday Things for a Healthier Planet*, the bicycle was one of the featured wonders. But it hadn't been a big part of the Durnings' life before they gave up owning a car. When they began their experiment, they got tune-ups for all of their bikes and began planning routes their children could take (Kathryn, thirteen, and Peter, twelve; a third son, Gary, nineteen, the one who had totaled the car, managed to borrow a truck and avoid much of the carlessness). Durning began riding downtown to work, at least on nice days. Unlike many of the hard-core cyclists with whom I've been spending so much time, Durning admitted he needed a push to get on his bike.

"There's something about the way we make decisions about our transportation that is not rational," said Durning, who has a friendly professor's way about him. "We say we want to exercise more, use fewer resources, particularly those of us in the Northwest. But when you have car keys in your pocket and a car parked out front, it's just like a groove ... So when you think about transportation, you say, 'I'll just hop in the car and go.' And the bicycle is hard to come up against that. Because it requires effort, whereas being in a car is sort of like flowing downhill."

Yes, the fuel is expensive, he added, "but only for that one time a week you have to go to the gas station. Psychologically, the next trip is free." With the FlexCar, of course, no auto trip felt psychologically free. He said that simple change led them to cut their auto mileage by two-thirds as they pondered the value of paying for each car trip. It made more sense to walk to a nearby restaurant than drive to an old favorite six miles away. The children realized they had to forget about asking mom or dad to drive to the video store. But, unlike the Petersons, they had not planned to be without a car from the time their kids were born. They were a successful, well-educated couple with ties across the region (in fact, Durning's father, Marvin, was an environmental lawyer who ran for governor of Washington in 1976). Durning's wife, Amy, teaches self-defense courses for women around the city and their youngest son was in a series of theater productions. As the dark and cold of the winter months set in, Durning ruefully said he was starting to spend as much on FlexCar as on a car payment. He was also appreciating all of the difficulties cyclists faced traveling in a city that made only sporadic provisions for bikes. That launched him on his next internet series, about what he termed "bicycle neglect" caused by this condition: "Car-head."

"Unintentionally and even unknowingly, we see the world as if through a windshield," he wrote. "We evaluate our surroundings as if from the driver's seat (obstacles to speed? places to park?). We consider 'automobile' almost a synonym for 'transportation.' And we consider such thinking utterly normal." As Exhibit A, Durning described what it was like to cycle over the Ballard Bridge, his most direct route to his downtown office. After carefully riding on a narrow pedestrian path over the bridge, he must thread through a gap in the curb of no more than six feet to merge onto a four-lane road with 40-mph traffic. It is "not impossible to bike this bridge," he added. "I do it on occasion. More often, though, I take a longer, hillier route to avoid these few hundred yards of anxiety. More often still, I don't bike at all, opting for a bus over this fearsome chokepoint." To hardened urban cyclists, of course, this is par for the course. Even in bike-friendly Portland, I know I can't ride on any street I feel like as I can in a car. Sometimes I'm assessing whether to risk my safety or—as in the case of the Ballard Bridge— how long you're willing to sit and stew while waiting for a break in the traffic. Durning also knew this, having been to European cities where bikes are routinely accommodated. But it was getting more personal as he figured out how to wean himself from the car. "Considering how little American cities do for bicycling," he told me, "it's astonishing how many do bicycle." In his own way, Durning had arrived at the conclusion reached by so many bike activists. They may cherish the bike culture they've created on the streets, but their goal, in the end, is for it not to be a culture at all, but to simply be one of the routine ways that we get around.

For now, I just cherish those times in my city of Portland when the weather is good and the bikes are crowding the streets, at least in the downtown and the inner neighborhoods. Like the day Rev. Phil and I left some meeting next to City Hall and rode down to a little Thai food cart several blocks away that is a favorite of the local bike messengers. We sat at a table waiting for our food and a woman in her forties rode up and sat next to us, frowning at some papers on a clipboard. She explained she was a state health worker who had to cram for an exercise on what to do if there was an anthrax attack at the post office. Somehow the conversation veered from there to Phil's upcoming trial and the woman asked, "Five hundred naked bike riders in Portland—how did I miss that?" Phil shrugged and began to explain how it worked. "You go as bare as you dare," he said. The woman considered. "If you're not going to get naked, what's the point?" she asked. We parted ways and I headed home, but I felt compelled to stop at Voodoo Doughnuts on the way to get something sweet to cut the spiciness of the Thai food. A couple of guys from Utah were in there, asking for directions to the coast. The young woman behind the counter said, "I don't know, I don't drive." And it didn't seem to bother her, what with being able to get around on her bike, as she later explained. How else do you think she can make ends meet while she works in a doughnut shop? And then I rode over the Burnside Bridge and headed up the Ankeny Bike Boulevard, falling in next to a woman on a gleaming Cannondale road bike, which looked way nicer than the Cannondale in my basement. "Nice bike," I said, being clever. I asked if it was all carbon fiber, and she said no, there's some aluminum in it, but it's pretty top of the line. Well, I said, you could get something even fancier. No, she replied, actually it's about the best there is. You see, she explained, she races mountain bikes for Cannondale and she gets the best stuff, and I'm thinking, okay, now I feel like a fool. But really, I was happy just being part of the bike scene on the street, even if I was having problems with the urban cool part.

4

Davis: Creating an American Bike City

I'm fresh off the turnip truck, so to speak, on my first morning cycling around Davis, and it doesn't take long for me to realize: the drivers here are incredibly mellow. They surrender the right of way with the same eagerness that people open doors for someone in a wheelchair. A couple of drivers even looked exasperated when I waved my thanks, as if they were saying, "Just get on with crossing the street." Bikes, of course, were everywhere. I rode past the Amtrak station downtown, watched a man get off a train, casually toss his briefcase in the basket of a bike locked in a nearby rack and ride off toward the campus of the University of California, Davis.

I pedaled onto campus past bollards that blocked cars and entered a world where bicycles filled the road and the only motor vehicle to be seen was a maintenance truck or two. There were racks everywhere and I was one of the few people wearing a helmet, making me feel like I was a medieval warrior gaping at the peacefulness inside the castle walls. Okay, I thought, but this is a college campus. Students ride bikes a lot. I headed toward the north side of Davis, population sixty-five thousand, with no particular destination in mind. In a bike lane, I fell in next to Ernie Biberstein, eighty-three, a retired microbiology professor, out for an exercise ride. "I remember when the town only had sixty-four hundred people and they put in the first stoplight," he said. "I've lived here for fifty years and I've always bicycled around." We parted ways and I pretty quickly found myself in a north Davis neighborhood honeycombed with off-street paved trails that linked several small parks tucked among suburban-style ranch houses. I took one path that led me to an overpass over a busy arterial—Covell Boulevard— and then dumped me in another park next to Davis High School and North Davis Elementary School. And there, in the elementary school yard, was an amazing sight. In a fenced-off area, there were racks with ninety-nine child-sized bikes parked in them. Around one of the buildings, I saw another set of racks with forty-seven more bikes. I soon attracted the attention of the principal, Judy Davis, who wanted to know why this man was standing on a picnic table taking pictures of her students' bikes. After she decided I was harmless, she explained that a quarter to a third of the four hundred sixty students regularly ride to school, as do many of the teachers. The school district doesn't bother with bus service. Many of the students can ride to school without ever getting on a street, she explained. "Most parents think it is pretty safe," Davis added, and it's good for the children as well. "We don't have much of an obesity problem" at the school, she said, as she and a custodian who had also wandered over agreed that they couldn't think of that many overweight kids. I walked back to my bike shaking my head in wonderment. Later, I was talking to Alon Raab, a Jewish Studies professor who moved from Portland to Davis to teach at the university. "It is just really relaxing" to ride here, said Raab, who also teaches a class on the sociology of the bicycle. "It is odd not to have this adversarial relationship with cars."

Davis, whose official logo is a high-wheeler, has that immediate impact on bike lovers. Through the years, it has often been billed as the Bicycle Capital of America and it is the first city in the country to win the League of American Bicyclists' highest award in its bicycle-friendly cities program—platinum. The 2000 Census said 14.4 percent of Davis residents commuted by bike, far above any other city. Davis may be the one place in the U.S. that almost looks like it could be a city in the Netherlands, where it feels safe for people of any age to cycle. In fact, despite its large number of cyclists, Davis has had just two bike fatalities in the last twenty years, another sign of the safety in numbers at work.

And yet, the story of Davis and bikes is much more complicated than you might think from my handlebar tour of the city. In one sense, Davis and a scattering of college towns around the country— Madison, Boulder, Eugene, Corvallis, Berkeley, Cambridge, and Palo Alto are among those that come to mind—have played an important role as laboratories of experimentation for bicycle transportation. With a large base of cyclists and a progressive political culture, they have tried things that would be harder to accomplish in most of America. In particular, Davis played an important role in pioneering the use of bike lanes and in building complete networks that helped cyclists of different skill levels move about the entire community. During the 1980s and early 1990s, when few thought much about bicycle transportation, Davis was like a bicycling Mecca preserved in amber, waiting to be discovered by a new generation of bike planners and advocates.

But Davis is also a cautionary tale. In recent years, many cyclists have felt the city has drifted—rested on its laurels, is a common expression—as ridership in the city ebbed. Critics cited example after example—such as the addition of new parking garages downtown and on campus as well as the refusal to put bike lanes on the main street through the center of town—of what they say is bicycle neglect by the university and the city. The 2000 Census confirmed some of the angst. As high as that 14.4 percent bicycle-commuting figure was, it represented a major decline from the 22 percent share reported in the 1990 Census. Part of the problem was the shifting demographics of the city. As the price of Davis housing skyrocketed, it attracted more people who actually worked in other cities and who seemed to appreciate Davis more as an affluent enclave with good schools and easy access to Interstate 5 than for the opportunity to get out from behind the wheel of a car.

"You have all these new residents coming to Davis and bringing their driving habits with them from L.A. or the Bay Area," said Tim Bustos, who was the city's bike coordinator from 1994 to 2006, "and they believe that is the way to get around." More parents are driving their kids to school, and Davis High School now has a parking lot crowded with the cars of affluent students who could easily bike or walk but prefer the status of driving.

The promise and perils of America's Bicycle Capital were on display one February night in 2007 in downtown Davis at the Varsity Theater, an old-fashioned movie house now used for a wide variety of events. The featured speaker was Ted Buehler, a graduate student presenting a synopsis of his thesis—and the 350-seat theater was just about packed. Outside, for the first time during my visit, I had trouble finding a place to park my bike that hadn't already been taken. All around me were clearly ardent cyclists with sturdy bikes outfitted with racks, baskets, and, in several cases, "one less car" stickers. Clearly, I had found the heart of Davis' bike culture. Inside, Buehler was getting ready to make a presentation about the history of bicycle policymaking in Davis, and to use the occasion to jumpstart a new advocacy group that would pressure the city and the university to do more for bikes. Buehler, who with his conservative haircut and unobtrusive glasses looked like a wonkish city planner, began by noting that even in Davis, "nobody studies bicycling here." And then he described the unlikely confluence of personalities, geography, and events that produced a city so unlike any other in America.

Many visitors to Davis assume there are so many bikes because it's flat and sunny most of the year. But so are many other cities in America where cycling is a decidedly minor activity. If not for the right people and the right conditions, said Buehler, Davis today would instead "be known as the square tomato capital of the world."[1] There is no doubt that weather and topography made the bicycle a useful tool for getting around the sprawling campus in the 1940s and fifties when it was the agricultural annex to UC Berkeley. Most students couldn't afford cars in those days and it was difficult to walk to many of the far-flung farm buildings. In 1959, the Davis campus became its own university and aggressive expansion plans were made. The school's chancellor at the time, Emil Mrak, was particularly fond of bicycling. He recalled how, as a teen growing up in the Santa Clara Valley, he would take off for hundred-mile rides through the Santa Cruz Mountains. And he liked to talk about how bike racers were famous when he was young. He told his architects to "plan for a bicycle-riding, tree-lined campus," and he urged new students to bring their bikes to school. Most critically, Mrak closed off the central part of the campus to automobile traffic, ensuring that bicycles would remain the easiest way to get around the school. The architects returned with a plan for a sprawling campus linked by gracefully curving bike paths. At one point, the school and the city even planned to close Third Street, which runs from the middle of campus through downtown, to cars. That never came to pass, but in 1966, the new bike-filled campus was celebrated in a famous Ansel Adams photograph showing students attending to their bikes at a parking rack that stretched toward a monumental building that almost looked like a religious shrine. Students established a bike shop in an old dairy shed called, logically enough, the "Bike Barn." When cyclists had a problem getting through busy intersections during the period between classes, the university solved the problem by installing roundabouts. Workers unrolled fire hoses to create the first traffic circle, fiddling with the circumference until it seemed right. Now, navigating a roundabout is one of the first things new students need to learn.

---

1. No, these tomatoes aren't actually square. But you've eaten them. The tomato with the firm skin that travels well (albeit at a sacrifice in taste) was developed at UC Davis.

Bicycling had become a big part of daily life at the University of California at Davis by the time Ansel Adams took this photo, part of a series he did for the UC system.

(Contemporary Print from Original Negative by Ansel Adams, UCR/California Museum of Photography, Sweeney/Rubin Ansel Adams FIAT LUX Collection, University of California, Riverside)

As the university and Davis grew, so did the number of car-bike conflicts on city streets. Bicyclists worried that it was becoming increasingly dangerous to ride in town, and, from the other side of the handlebars, there were also complaints about cyclists riding on sidewalks and disobeying traffic laws. Frank and Eve Child—he was an economics professor at the school and she was a dancer—had spent the summer of 1964 in the Netherlands and became convinced that the city needed to do more to accommodate bikes. (Ironically, Holland's big push to preserve biking and make it safer didn't come until the 1970s. But even before that, there was enough to impress a visiting American couple.) Frank Child wrote a letter to the editor urging that the city provide dedicated rights of way to cyclists on city streets. That kicked off a small but dedicated movement to push the city into action. "None of us had ridden in a double century or ever would," wrote Dale Lott, another UC professor who with his wife, Donna, was another key bike advocate. "We liked to do our daily travel around town by bike, and wanted to preserve that feature of life in Davis."

These newly minted activists were largely rebuffed by the council and city staff, but they managed to make bicycle accommodations in the city the major issue of the 1966 city council campaign. They elected two newcomers who supported bikeways and ousted an incumbent who derided bikes as outmoded relics. Within months, the city council agreed to put bike lanes on several streets and a new era was launched. It was so new, in fact, that nobody was quite sure what the bike lanes should look like. They tried several different ideas (including two-way lanes and lanes between parked cars and the sidewalk) before settling on the familiar striped bike lane seen around the country today. "There didn't seem to have been much controversy," said Buehler. "There wasn't much fanfare. It just all came together."

The city was even able to quickly change state law so that it could legally install the lanes, and the emerging Davis bikeway standards were largely adopted by the Federal Highway Administration when it put out its own guide to bike facilities in 1974. In many ways, the city quickly achieved just what the Netherlands was attempting to do: preserve and expand a bicycle culture that already existed. In 1970, the university surveyed its 12,323 students and found that 78 percent had bikes with them at school, according to a city history by Mike Fitch. In addition, Fitch said, another study, from 1972, found that 30 percent of trips in Davis were by bike. Buehler's thesis contains another interesting parallel to the Netherlands that speaks to the depth of the bike culture in Davis. He found a promotional ad that the local newspaper, *The Davis Enterprise*, had run in 1964. It featured a sketch of a woman in a dress pedaling on a bike with front and rear baskets filled with packages. She's also pulling a trailer with a child in it, and the headline reads, "Shop Davis First!" It's hard to imagine another American city in the mid-sixties where an advertiser would expect a housewife to shop by bike. "It helps to be going with the tide than against it," said Donna Lott, "and in Davis we were preserving a tradition."

Two city staffers—Dave Pelz, the public works director, and Duane Copley, the city engineer—also played crucial roles. Avid cyclists themselves, they plunged into the fine details of making the bikeways work. In a 1999 paper titled "It's All About Connections," the two laid out their philosophy. "[T]he message must be clear," they wrote. "A bicycle facility has to be part of a totally connected route on a grid that serves the population. We would no more build a system for the bicycle that ends every few blocks than we would build an arterial for motor vehicles that detoured traffic every 800 meters." Pelz, who worked for the city from 1964 until his retirement in 1999, "rode his bike to work each and every day," Bustos told me. "That is going to send a message." Pelz, who had biked around Europe as a young man, went to bicycle conferences in Groningen in 1984 and Amsterdam in 2000. He shared the Davis story abroad and brought back new ideas for potential adoption. Bustos said that when he wrote the application for the bicycling league's platinum award, which the city received in 2005, he did it as a tribute to Pelz, Copley, and other former city leaders, rather than for anything the city was currently doing. "That award was upmost an historical award," he said.

Also because of the university's influence, Davis was in the forefront of the environmental movement as it gained steam in the 1960s. The city adopted a groundbreaking energy conservation plan for buildings that attracted national attention. Residents experimented with different kinds of housing and debated how they wanted the community to look. The Village Homes and Northstar developments were each built with greenbelts that included off-street bike paths. Eventually, the city required greenbelts for new developments, thereby creating a system of developer-built trails as the city expanded. Some developers and homebuyers initially resisted the paths. But those trails, now totaling some sixty miles, have since become big selling points with homeowners. I noticed that real estate ads were filled with references to them, such as, "Located near shopping, parks, bike paths & schools in South Davis." Developers still built subdivisions with suburban-style cul de sacs, but the greenbelts helped preserve connectivity for cyclists and pedestrians. The city also helped pioneer traffic signals that were sensitive enough to be activated by cyclists and, at one problematic intersection, a green-light phase for cyclists only.

The city also constructed several side paths, essentially sidewalk-like paths that run along streets. They're disliked by many traffic engineers (as I discuss in Chapter 7) and even some cycling advocates in the city. Pelz, now retired, was not known as a big fan of them either. But as he put it when he talked to me: "What you are experiencing is our attempt to satisfy the full range of people who make trips on bicycles." The city also wangled money from the state and impact fees from developers to improve connections across Interstate 5 to new neighborhoods to the south. There are now five bike-friendly crossings over and under the freeway, a remarkable achievement for a stretch of freeway less than five miles long. "Davis got into the bike thing at a very opportune time," when the city was still in a rapid growth phase, Pelz explained. "If you're in a small community," he added, "all you've got to do is incorporate bicycling into your specifications for new development, and you've got it made, and you didn't have to spend millions of dollars. ... You've just got to be patient and build it one new subdivision at a time." But there is one big caveat, he added. "It takes a lot of political will to do it, a lot of guts."

As developers learned the value of the greenbelts and bike lanes, they became less resistant. The idea that children could safely bike in the community helped build an image that made the city attractive to newcomers. (Although it should be noted that, just as has happened elsewhere, parents in Davis now drive their children to school in greater numbers. The elementary school I visited happened to have the highest share in the city of students who bike and walk to school, perhaps because it is so accessible by off-street paths.) The city also planned for neighborhood grocery stores that are easy for cyclists to reach and some of them usually have quite a few bikes parked in front.

One of the most remarkable things about the Davis experiment has been the impressive traffic safety record for all users. Norman Garrick, a civil and environmental engineering professor at the University of Connecticut, analyzed traffic injury and fatality data for a 2004 paper about the city's bicycle planning. He found that, between 1998 and 2002, Davis had the lowest pedestrian, bicycle, and vehicle fatality rates of sixteen similarly sized California cities. In fact, the city didn't have a single bike or pedestrian fatality during that period. He also found it had the second-lowest injury rate for all users. "This finding is probably indicative of the fact that crashes between vehicles and between people and vehicles occur at lower vehicle speeds in Davis than in cities such as Irvine and Turlock," he wrote, adding that, "one important street design goal in Davis is to reduce vehicle speed, especially at locations where vehicles are likely to encounter pedestrians and bicycle users." Garrick also noted that Davis decided not to build any streets wider than four lanes, unlike so many suburban-type cities that built wide arterials that have such a "corrosive effect" on bicycle and pedestrian travel. He pointed out that College Station, Texas, is a similarly sized agricultural university town that is also separated from other large urban areas. That city, though, has eight intersections with more than forty thousand vehicles a day, compared to none in Davis. He attributed it both to the much higher rates of cycling in Davis and to the lack of a connected street network in College Station, which forces more motorists onto the arterials.

As Buehler brought his narrative toward the present day, the clouds figuratively darkened. As the city expanded, it became less of a company town dependent on the university. By 1970, the city's population had grown to just under twenty-four thousand, more than two times what it had been a decade earlier. And local officials were making plans for a city of a quarter million people by the turn of the century. That spawned a strong anti-growth movement that voted in a like-minded council in 1972. Unlike in most cities, you won't see the suburbs here gradually tapering out in the countryside. The city comes to the edge of farmland and then abruptly stops, thanks to an agreement the city worked out with the county aimed at preventing leapfrog development outside Davis boundaries. Since 1972, the modern political history of Davis seems to consist of one pitched battle after another over proposed commercial and residential development. For cyclists, this was a mixed blessing. Successful developers generally knew their projects had to have good bicycle connections. And the city's attempt to restrict big-box retail helped preserve a lively downtown shopping district that was easily accessible to cyclists. But the restrictions on growth helped drive up the price of housing, especially since the city was such a desirable place to live with plenty of jobs. Davis became a bedroom community for many affluent workers, particularly from nearby Sacramento, who appreciated the small-town way of life, and they often had long commutes and little interest in bicycling. From 1990 to 2000, the number of Davis residents with out-of-county commutes increased from two to twelve thousand, which is one big reason why the percentage of bicycle commuters declined during that period. At the same time, many workers at UC and other businesses in town were priced out of Davis—where the median home price topped $550,000 by 2006—and were forced to commute in by car. The ten-square-mile city is eminently bikable, but only by those who can afford to live there. I found cyclists were also split in fights over commercial development. In November 2006, for example, Davis voters narrowly approved the construction of a Target department store. Some cyclists feared the Target store would weaken local retailers, particularly in downtown, that were easily accessible to cyclists. But others argued that Davis residents were already driving to other cities to shop at Target and other big-box retailers. Putting one in Davis would reduce vehicle miles and give people the option of shopping at one by bike.

Bustos said the city's drift on cycling after the turn of the century was caused in part because Davis had neared full "build-out"; in other words there was no developer to pay the bill for more infrastructure. Susan Handy, a transportation and land-use researcher at UC Davis, recalled how residents recently voted down a development that would have been placed at the edge of the city between two existing neighborhoods. Some people voted against it because they didn't think it had the right mix of affordable housing, she noted, "but I voted for it because I thought it was better to have the housing here than in Woodland," some twelve miles away. In fact, in the fall of 2007, a Woodland resident who worked at UC Davis was killed on a country road during his bicycle commute. Buehler said one of the goals of the new bicycle advocacy group he helped start—called Davis Bicycles!—was to pressure Yolo County to provide better cycling conditions on the roads leading to and from Davis. While this was a laudable goal, it didn't get to the root of the problem.

Daniel Weintraub, a political columnist for the *Sacramento Bee*, was not talking about cycling when he wrote this July 2007 column about Davis. But the point he makes is relevant:

Davis has a reputation as a liberal bastion. But the city is truly conservative, fighting change with every ounce of its political body. While the rest of California becomes more ethnically and economically diverse, Davis remains a mostly white enclave for wealthy, highly educated people … The children who grow up in Davis cannot afford to live in town once they leave their parents' homes, but their parents refuse to consider just about any project to build more houses. Anyone lucky enough to get a job in the city has to live elsewhere and commute in, causing more traffic congestion, smog and global warming. Wonderful.

This all raises the question of whether the Davis bike model could have been preserved even if the community had been allowed to grow much larger. We'll never know because it is a road not taken. But I don't see why not if the city had continued to insist on greenbelts, good connections for cyclists, and grocery stores for each neighborhood. And, in fact, some additional growth is coming. The university, responding to the needs of its workers, is working on its own housing development out of the reach of city control (the campus is just outside city limits). And there is talk of allowing higher-density housing near downtown that could encourage a walking- and biking-oriented lifestyle. Many Davis residents fear, of course, that they will be overwhelmed by traffic that will ruin the city's small-town ambience. But it wouldn't necessarily have to be that way if cycling levels were to begin going up instead of down.

By the 1990s, the student body at UC Davis was also changing. They were becoming more affluent, more likely to bring a car with them, and more likely not to have had much childhood experience with cycling. Many found a ready alternative to the bike in the Unitrans bus system, which was started by students in 1968. It was greatly expanded in the 1990s when a portion of undergraduate student fees was dedicated to the system and students were no longer charged to ride. So the bus essentially became a free means of travel, which was particularly attractive to students who increasingly lived further from campus. Although the city was still relatively compact—it's only about five miles from one side of Davis to the other, which seems like an easy ride to me—Buehler said many students and residents complained that the city was getting too big for biking.

By 1999, Pelz and Copley had both retired and "things changed a lot," said Bustos, the bike coordinator. "You had people [in City Hall] more inclined to manage for motor vehicles than for bicycles." Buehler said such cities as Portland and Boulder had become the real innovators, willing to take risks to increase cycling and other forms of alternative transportation. In contrast, bicycling education was no longer offered at the Davis schools and I had to work some to find a bike map of the city.

For cycling advocates, the new attitude at City Hall seemed to be summed up by a fight in 2006 over Fifth Avenue. The street, running along the north edge of downtown, is the main east–west thoroughfare through the central part of the city. Many people had complained for years that the four-lane arterial was dangerous for cyclists and pedestrians who tried to cross it. The North Davis Neighborhood Association, which represented the area on the other side of Fifth Street from downtown, pressed for changes that would reduce the number of motor vehicle lanes and provide room for bike lanes. By having one auto lane in each direction, plus left-turn pockets for motorists, the new plan would reduce crashes and keep traffic moving at a safe pace, proponents claimed. But the city staff—as well as the local chamber of commerce—opposed the "road diet," saying it would worsen congestion, particularly on the side streets, and the city council voted not to proceed. City officials argued that cyclists could easily take alternative routes just a few blocks away. And, to be honest, I rode on Fifth Street for several blocks and didn't find it particularly scary, at least by the standards of what I see on many arterials in other cities. But it was one of the few places in Davis where cyclists really have to mix it up with cars, and the neighborhood association saw it as a real barrier between downtown and nearby residents.

"If Dave Pelz was still public works director, he would have made [the road diet] happen," said David Takemoto-Weerts, a member of the city's bicycle advisory committee and the bike coordinator for UC Davis. "It would have been a no-brainer." Pelz himself was more diplomatic, saying he didn't have the proper data to judge. The Fifth Street issue came up after Buehler's talk, when several people were asked to comment on his presentation, and Davis Mayor Sue Greenwald said she would have gone ahead with the road diet but lacked a majority on the council. That won her big cheers. The real issue, she said, was reassuring people from the outskirts of the city that they would still be able to get through the middle of town okay. "It's a challenge to convince citizens and their elected representatives that it would in fact have worked," she said. As Buehler told me later, even in the Bicycle Capital of America, nobody wants to make things more difficult for the motoring majority.

Still, there have been some recent positive signs. The local soccer league has encouraged parents and kids to ride to soccer games, and a 2006 survey found that nearly 20 percent did. Some cycling advocates were discouraged by that percentage, but it would be remarkable in almost every other U.S. city. A new city engineer, Bob Clark, began to establish a good working relationship with bike advocates. The League of American Bicyclists renewed Davis' standing as a "platinum" city. Buehler and his group began lobbying the council and quickly won some small victories. The city agreed to restripe several bike lanes before a group of bike and pedestrian planners met in Davis in the fall of 2007, and it also marked a bicycle loop around the city that could serve as the beginning of a signed route system (One thing that had struck me on my rides around the city was the lack of signage on the bikeways.) But the city council refused to end the long tradition of allowing residents to dump their grass clippings and other yard debris on the edge of the street, where it often becomes a hazard for cyclists. That didn't strike me as particularly important until my talk with Raab, the UC professor. It can get really dark at night in Davis because the city keeps street lighting to a minimum to maximize star views, and he rode into a pile of yard debris one night that sent him tumbling to the asphalt.

The university, which once spawned the bike culture, has also come in for its share of knocks. Buehler said in his thesis that the school has not always followed its 1994 long-range development plan that calls for bicycle improvements to be incorporated into campus growth. For example, Buehler noted that three main bicycle paths once served residential units to the north of campus and all were eventually displaced by construction. One of the paths "was removed entirely, one was replaced with an inferior path, and one was carefully rebuilt to its prior quality," he wrote. Takemoto-Weerts, the UC Davis bike coordinator, acknowledged that he's had to make compromises on bike facilities as construction changes the campus. But part of it is also a philosophical difference. One of the paths runs parallel to Hutchison Drive, a street that brings cars into a huge new parking garage, and Takemoto-Weerts said he believes that bike lanes are safer than these side paths. He said the school was also planning to widen the bike lanes after getting clearance to move the curb closer to some large trees.

Takemoto-Weerts said the school has taken some steps that helped preserve the bicycling culture. In recent years, freshmen have not been allowed to bring cars with them for their first year in the dorms because of the shortage of parking on campus. That's made it more likely, he said, that they'll bicycle when they go downtown or somewhere else off campus. "One of the things I want to instill in their first year is the benefits of using the bike as much as they can," he said. "None of them have lived in a community where bicycling is as popular as it is here."

And, indeed, I met several students who said their cycling experience in Davis gave them a new-found sense of the usefulness of the bike. I chatted with Kate Wright and Jason Moore at Buehler's event. Wright, a graduate student in community and regional development, said she had only biked a bit in her hometown of Santa Rosa before coming to Davis. "But after being here, I just realize how much I love it: the exercise, the not sitting in traffic, the not whining about parking." Moore, a graduate student in mechanical engineering, chimed in, "It's the first city where I could put out my hand for a turn and a car would slow down." Wright nodded. "It's caused me to look at my hometown in a whole new way and I realized there were other reasons why I never biked much before," she said. Both said they were interested in promoting bicycle transportation wherever they ended up. Chris Dearth, who now works for the City of Portland's planning department, was a student at Davis in the 1970s. "I grew up in Long Beach, where I drove everywhere," he said. "I drove if I had to go one mile." But in Davis he didn't have a car at first and he fell in love with the easy biking on campus and in the city. And when he got a job in Sacramento as a legislative aide, he commuted by bike fifteen miles each way. "I was in the best shape of my life," he said. After leaving, he continued to ride and is now a daily bike commuter in Portland. "I've been passionate about biking ever since Davis," he said. "Davis has been formative for me."

Still, many students buy cheap department-store bikes that they abandon when the school year ends and they return to an auto-centric culture. Some former students told me that bicycling in Davis represents a pleasant interlude that is hard to repeat when they move on. Michelle Sandhoff was a regular cyclist in Davis and enjoyed it enough that she took her bike with her when she moved to Alexandria, Virginia, after graduating in 2005. However, "I haven't biked a lot here because I'm so terrified of the drivers and vehicles," she said. "People just freak out when they see a bike." She complained about motorists who didn't seem to see her and would routinely cut her off. "It's like they don't understand. They don't know what the etiquette should be."

After Davis' polite drivers, it makes sense that much of the rest of the country could be a shock. It made me remember that, in addition to being called the Bicycle Capital of America, Davis is also often referred to as, "Ten square miles surrounded by reality." Despite its challenges, Davis remains an almost unparalleled place to ride a bike. As gas becomes more expensive, Davis residents are able to adjust more easily than most Americans—as long as they don't have to leave the city limits.

Madison, Wisconsin, and Boulder, Colorado, are also often described as islands surrounded by reality, which is probably a characterization of many college towns that are more politically liberal than the surrounding area. But they're also important laboratories of innovation that have sought to compete with Davis' claim of bicycle supremacy. In addition to large numbers of student cyclists, both cities are also important centers of the bike industry. About 20 percent of the country's bicycle manufacturing and distribution business is in the Madison area. Boulder is an important center of the outdoor recreation industry and is headquarters of two of the country's major bike lobbies, Bikes Belong (the bicycle industry trade group) and the International Mountain Bicycling Association.

In Madison, the big player is Trek, which dominates the high-end bicycle market in the U.S. The company is headquartered in nearby Waterloo and Trek's chairman, John Burke, has become the industry's most powerful advocate. Burke, who served on the president's council on physical fitness, has become close to politicians as diverse as President George W. Bush and House Transportation Chairman James Oberstar, D-Minn. Burke says his goal is to increase the percentage of trips made by bike in the U.S. from 1 percent to 5 percent over the next decade. And he's taken a powerful interest in notching up bicycling in his hometown. Trek, followed by three other cycling companies—Pacific Cycle, Saris Cycling Group, and Planet Bike—has helped finance the City of Madison's effort to figure out how to improve its bicycling climate to win a platinum award.

Madison Mayor Dave Cieslewicz, a former land-use and transportation activist, was one of the first of more than seven hundred U.S. mayors who, following the refusal of the Bush administration to agree to international limits on greenhouse emissions, signed an accord agreeing to their own limits. And in the fall of 2006, at the urging of bike activists, Cieslewicz—known universally around town as "Mayor Dave" because of his hard-to-pronounce last name—announced the formation of a platinum committee. "All of the great cities for bicycling—such as Copenhagen, Amsterdam, Boulder, Portland, and Davis—have become great cities for bicycling because of the visionary actions of citizens and government," he said. "The time is ripe for Madison to become the best city in America for bicycling."

When I was in Madison in June of 2007, the city's bike coordinator, Arthur Ross, gave me a tour of the city's bike network. Unlike in Davis, where developers and the university built most of the trails, in Madison the city has been aggressive about converting lake frontages and old railroad rights of way to bike paths. And unlike in many places, these "rails to trails" have "always been transportation oriented," Ross said. Most of the residents within two or three miles of downtown are close to trails that will take them to the state capitol or the university, which stand at opposite ends of State Street. In 2006, the city completed a $1.8 million "missing link" bike trail project that provided the final key connections downtown.

While we were riding around, Ross also took me along one particularly inventive bikeway on University Avenue on the south side of the main section of the University of Wisconsin campus. The wide boulevard contains three westbound lanes for cars, a bike lane, and a bus lane. But on the left side of the street, protected by a curb, is a "contra-flow" lane that allows cyclists—alone among all vehicles—to travel in the opposite direction. Cyclists had previously used a contra-flow bus lane on that street. But when the buses were moved a block away, to an eastbound one-way street, cycling advocates persuaded the city to keep the special lane for bikes. They argued that if the city didn't, many cyclists would be likely to ride on the sidewalks or the wrong way in the street. Ross said he was particularly proud that the city had designed the lane carefully enough that it won the blessing of John Allen, the vehicular cycling expert who has been critical of many of the bikeways built around the country. Overall, about 3 percent of work trips in the city were made by bicycle, according to the 2000 Census. But Ross said some counts by the city suggest that 7 to 10 percent of trips in the closer-in parts of the city are made by bike. He said that the city has counted up to twelve thousand bike trips a day along University Avenue in the fall, which is usually the most active cycling season, since students are back in school. That's about double where it was a decade ago, he said.

Later, I watched as members of the platinum committee and city staffers met to work on a draft copy of the report. They sat at a long table, passed around snacks (including one local delicacy, cheese curds), and tried to figure out what they could sell to the council and Mayor Dave. The report called for expanding Madison's system of multi-use trails—already one of the best in the nation—and improving connections to make bicycling in the city feel more comfortable for beginning and timid riders. They talked about making sure that the city's pledge to reduce greenhouse emissions was prominently mentioned and about how they expected action during a timeline that fit within the mayor's current term of office. "The nice thing is this puts gentle pressure on him," said Mary Rouse, the retired dean of students at the University of Wisconsin and co-chairwoman of the committee. John Coleman, a citizen bike advocate, noted the $72 million a year lost in damages to auto crashes and suggested that a shift to bicycling might help that. "Maybe we could get the insurance industry to chip in a bunch of money," he said, realizing that probably wouldn't happen.

Afterwards, I had dinner with Jay Ferm, the advocacy coordinator for Planet Bike and the other co-chair of the committee. "I don't give a damn about platinum," he said. "But I give a damn about what it takes to get platinum. I want people from Copenhagen to come to Madison to figure out how to do stuff." While the city has steadily expanded its path system, he noted, it hasn't done everything it could to make cycling easier on the streets. The platinum report talks about looking for opportunities to create such facilities as low-traffic bike boulevards and bike-friendly improvements at difficult intersections. The major goal, Ferm said, was to simply increase the percentage of trips made by bike, which the bicyclists' league has cited as its main measurement of a city's friendliness toward cycling. But he said the committee had largely tiptoed around what he called the "elephant in the room."

"We've got to discourage car use," Ferm said, "and a lot of people in the bike community are intimidated by that." He talked about how UW football fans often park miles away from Badger Stadium on game days and enjoy the celebratory atmosphere of walking in. "On Badger Saturdays they walk two miles and they love it," he said of the fans. "But would they advocate a car-free zone [around the stadium]? No way. No way."

In Boulder, city officials have been more explicit about trying to limit the use of cars. They've stuck to a goal of keeping vehicle miles from growing, although they've used more carrots than sticks. They poured millions of dollars into a bus system—which many local residents ride for free through passes bought by their employers—and into an extensive bikeway network. The city has also tried to accommodate a wide variety of riders, sometimes providing both bike lanes in a road and side paths next to it. The city has also been able to use flood-control money to build bike paths along Boulder Creek, which runs through the city. The 2000 Census found that 7 percent of commuting trips were by bike. The city conducts its own surveys and concluded that, in 2003, some 21 percent of all commute trips by Boulder residents were by bike. That figure attracted no small share of controversy, especially after it was picked up in a *Wall Street Journal* article and touted as higher than the mode share in Davis. Even many cycling advocates scoffed. "Nobody buys the 21 percent mode share," said Ray Keener, a cycling industry consultant based in Boulder.

Martha Roskowski, who runs the "Go Boulder" alternative transportation program for the city, defended the numbers but said they needed to be put into context. Boulder—like Davis—has strict growth controls. It also is a big employment center, with the University of Colorado, the National Center for Atmospheric

Research, and several high-tech employers. As a result, some 65 percent of the city's workforce actually lives outside of Boulder and Roskowski said the vast majority of those workers commute by car. The survey only covered city residents, so it's missing the majority of work trips made within the city. In short, Boulder is one of those bike-friendly college towns, surrounded by reality—and reality commutes in every day.

5

Portland Built It and They Came

For one ridiculous moment, I felt like a teenage girl rummaging through her closet looking for the right top. Should I wear my spandex and enjoy the rush of speed on my feather-light road bike? Or should I go in casual wear on my comfortable hybrid, which I usually ride to work? Nope. I finally settled on a T-shirt, hiking shorts, and my mountain bike. After all, the sucker eats potholes for breakfast and it seemed like the jauntiest way to take a sunny Saturday spin to the Multnomah County Bike Fair.

As I came within a few blocks of Colonel Summers Park in Southeast Portland, the urban ecology started to change. Cyclists, alone and in clumps, approached from all directions. You could see several motorists swivel their heads, suddenly realizing they were going to have to think a bit more while they navigated the narrow streets around the park. I bounced my bike over the curb and rode over a grass field to a roped-off parking area rapidly filling with bikes of all descriptions. Parents lifted toddlers out of trailers and couples dismounted from tandems. I walked to the fair's entrance, an archway made of old bicycle rims and strolled along a midway lined with booths. A handful of riders on ludicrously tall bikes made of two or three frames welded together wobbled through the park, like circus clowns on stilts. I stopped to talk to a group of guys who always made me smile every time I saw them: the

Belligerantes. They swaggered in their red letterman jackets in good cheer, with beers in hand. This tongue-in-cheek bike gang rides homemade, super-sized versions of that favorite baby boomer bike, the Schwinn Sting-Ray. They were shy about giving their names. One man introduced himself as the "commander." One of his pals rolled his eyes. "Mike always wanted a Sting-Ray when he was a kid and he could never have one," the friend teased. Commander Mike said they like to ride in small-town parades, but that was about the extent of their civic-mindedness. Mostly, he explained, "We're into no helmets and drinking."

Next door, I bought a smoothie. But first I had to ride the stationary bike that powered the blender that made the drink. While I slurped my slush, I watched the bike games on the asphalt playground, lined for the day with bales of hay and temporary metal bleachers. Most amusing was the "eating by bike" competition. Contestants lazily circled the playground while eating noodles, an apple, licorice, a banana, and a paper cup of juice. No putting your foot on the ground allowed. Soon, the arena was a whirling mess of grunge cyclists, splattered food, and a crowd hooting its approval. While the banana peels and other discards were cleaned up, word circulated that the Sprockettes would be up next. "They're like a mini-bike dance team," one awestruck young man told a friend. "I met them at a party last night. They're really cool."

Perhaps it wasn't the slickest entertainment in the world. But you could see it as Portland's answer to the Southern California car cultists of the sixties. In a sense, those "Kandy-Kolored Tangerine-Flake" hot rodders, to borrow a phrase from Tom Wolfe, were experimental artists celebrating a vehicle that was remaking just about all of American life. Now, Portland's fertile mixture of artists, hipsters, liberal professionals, deep-green ecologists, outdoor recreationists, urban planners, liberal politicians, and various combinations of two or more of the above are creating a new kind of culture surrounding the simple idea of getting around a city by bike. Portland residents use the bike for transportation more than any other large city in America, and the city has gained an international reputation for encouraging bicycling. And you'll be hard-pressed to find any city with as rich and varied a bike culture, from jam-packed cyclocross events at the local raceway to what has become North America's largest annual naked bike ride.

Portland certainly has its oddities. For one thing, most American cities would resist celebrating anything like the Rose City's unofficial logo:"Keep Portland weird." But much of what Portland has done to mainstream bicycling could be easily copied. And unlike Portland's light rail and streetcar systems, which cities around the country are rushing to emulate, a bikeway network is a cheap investment. Even if you throw in the city's trail network and a waterfront esplanade, both of which serve recreation and scenic purposes as much as bike transportation, the cost of building Portland's bike network between 1993 and 2008 clocked in at less than $100 million. It cost more than that—$143 million, to be precise— to rebuild just one of the city's freeway interchanges, the Sylvan exit on Highway 26.

Even in Portland, though, bicycling is still very much a subculture. A big majority of trips in the city are by car, and Portland, by population, is only about a third of a much larger metropolitan area dominated by a suburban, auto-oriented lifestyle familiar to most Americans. Many Portlanders share the same disdain for cyclists you'll too often find all over America. But the signs of change here are unmistakable. Ridership over the city's main bridges that are open to cyclists into downtown—one of the best measures of bicycling's popularity in Portland—more than quadrupled in the fifteen years since the city began seriously expanding its bike network in 1993. The U.S. Census' annual American Community Survey found that about 5 percent of the city's commuters traveled by bike in 2007 (and that survey's methodology may actually underestimate bike usage; the survey asks for the primary mode of transportation commuters used in the last week. So people who ride one or two days a week would not be picked up, nor would people who combine a bike trip with a longer bus, train, or car trip). The Portland city auditor, who also conducts an annual survey, found in 2008 that 8 percent of residents listed the bike as their main means of transportation and another 10 percent said it was a secondary form. In some areas, such as the largely flat, grid-street neighborhoods of the inner east side, more than a quarter of residents say they use their bicycle as a primary or secondary means of transportation. I've noticed that there is literally not a time of day or night, or of any season or in any weather, where I can go for a trip of more than a few blocks without at some point seeing a cyclist. And that includes the last time Portland had a good snowstorm.

In a little more than a decade, Portland tripled the mileage of its bikeways and renovated most of the bridges over the Willamette River—which runs just east of the compact, thriving downtown—to make them safe for cyclists. The city is dotted with directional signs and pavement markings for riders. Downtown signal lights are set at speeds between 12 and 18 mph, slow enough for cyclists to keep up with the flow of traffic, except on the uphill stretches. Some thirty miles of low-traffic bike boulevards provide pleasant cycling through several neighborhoods and an off-street path stretches almost unbroken all the way from the east bank of the Willamette River to Gresham, some twenty miles to the east. TriMet, the region's transit agency, was one of the first in the country to put bike racks on all of its buses. The city launched one of the country's most successful social marketing programs to encourage residents to bike, walk, or take transit instead of driving. On some commercial streets, the city is taking out car parking to put in rows of bike racks—and this is at the request of local store owners who think the bike racks will attract more customers. In early 2008, the League of American Bicyclists designated Portland as only the second platinum city in the country, after Davis.

Just a few weeks later, Portland voters elected Sam Adams—who as a city council member in charge of transportation, was one of the most aggressively pro-bike officials the city had ever seen—to be mayor. While bicycling wasn't the biggest issue in the race, it was striking that voters didn't seem concerned by criticism that Adams was too apt to favor bicycling and rail transit over the automotive majority. Even Adams' chief opponent, businessman Sho Dozono, said in one televised debate that Portland "ought to be equal" to Amsterdam as a haven for cycling.

Cyclists and other transportation reformers also hold sway on Metro, the elected council in charge of the region's planning. One of the councilors, Rex Burkholder, chairman of a powerful intergovernmental committee that doles out federal transportation money, is a founder of the Bicycle Transportation Alliance, the state's major bike lobby. And the state of Oregon also plays an important role. Long before the "complete streets" movement began to take off nationally, Oregon—in 1971—adopted its own law requiring that at least 1 percent of road money be spent accommodating cyclists and pedestrians. That law continues to be one of the most powerful tools in the arsenal of bike activists.

Just as importantly, the region—on the Oregon side of the Columbia River, at least, where the bulk of the population lives— has committed itself to compact development. That has helped make the bicycle a viable transportation tool. The metropolitan region is ringed with an urban growth boundary that limits suburban sprawl, and for years the number of downtown parking spaces was capped to discourage commuters from driving. The area's leaders have largely avoided pushing for massive new highway projects,[1] to the point that a local Federal Highway Administration official complained in

---

1. A big exception is the proposal for a new Interstate 5 bridge over the Columbia River between Portland and Vancouver, Washington. The project, estimated in 2008 to cost $4.2 billion, has stirred major debate over whether it would ease congestion or encourage more suburban sprawl on the Washington side of the river. Burkholder, who supports the new span, has found himself on the opposite side from many of his old cycling allies. However, all of the proposed bridge plans include state-of-the-art bicycling and pedestrian facilities.

2007 that Metro's transportation plan failed to "acknowledge that automobiles are the preferred mode of transport by the citizens of Portland."

That's not the first time the region has fought the highway builders. The city tore up a waterfront highway in the 1970s, replacing it with a park that included a wide bike and pedestrian path. In the same decade, local officials killed a big freeway project that would have cut an eight-lane-wide swath through Southeast Portland. Instead, the region diverted nearly $500 million in federal highway funds into the start of a new light-rail system and dozens of smaller road projects. TriMet now operates one of the country's largest new commuter rail systems—forty-four miles, with more on their way—and the city is expanding its own streetcar line that promotes dense multi-family housing. Portland has been celebrated in urban planning circles and routinely lands at the top of various rankings of livability, walkability, and environmental sustainability. *Bicycling* magazine has repeatedly rated it the best bicycle city in North America.

Portland's livability has made it one of the most sought-after destinations in the country for college-educated people in their twenties. This "creative class" transformed Portland's art, music, theater, and restaurant scene, and many of these young people, not surprisingly, liked getting around by bike as well. Alone among the major West Coast cities, Portland was a place that offered relatively cheap rent and decent transportation alternatives. I frequently meet people like Trish Kimbell, who moved here in 2006 at the age of twenty-six after touring with a children's theater company for four years. She could live anywhere, she said, "but I wanted to have a simple lifestyle where I could get around without needing a car. The way Portland is organized, you can do that." She mostly bikes the four miles between her apartment and her call-center job downtown, hopping on the bus in bad weather and, on occasion, tagging along with friends who do have cars. Perhaps most importantly, in Portland, she doesn't feel like she's a misfit or in danger because she relies so much on a bike. "I like the fact there is a bike community," she said. "I will be riding to work and there is a caravan of five or six bikes. There's something about strength in numbers."

Besides working to attract young people like Kimbell, cities around the country are beginning to follow the Portland model, with newly vital downtowns, urban rail systems, and growing interest in alternatives to single-home suburbia. It's not lost on many urban thinkers that Portland could adapt to six-dollars-a-gallon gas and big reductions in greenhouse emissions much easier than Phoenix or Atlanta. So it is no surprise that Portland is also looked upon as a kind of test market for bicycle transportation. Other cities will find that they may not be able to replicate some of the factors, such as Portland's moderate weather, strong street-grid network, and outdoor-oriented lifestyles. But there seems little doubt that the city's willingness to carve out space for cyclists helped spark the boom.

"Portland was the first city of its size that created a bikeway network and took bicycle transportation as a serious alternative," said Roger Geller, Portland's bicycle coordinator. "It was sort of a 'build it and they will come' idea." Of course, the rise of bicycling in Portland was much more complicated than that. But it's a story that, in many ways, will sound familiar in cities like San Francisco, Seattle, or Minneapolis, where bicycling has also grown in fits and starts but is now an established part of the local culture and transportation establishment.

Portland—and much of Oregon, for that matter—was part of an earlier cycling boom back in the late 1960s and early 1970s after the rise of the environmental movement and the first Arab oil shocks. A Portland State University professor, Sam Oakland, founded the Bicycle Lobby in 1968 with the manifesto of sealing "off downtown Portland from personal automobile traffic." That didn't happen, but the group helped a small-town legislator from Southern Oregon, Rep. Don Stathos of Jacksonville, pass the 1971

"Bicycle Bill" that required the 1 percent set-aside to accommodate bicyclists and walkers. Stathos, a Republican businessman who happened to like to bicycle, had been upset that his kids couldn't safely ride to school, something that to him seemed like a normal rite of childhood. Portland was one of the first cities to hold a Bike-to-Work day and to hire a bike coordinator. Bill Walton, the Portland Trail Blazer star who led the team to its only NBA title in 1977, came to symbolize the Northwest outdoor lifestyle as he pedaled around town on his ten-speed (including in the parade the city threw for the championship team). The money from the Bicycle Bill helped build a rudimentary system of bikeways in various parts of the state, including a path that ran alongside a new freeway through Portland, Interstate 205. Eugene, a college town south of Portland, built a particularly impressive system of paths that made it a national bikeway pioneer in the 1970s and 1980s.

At the same time, Oregon was earning a national reputation for its ambitious effort to control leap-frog development. In 1975, the Legislature approved a statewide land-use planning program that, among other things, required each city to draw an urban growth boundary around its fringe and direct new development inside of it. Critics were quick to say the line was more akin to a noose, and the landmark law survived a voter referendum only after a dying Tom McCall—who, as governor proclaimed of Oregon, "Visit but don't stay"—vigorously campaigned to preserve it. The new land-use limits were enthusiastically embraced by the political leadership of Portland (and to varying degrees by the leadership of the suburbs). These leaders pushed for a compact city that would maintain a strong, lively downtown and close-in middle-class neighborhoods. However, the nascent bike boom of the 1970s fizzled in the Reagan years as it did in much of the country. Cheap gas and big SUVs, which multiplied faster than the McMansions being tossed up on the suburban fringes (the original urban growth boundary actually left lots of room for development), made the streets busier and meaner. Road rage entered the lexicon. In 1984, Portland did elect a bike-loving mayor, Bud Clark, a former barkeep with a bushy beard and an ever-present rose in his lapel. But besides occasional news photos of Bud cycling around the city, looking like Hollywood's idea of a French provincial mayor, the bike scene was largely somnambulant.

Two decades later, on a pleasant day in early spring, I rode through Portland's leafy Irvington neighborhood, appreciating the nicely restored mix of Craftsmen homes, bungalows, and stately early twentieth-century mansions, all fronted by green lawns and ample sidewalks. It's a neighborhood that dates from the turn of the twentieth century, developed with the streetcar in mind on acres and acres of square blocks. It was easy to bike on low-traffic streets as I savored the spring blooms. Except for the apartment houses on its edges, Irvington isn't really denser than many suburban housing developments, but its street grid is connected to everything, and that makes all the difference to cyclists. Schools, stores, and churches are all easily accessible without having to travel much on busy streets. Even one of the region's largest shopping malls, Lloyd Center, is a short ride away. I was on my way to visit with Burkholder, the Metro councilor, to talk about how the city has changed since the 1980s. From early on, he had a European sensibility toward bikes, seeing them as something you hopped on in your street clothes to get where you're going—not as a thrill ride. I can't remember how many times I had driven past him over the years as he pedaled along, his back stiffly upright, garbed in nice slacks and wool sweater, a plaid cap upon his head. He moved with such stately deliberation that motorists just seemed to go around him with a shrug, the same way they do a truck lumbering up a hill.

On one side of Burkholder's wood-frame house is a wire cage filled with a jumble of bikes. We settled in his living room, mugs of tea in hand. "I remember riding my bike to work in the early eighties and knowing every rider on the Broadway Bridge," he said, noting that he may have looked unruffled but that he was sometimes seething inside. The bridges over the river were an obstacle course, either because riders had to ride over metal grating next to cars or because of the welter of on-ramps that funneled cars onto the spans from several angles. Most of all he was angry that he didn't feel safe letting his children ride downtown with him. "Why should it be dangerous for a young kid to ride a bike?" he remembered thinking. "It's a basic human right." Throughout the city, traffic speeds were high and the city seemed to have little interest in doing anything for bikes that would cost money or inconvenience a motorist.

In the fall of 1990, Burkholder spotted a flier on a telephone pole advertising a meeting at the library to form an organization of bicycle riders. He was one of about forty who showed up, including an organizer from Greenpeace. The meeting had a decidedly anti-war fervor to it; at the time the U.S. was preparing to launch the first Gulf War. The political left, organized for so long in opposition to the Cold War, was now beginning to grasp what it saw as a dangerous new folly: fighting for oil to fuel behemoth automobiles. It was an eclectic group, though, and people had plenty of local gripes as well. Jim Ferner, a carpenter from nearby Beaverton who became a key bicycle activist, was ticked that TriMet wouldn't let him take his bike on the bus. Eventually, a new organization emerged, the Bicycle Transportation Alliance. Thanks to a family inheritance, Burkholder and his wife, Lydia, could pursue their passions as much as any career. And Burkholder threw himself into the new group. "He was the rational guy, the more politically savvy one," said Karen Frost, who later became the BTA's first executive director. "He had training in public administration and he had the time … He was the guy who held it together." The organization made quick progress with TriMet, which became one of the country's first major transit agencies to install bike racks on all its buses. And the new group found that it had a market for its advocacy. "Bicyclists have this rabid sense of self-identity, so they're sending us money," said Burkholder. Out of the blue, Jay Graves, owner of the Bike Gallery, which would grow into the city's largest chain of bike shops, started giving $200 a month, enough to begin paying staff. But the BTA foundered when it also tried to organize pedestrians. It turned out that people who liked to walk around town didn't seem to see it as an activity that needed a lobby.

From the start, Burkholder said, the group realized it had a powerful ally in the Bicycle Bill. Over the years, the local and state bureaucracy had learned how to work around the law or to simply ignore it. "We were looking for a test case," he said. "We wanted it to be big enough to catch the public's attention." As it happened the Trail Blazers were building a new basketball arena and accompanying complex of offices, retail, and parking garages just east of the Broadway Bridge. As its part of the deal, the city had agreed to put in a new street system. The BTA demanded that the city install bike lanes along the new streets. City officials refused and the two sides trooped off to court. After the BTA won a favorable ruling before the state Court of Appeals (which the state Supreme Court declined to review), the two sides agreed to an accommodation. What the court case demonstrated was that the Bicycle Bill had teeth, and that helped give the BTA the clout it needed to become a player on the local transportation scene. It also made all layers of government in Oregon more sensitive to the need to put in bike lanes and sidewalks on major street projects. The BTA, which by 2008 was a five-thousand-member group with seventeen staffers and a $1.4 million budget, occasionally raises the specter of a lawsuit, but as of mid-2008, it had never actually filed another one. The organization was wary about losing the goodwill it has built up with city, regional, and state government or of taking on a cause it could lose.

Ironically, the city's transportation commissioner at the time of that lawsuit was Earl Blumenauer, who has since been elected to the U.S. House and become nationally noted as one of the foremost bike advocates in Congress. Although he is now frequently profiled for traveling around D.C. by bike, he was more known as a long-distance runner in the late 1980s and early 1990s. And caught up as he was in epic battles over mass transit and compact development,

Blumenauer hadn't paid much attention to the emerging bike lobby. But somewhere in there, the bicyclists won him over. "I wasn't doing anything about bikes and I got nailed," Blumenauer said years later. "It was interesting and they were right."

Under Blumenauer's watch, the city beefed up its bicycle program and Mia Birk, an intense young woman who had worked on third-world transportation issues for a Washington, D.C., think tank, was hired to run it. Blumenauer gave her strong political backing and a mandate to build a complete bicycling infrastructure. The idea was that the city would not only draft a bike master plan, it would actually try to follow it. Portland would not just be a city that stripes in a few bike lanes under pressure and then leaves cyclists to fend for themselves at dangerous intersections. It would try to think through the problems of how to make it easier for bicyclists to travel throughout the city. Birk knew one of her first jobs was to change the car-oriented culture of the transportation department. "A woman coming into an engineering department is one thing," said Burkholder. "A bike advocate coming into a road department is another. But she was tough and she had Blumenauer's support."

"We tried to light a fire around biking as a mainstream form of transportation. It needs to be part of daily life, so it's not a fringe thing," said Birk, who later became a principal at Alta Planning + Design, a fast-growing firm specializing in bike and pedestrian planning. She went to service clubs, churches, neighborhood associations, and anyone else who would listen. "I'd have 90 percent of the room staring at me, like, are you from the moon?" she recalled. "But in every group there would be a few who came up and were interested. We'd get them on an e-mail list and pretty soon we could get a crowd at city commission meetings."

Birk took the same evangelistic attitude with her when she met with the city crews who actually swept the roads, laid the asphalt, and painted the traffic stripes. If the sermon about accommodating bikes didn't work, she hoped the doughnuts she brought along might win them over. Under her tutelage, the bike network began to grow and the city, in 1996, adopted a master plan that called for a 630-mile system. Birk and her team stole ideas from the New Urbanists, the Netherlands, college towns, and from whatever else seemed to work. "It's an evolutionary field," she explained. "We're kind of creating it as we go." The city took Northeast Glisan, a four-lane street with plenty of excess capacity, and put it on a road diet. They shrunk it to one lane each way with a turn lane in the middle. That freed up room for bike lanes, slowed speeders, and prevented congestion by giving motorists a safe haven for left turns. On bridge approaches, the city put in blue-tinted lanes to warn motorists to surrender the right of way when they had to cross over bike lanes (the blue lanes were also tried at a few other problematical intersections). And the city even closed one entrance ramp to the Hawthorne Bridge that was causing difficult bike-car conflicts. Today, it sits empty and blockaded, a concrete memorial to 1950s-style traffic engineering.

Portland also created a handful of bike boulevards that were inconvenient for motorists but were quick thoroughfares for bikes. Some of the best bike boulevards were in an area of Southeast Portland where the city had launched a major traffic-calming project in 1990 that funneled traffic to two major commercial streets—Hawthorne and Division—and away from the nearby residential streets. Several residents bitterly protested, but years later these quiet neighborhood streets are highly prized, and Division and Hawthorne have become lively shopping and restaurant corridors. After having torn down the highway on the west side of the Willamette River in the 1970s, the city reclaimed the river's east bank in the late 1990s by building an esplanade in the shadow of Interstate 5. The $30 million project (mostly financed with federal money, thanks to ISTEA) included a new pathway on a bridge owned by Union Pacific that now carries cars, light rail, Amtrak, freight trains—and thousands of walkers and bicyclists every day.

One day, Birk recalled, she received a call from a crew chief explaining that he was going to repave a stretch of Southeast Seventh Avenue. It was marked as a bike route on the master plan, he said, what should I do? Birk and a traffic engineer hustled down to meet with him. At this point, it was just a line on the map. But they quickly sketched in the same kind of plan they had used for Glisan, and the road crew did the work over the weekend. On Monday, the city phones lit up with complaints from businesses fronting the street. "It wasn't the Portland way where you talk everything to death before you make a decision," she said. She made the rounds of the merchants to apologize for the hasty action. But she told the story with glee for years afterward. "We had two mottoes that guided us in those days," she once explained. "One was, go like hell until you can't go no more, and the other was, it was easier to ask for forgiveness than to ask for permission."

Rob Burchfield, the city's chief traffic engineer, was a cyclist himself. He said the city found a lot of easy projects it could do at first to carve out space for bike lanes without having much impact on overall traffic capacity. "Our strategy to date for the most part has been to try to balance the needs of all of those modes and not really take away from capacity for automobiles," he said. "We may have in some cases capped it and said there is not going to be any more capacity in this corridor for cars. There have been a few places where we have taken away capacity, but in general those are in cases where I would say the capacity has been under-utilitized."

As the network grew, Burchfield said the money spent on bicycling proved to be a wise investment. "I think the economics, the dollars and cents, the cost-benefits of bicycle transportation make a lot of sense," he said. "I mean, bicycles are just so undemanding of the system, you know? They are the small vehicles that don't wear the pavement." That compares favorably to "all of the external negatives that go with a transit bus that pounds your pavement, to inefficient automobiles that don't move many people relative to their mass, to high capacity transit systems, which we love, but take a major investment of energy and materials and construction cost ... For simple transportation, the bicycle is very elegant and very cost-effective. So I think there are reasons why it makes good policy to go as far as you can with bicycle transportation."

Not everyone agrees with that. But it is instructive that the city has had much bigger battles over renaming streets (one proposal to rename a major arterial for labor leader Cesar Chavez sparked a doozy of a political fight) than it has had about striping in bike lanes.

Still, Birk did get plenty of attention, both positive and negative, to the point that some City Hall leaders worried that residents were getting the idea the city wasn't doing much for transportation besides encouraging bikes. In 1999, her program was "mainstreamed" into the regular transportation staff. By then Blumenauer was in Congress and she felt that she no longer had the same political backing. She left the city the same year, after having helped increase the bikeway mileage from about sixty-five to around two hundred. Still, progress continued, albeit at a slower pace, under transportation commissioners who paid less attention to bikes. There were still plenty of gaps in the bicycle master plan, particularly in the hilly Southwest neighborhoods and on the eastern edges of the city where the grid network began to break down. And even in the best east side neighborhoods, there were gaps in the system and difficult intersections that city bike officials said they didn't have the resources to fix. Still, ridership continued to steadily rise. The city counted bike traffic over the bridges into town during the peak summer riding season and found that it had climbed from about 3,600 daily trips in 1993 to more than 16,700 trips a day in 2008. At times of the year, bike traffic on the Hawthorne reached 20 percent of all vehicle trips. Perhaps best of all, as cycling increased the bike crash rate declined—further evidence of the safety in numbers theory.

In part, ridership continued to grow for reasons other than the bikeway network. One was the Transportation Options program, which moved from neighborhood to neighborhood, plying residents with information, small gifts (such as pedometers), and strategies for reducing their driving in favor of biking, walking, and transit. Before-and-after surveys showed reductions of 9 percent in drive-alone trips. Gas prices, which began spiking in 2005, also played a role. And bicycling came to take on a certain cachet, particularly among the city's young new arrivals. And that in turn attracted more people to the city who were interested in living a bike-centric lifestyle.

🚲

The disparate strands of the city's bike culture were also coming together. In 2002, Portland hosted Bike Summer, a month-long series of bike events held in a different city each year. Bike Summer produced dozens of enduring friendships and a new group—Shift—that knitted the bike community together through a lively listserv and a calendar that rarely had a day bereft of some kind of ride, party or other "bikey" event. "We just had this feeling of a community being born," said Phil Sano. "The back of my neck is tingling right now thinking about it. You knew in your soul it was going to be right."

Rev. Phil said he would never forget the bike summer's finale party. Several cyclists had been talking about a naked ride after the farewell party and someone had printed up fliers advertising just such an event. "At this party at City Bikes [a local bike repair cooperative] there was tons of beer and lots of sexy bikers," he recalled, "and it was about 1 a.m. and people were still coming and then people started stripping. I think about fifty bikers were rolling and at one point we saw some cops. But they just chuckled at us and waved us off … Then there was a naked dance party afterwards." (Well, it was somewhat tamer than this description; most people had put their clothes back on.)

In this tight little world, people found all sorts of ways to express their style. C.H.U.N.K. 666 was a clannish group of mutant bike builders, noted for their post-apocalyptic vision of a world without oil. Each year they held a Chunkathalon, which included everything from jousts to fireworks-laden bikes after dark. The Zoobombers would take little-kid bikes on light rail every Sunday night up to a hilltop above the city's zoo, party under the stars (or more often, this being Portland, under clouds), and then race down through some of the city's wealthiest neighborhoods at breakneck speed. The Sprockettes, the bicycle dance team, produced their own pinup calendar and became an established dance troupe. "There's something about bikes that people want to make them into art forms," said Ayleen Crotty, who hosted a monthly bike show on KBOO, a community radio station. "Our city is just completely saturated with bike stuff." While the BTA was all about political advocacy, this new generation of bicyclists was simply going to take to the streets and have fun. "If people aren't motivated by the environment or by health, probably the only thing that is going to get them out there is having a good time," said Rev. Phil.

The Shift calendar became so full that the city's monthly Critical Mass ride, a prominent part of the bike culture in so many cities, withered to the point of not even being held some months. A big part of it was that the police devoted major resources to regulating the ride and were quick to crack down on any infractions. (The police, however, did so with a cheerier attitude after Mayor Tom Potter participated in the ride shortly after being inaugurated in 2005, saying he wanted to ease tensions between police and participants.) I went on a couple of Critical Mass rides and couldn't remember being so closely escorted by police outside of the times I've been in presidential motorcades. The last time I checked out the ride, on a sunny evening in May of 2007, there were nineteen riders and ten officers at the start, and when I left, the police outnumbered the participants. "No matter how nice they are, people just don't want to hang with the cops," explained Sara Stout, a veteran Critical Masser who co-hosted the KBOO bike show with Crotty.

Beyond that, many cyclists questioned why they even needed the polarizing ride. One night I talked with several cyclists who deliberately scheduled a "people's ride" on the East Side at the same time as Critical Mass, which always started downtown. "I think people are trying to reinvent Critical Mass," said Dat Nguyen, one of the mainstays of Shift. "It's rebranding is all it is. Families don't want to ride in Critical Mass any more, it's too much hassle. But look at this." He pointed to a small knot of parents with young children waiting to ride. "People respect us more on this side of the river. Over on the other side they are commuting. They're tired, they just want to go home." And in fact, the ride, bereft of the police, did seem to mostly attract waves and smiles from bystanders as it wended its way through mostly residential neighborhoods.

One of the things I found most intriguing about Portland's exploding bike scene was how it could build community in the unlikeliest of ways. For example, I had been reading on the Shift list for more than a year about people moving—as in literally moving from one residence to another—by bicycle. It was hard for me to think of a more unimpeachable use for an internal combustion engine than renting a truck to carry furniture across town. But then I decided to help out on a bike move.

Babs Adamski, who worked at a used bookstore at the central library, was moving out of a house she shared with a couple of roommates into a smaller home about six miles away. She had only a fraction of the furniture of the typical suburban homeowner, but she did possess a bed, a chest of drawers, a couch, and a lot of boxes, among other things. I showed up around 11 a.m. and found that I wasn't alone. There were more than twenty of us, and we spent more time eating doughnuts and drinking coffee than carrying furniture. With so many people around, getting the stuff out to the bikes was pretty quick. "The thing is, I've never seen a truck move attract fifteen or twenty friends," explained Steve Kirkendall, a computer programmer, as he cinched boxes into his bike trailer. "It's like a barn-raising," added Timo Forsberg, who managed to secure the mattress to his trailer. "Everybody loves to help their friends, but they don't realize that until they do it."

The best part, however, was after we started on our six-mile journey. There were eighteen cyclists with loaded trailers, and another three or four of us with various items on racks and in panniers. Despite the drizzly weather, we enjoyed the surprised looks and smiles from onlookers. And I saw just one angry motorist, who yelled something after being delayed at one intersection. "There's something about being out there on the road with a bunch of funny-looking goofy vehicles filled with stuff hanging out," explained Forsberg, who kept up a steady stream of banter during the ride. "Do you think it makes my bike look fat?" he asked in mock concern at one point as his trailer swayed back and forth under the weight of the mattress. At the other end, we had the trailers unloaded in a flash. I only carried two armfuls of stuff. Then we started eating pizza and drinking beer. In the merriment, nobody noticed one friend of Adamski who brought over a folding table in her pickup truck. And then Adamski realized she'd have to use the truck to get her couch, which accidentally got left behind. But it was certainly the easiest move I've ever participated in, and now I understand why I see a notice on the Shift list for one almost every week.

Jonathan Maus, a young Californian who consulted for the bike industry, moved to Portland and was so taken with the local scene that he dropped his other work to write the blog, bikeportland. org. "It's like Paris early in the twentieth century when all the great writers and artists are there," he says. "What we have here is this great bike culture, all these people riffing off of each other." Maus has become the twenty-first-century equivalent of a frontier newspaper editor, both a booster of the local bike scene and its chronicler. He's not alone. Filmmaker Dan Kaufman produces regular video reports on the "Crank My Chain" Web site. At

Portland State University, officials began developing an institute devoted to bicycle and pedestrian research. City officials also sought to stoke the bike culture by holding its first Sunday parkway event in 2008, copied from the weekly *ciclovias* held in Bogota, Colombia, and Guadalajara, Mexico. The city closed off a six-mile loop to cars that attracted thousands of cyclists and pedestrians.

Portland was also increasingly becoming an important home to custom bike builders, whose businesses resembled the small beer makers that made Portland a center of the microbrew industry. As of December 2007, Sacha White, the builder of Vanilla Bicycles, had a five-year waiting list for his bikes, which can cost up to $8,500 but have gained a national reputation for their fine workmanship. "Cycling for transportation is becoming more a part of peoples' lives," he said. "Investing in a really good functional vehicle makes a lot of sense to me." Todd Fahrner and Dean Mullin took that practicality a step further by opening Clever Cycles, which featured Dutch *bakfiets,* which are cargo bikes capable of carrying a couple hundred pounds of kids and/or groceries. The boxy bikes are now a common sight around Portland.

In 2006, the city commissioned a study that found that the city's bicycle-related businesses were generating $63 million a year. Bike advocates touted it as a sign of the industry's growing importance to the city. But Portland economist Joe Cortright said the city was looking at the wrong metric. The economic activity generated by bike businesses is a tiny fraction of the city's economic output, he noted, probably exceeded by a car dealership or two. The larger point, he said, was that bicycling allowed residents to save vastly larger sums of money. He explained this in "Portland's Green Dividend," a paper commissioned by CEOs for Cities, a pro-urban group. "Being green means Portlanders save a bundle on cars and gas," he wrote, "and local residents have more money to spend on other things they value, which in turn stimulates the local economy." All told, residents of the Portland region drive about 20 percent fewer miles per capita than residents of the average large metropolitan area, he calculated, producing annual savings of $1.1 billion, or 1.5 percent of the region's regional income. He explained that those savings have a higher chance of staying and circulating in the region than money spent on gasoline, of which at least 73 percent of its value is immediately exported. It should also be noted that these calculations are based on three-dollars-a-gallon gasoline, so the savings only escalated as prices rose.

Somehow, though, cyclists are not always seen as saviors of any kind. Portland's biking revolution has not been universally welcomed. Motorists are often unhappy about having to share the road with cyclists and they frequently complain about the bad behavior they see from riders. One woman who moved from Portland to Monroe, North Carolina, told a local columnist there in 2006 that, "We are thrilled that we have left the massive amount of bikes on the roads in Portland ... People who ride bikes to work or just on the weekends in Portland have taken over the street." The former Portlander, Sandy Harmon, went on to say that, "They are suppose[d] to follow the same rules as cars but they don't. They weave in and out of traffic, run red lights, ride right in front of your car or two abreast—putting one of them in the way of cars approaching from behind, which forces cars to slow down to their speed or try to pass them by having to get into oncoming traffic."

While that may be a fanciful account that exaggerates the impact of bicycles, there is no doubt that the growth in bicycling has been an adjustment for the motoring majority. There have been some nasty flare-ups. In 2006, cyclist Randy Albright became big news after *The Oregonian* obtained a TriMet security tape of his confrontation with a bus driver. On a cold winter morning, Albright moved out of the bike lane on the east approach to the Hawthorne Bridge to avoid gravel that had accumulated on the side of the road after it had been laid down during a recent snowstorm. A bus zoomed by that Albright felt missed him only by inches. The cyclist caught up to the bus in heavy traffic on the other end of the bridge and swung his bike in front of the vehicle to block it from moving while he berated the driver. The security tape shows a bald, barrel-chested man push his way through the standing-room-only crowd on the bus and get off. Then he is seen, after a short confrontation, punching Albright and pushing him and the bike out of the way. The rider then calmly got back on the bus, and the driver put the bus in gear and moved on. (The attacker was never identified; Albright sued TriMet and the case was settled in arbitration, with TriMet agreeing to revise its manual for drivers.) Even some bicyclists on the Shift listserv thought Albright had acted hastily, although not as abysmally as the attacker or the bus driver, who blithely ignored the assault. But some readers reacted with their own thoughts of violence. The reporter who wrote the story played me some of his voice mails, including several from men volunteering to punch the cyclist themselves. One, creepily enough, said he'd simply like to run bicyclists off the road.

But for all of that, there also seem to be increased numbers of motorists who drive with an eye out for cyclists, and they often surrender the right of way when they don't have to (and maybe even shouldn't). That's not surprising since, increasingly, many motorists are cyclists themselves. I've found that a car with a bike rack is often a good clue for gauging a driver's affability toward cyclists. Greg Raisman, a traffic safety expert for the city, said he was convinced that bikes have played a role in calming traffic and have helped drive down the city's overall crash rate.

With more bikes on the streets, the city has come under pressure to crack down on the bad actors. The city unveiled a "share the road" campaign after the Albright incident. And the police routinely conduct stings targeting both motorists and bikes for rolling through stop signs. Not surprisingly, many cyclists have claimed the city has been overzealous about ticketing cyclists, and the hefty $242 fine[2] for running a stop sign has certainly captured their attention. They

---

2. First-time offenders can typically get the citation dismissed by attending a two-hour road safety class.

were particularly upset about one sting—along one of the city's bike boulevards—that targeted cyclists running a stop sign as they entered a wide traffic circle in the Ladd's Addition neighborhood. They saw the stop sign as one that they could safely ride through because the road was so wide in the generally quiet traffic circle. But Curt Dewees, a long-time bike activist and a resident of the neighborhood, said that all too many cyclists failed to realize how they were endangering pedestrians in a neighborhood that is particularly attractive to walkers.

"When a bicyclist is riding at 20 mph and cuts off a pedestrian, they're not thinking that they are doing the same thing to a pedestrian that a car does to a bicyclist," Dewees said. "I think that's a perspective most bicyclists don't like to think about … It's just human nature. When you're traveling somewhere, it's easy to justify doing what you're going to do. I think motorists do it to bicyclists and bicyclists do it to pedestrians. You think, 'I'm important, I'm in a hurry.'"

Some cyclists also grumbled when officials put new markings on the Hawthorne Bridge to separate bikes and walkers, although something like that had to be done on the increasingly crowded bridge pathways. The bike messengers, who favor one-speed, fixed-gear bikes, griped about a local judge's ruling that they had to have a mechanical brake on their bikes. They insist they can stop just fine by pedaling backward to halt their rear wheel's forward movement.

Portland's bike-friendliness has also come under fire from conservative activists who tend to lump it in with what they see as the city's other ills: too much money spent on transit and too little on new roads, subsidies to downtown condo developers, and misguided efforts to discourage driving. John Charles of the libertarian Cascade Policy Institute has been a particularly vociferous critic of light rail, saying it sucks up vast amounts of money for little benefit. "You have to observe consumer demand," he said. "I object to what the city is doing with this whole mania of trying to get people out of their cars." He's skeptical of bike lanes in any case, but he argued that they are particularly inappropriate if they take away any capacity from the transportation choice of the majority: the motor vehicle. Jason Williams of the Taxpayer Association of Oregon said he thinks bike lanes merely anger taxpayers who see them as wasteful spending when so many "basic" road projects go unfunded. Neither sees bicycling as a real solution because of the relatively small number of riders, particularly in the suburbs, where those two spend most of their time.

Critics of compact growth note that what Portland has done in part is push more people across the Columbia River to Washington State, where land-use controls are less strict. All of these complaints aren't surprising. What is striking, though, is that they have not reached—pardon a little bicycle pun here—critical mass in the Portland area. The oppressed auto majority has not risen in protest. Burkholder, the cycling advocate-turned-politician and his like-minded colleagues on the seven-member Metro Council have for the most part faced little opposition at election time (and I was struck that five of the seven councilors participated in a day-long bike ride held in 2007 to give local public officials a feel for the local bikeway system). On the Portland city council, none of the five members profess anything but support for bicycling. And the city's new mayor, Sam Adams, has made the cycling community one of his key support groups.[3]

---

3. Another member of the council, Randy Leonard, has been the biggest surprise for bike advocates. Leonard is a retired firefighter who once headed his union local. He favored large pickup trucks when he was first elected in 2002. But, tired of the cost of commuting downtown from his home in outer Southeast Portland and feeling like he needed more exercise, he became the council's most committed bike commuter. Given Leonard's blue-collar, macho image, his conversion still leaves many local bike advocates shaking their heads in pleased amazement. Leonard said his staff and friends tell him he is a nicer person when he rides—and politically he's become a reliable vote for more money for

Adams apprenticed in Portland politics as the chief of staff to Mayor Vera Katz during her twelve years in office, from 1992 to 2004. He was known as a Machiavellian figure who shared his boss's benign disinterest in bikes. When he ran for the city council in 2004, Adams, who is gay, had the backing of the city's powerful gay-rights community. What was less well known was that he also courted cycling advocates. His campaign manager, Tom Miller, was a BTA board member firmly steeped in the bicycle-as-transportation culture. Adams promised during the campaign to seek to run the transportation department if he was elected. And he promised to launch an effort to earn the League of American Bicyclists' top platinum award.

Adams won a narrow victory, took over the transportation department, and launched a platinum planning effort; at one point, he had to fight Katz's successor, Tom Potter, to get $100,000 in the budget to pay for it. Miller became his chief of staff and Adams' office turned into a hotbed of bike advocacy. Adams told me that the city couldn't continue to make space for an ever-growing number of single-occupancy vehicles while still maintaining its livability. "I can't tell [residents] to get out of their car," he said. "I can't order them to do that. But I can give them safe alternatives."

"There is a lot you can get done when you have the political support," Geller, the city's bike coordinator, told me one day over lunch after Adams had been in office nearly two years. Adams—and Miller in particular—were pushing for projects that could continue the increase in the mode share for bikes. The biggest hope Geller had was that bicycling could get some real money from the city. "We've had a poverty mentality," he said. "We've been trained not to ask for a lot of money." Increasingly, Geller talked publicly about building a "world-class bicycling city."

---

bikes. Leonard, who was used to asking for a lot as a union boss, said it's pretty easy to get on the right side of cycling advocates. Really, he said, shaking his head, "they ask for so little."

Adams showed that he was willing to move quickly when he saw an opening. After two cyclists were killed in the fall of 2007 in collisions with right-turning vehicles, Adams brought together a large group of city officials and transportation representatives from the private sector to hammer out safety improvements. The police agreed to become more aggressive in investigating bike crashes, and the police chief put new leadership in place at the traffic enforcement division after cyclists complained that one of the top enforcement officials was biased against cyclists. More noticeably, the city installed bike boxes at fourteen intersections where there was a high crash risk. The green-colored bike boxes, a common feature in many European cities, require motor vehicles to stop several feet before an intersection while cyclists are allowed to gather in front. That gives cyclists a chance to get through the intersection before right-turning vehicles. Some cycling experts, such as John Allen, questioned whether cyclists would face increased danger as they tried to enter the box just as the light is turning. But Portland officials were confident they would work, and they launched a billboard campaign to educate motorists to stop before the boxes— bringing further attention to the role of bicycling in the city.

As the platinum planning process got underway, there was a lot of talk about Netherlands-style cycletracks and bike paths. But the discussion kept coming back to expanding the city's network of bike boulevards. When Portland was first building its bikeway network in the 1990s, cyclists were most interested in bike lanes. They were mostly hardened riders who wanted to travel on the same arterials for the same reason as motorists: because they are the fastest routes to the most popular destinations. "We thought bike lanes would do it," said Geller. "They'd work for everyone. But there are a lot of people who don't feel comfortable riding on busy streets." In contrast, the most popular bike boulevards were in Southeast Portland, where the bicycling mode share in some neighborhoods was over 10 percent. For the most part, the bike boulevards had also become well accepted by residents. "I like it because it's a community feel," explained Jon Berry, who lives on Southeast Lincoln Street and frequently bicycles to his work at a brewery in Northwest Portland. "My wife and I often sit out in front and have a cocktail and watch the bikes go by. I guess I like looking at bikes more than cars."

As Adams prepared to run for mayor in 2008, he spent much of 2007 assembling a $464 million package of street repairs and improvements that would be financed by a new fee on households and businesses. He hoped for a bold stroke that would enhance his leadership credentials while also getting rid of a huge maintenance backlog that had plagued the city's streets (a problem, it should be said, endemic to most cities, which find it hard to keep their networks in good repair).

Adams had plenty in the package for his cycling constituency, including $3.2 million to expand the Safe Routes to Schools program and $24 million to build another 114 miles of bike boulevards, which he advertised to the broader public as bike and pedestrian "safety corridors." Polling, he said, showed that while residents didn't list bicycling as one of their top concerns, they were very interested in reducing the safety conflicts between bikes and cars. When Adams presented his plan to the city's Bicycle Advisory Committee, he told the assembled cyclists he thought the expanded boulevard network could double bicycle's mode share. "This is about getting more people on bikes," he said, adding that cyclists will then "have a bigger constituency base and we can go from there."

By the beginning of 2008, it was clear Adams would not be able to simply send his plan through the city council and then focus on running in the May primary for mayor. A lobbyist for gas dealers and convenience stores threatened to refer the measure to the May ballot—and Adams didn't want voters considering both him and his tax increase at the same time. Instead, as the economy worsened, Adams backed away from his plan and said he'd instead try to make piecemeal improvements to the bike network.

Cyclists loudly backed Adams in his mayoral race, with the BTA's executive director, Scott Bricker, organizing a fund-raiser for Adams. Several of the candidates for city council also competed for the support of cyclists, with Jonathan Maus, the bikeportland. org editor, treated with the same deference given the mainstream media. Still, the candidates endorsed by the cycling lobby in two of the city council races lost to better-known rivals. Cyclists still have only so much power in Portland.

However, there's a certain kind of fervor to the bicyclists in Portland that sticks with the political writer in me. That seemed on perfect display at the BTA's annual fund-raising dinner in 2005. Since then, the event has moved to the larger—but much more sterile—Oregon Convention Center. I preferred the event when it was still in the Melody Ballroom, an aged stone building with an ornate wood-and-plaster interior that felt like a witness to Portland history. Mayor Potter, then newly elected, was there, along with Blumenauer, Adams, a passel of legislators and small-town mayors, and some five hundred other guests.

"We need a group consciousness: when they are harassing one of us, they are harassing all of us!" intoned Ray Thomas, a local bike lawyer and the night's emcee. "Bikes are the most efficient form of transportation ever devised," exulted Blumenauer, to the cheers of dozens of tinkling bike bells, handed out for just this purpose. As the speeches wore on, I looked around the faded ballroom and felt like I could have been at an Irish-American dinner in the 1920s. Or a civil-rights event in the 1960s. Or a gay-rights banquet in the eighties. Somehow, in Portland at least, bicyclists have become part of that great American melting pot.

6

Biking in the Big Apple

Islowly pedaled over the Brooklyn Bridge, dodging photo-snapping tourists as I watched the skyscrapers of Wall Street grow closer on a fine spring day. Still uncertain of my safety on the Manhattan streets, I planned to play it safe by scurrying over to the East River bike path as soon as I came off the west end of the bridge. But I saw a cyclist ahead of me ride straight down Centre Street, into the maw of Manhattan traffic. On the spur of the moment, I decided to follow. As I pedaled, the city became kind of a blur. Bike lanes seemed to come and go, but I found room to maneuver on the one-way street. Centre took me to Lafayette and then to Fourth as the blocks reeled by. I swooped around Union Square and suddenly found myself on Park Avenue, three lanes each way, moving toward midtown. The buildings became grander, the sea of pedestrians more expensively attired. I tucked in behind a cab, which slowed me some, but felt safer. I was content not to compete with the bike messengers hurtling between cars in the faster lanes. I was starting to enjoy myself. Almost before I realized it, I reached West 26th Street, my intended destination. I was way early for my appointment.

By accident, I had experienced what others have known for decades. New York City, with its dense forest of high-rises, flat topography, and short distances is ideal for bicycling—except, of course, for the danger of competing with the hordes of adrenaline-charged motorists fighting for a share of the limited space on the street. Just as in other cities, New York traffic engineers have spent most of their time over the last several decades trying to figure out how to ram more cars through a city once built for people on foot. But unlike in most places, where town fathers gleefully pushed Uncle Sam-paid interstates through their old downtowns, New Yorkers never gave up on other forms of locomotion. That was particularly true in Manhattan, where car owners have always been a relatively small minority (only about 22 percent of households) and the subway will get you almost anywhere, often with surprising speed, if not comfort. While the motor vehicle insinuated itself into every nook and cranny of the city, it was never welcomed uncritically. And even back in the days when bikes were marketed almost solely as children's toys, cycling for the sake of transportation seemed to get at least a little respect in the otherwise brawny world of local politics. Novelist Norman Mailer, who made a semi-serious run for mayor in 1969, wanted to seed lower Manhattan with free bikes, build a monorail around the island, and eventually ban the private car. In his own quixotic run for mayor in 1965 from the other side of the political spectrum, conservative commentator William F. Buckley Jr. proposed placing bikeways on Manhattan's major north-south boulevards. John Lindsay, who *was* elected mayor in 1965 and again four years later, held periodic car-free holidays on Park and Madison avenues, curtailed auto traffic in Central and Prospect parks, and restored the Brooklyn Bridge pedestrian path. And he practiced what he preached, often joining in bicycle rides around the city. What is now New York's major bicycle lobby, Transportation Alternatives, was started in 1973 by fiery anti-car activists whose first demonstration was a march on General Motors headquarters in Manhattan. In 1980, Mayor Ed Koch, enthralled by the hordes of cyclists he had seen on a trip to China, ordered barrier-separated bike lanes on Fifth and Seventh avenues and Broadway. The experiment went awry (more about that later) and the barriers were ripped out within a few months. But the thought was there, which it almost invariably wasn't in other U.S. cities.

Now, as the bicycle movement has gained a foothold across America, New York City suddenly roared back into the forefront in 2007. Mayor Michael Bloomberg, who had previously not shown any great interest in cycling, appointed a new transportation commmissioner, Janette Sadik-Kahn, who was designated to help lead the charge for a London-style congestion pricing plan aimed at discouraging traffic into Manhattan and at raising hundreds of millions of dollars for mass transit. Sadik-Kahn, who saw the overall value of a bike-friendly city, made sure that bicycles were part of the new order on the streets. She pushed forward with an aggressive bikeway plan that included a test of a European-style protected cycletrack. Sadik-Kahn liked to say that she got her job description from her son:"reduce the trucks, increase the bikes, and plant more trees."

Sadik-Kahn had a long way to go if New York was to rival Copenhagen, where cyclists account for 34 percent of commute trips, a city that she happened to visit shortly after she was appointed to the job. But cycling is on the upswing in New York and it has

Janette Sadik-Kahn, New York City's groundbreaking commissioner of transportation, talks to fellow riders at the 2007 Tour de Bronx, an annual ride sponsored by Transportation Alternatives and the Bronx borough president. (Photo by Clarence Eckerson, Jr.)

become a visible part of the fabric of the city. That's important, not only for the city, but for the bike movement in the entire country. As America's largest city and the media capital of the nation, New York is, despite its uniqueness, a trend setter. New York's urban renaissance—which has made parts of the city almost a theme park for adults—has been admired and copied throughout the nation. If the streets became crowded with bikes, you'd see it in countless movies, television shows, and news stories. To rework the old slogan, if bikes can make it here, they can make it anywhere.

Well ... maybe not everywhere. Suburbia, with its long distances, isolated subdivisions, and wide arterials, is still the toughest nut for cyclists to crack. But it's striking how cycling is reaching the tipping point in pre-automotive cities like New York, Chicago, and San Francisco, where vehicle congestion, the environment, health concerns, and progressive politics are combining to give cycling a boost. Never before have so many large cities set ambitious goals for making bicycling a serious part of the transportation mix.

Despite New York City's grand scale, or perhaps because of it, nothing is easy here. If there have always been New Yorkers who have seen what cycling could be for the city, opposition has also been easy to find. In such a crowded city, squeezing in more bicycles has to come at the expense of something else. I've seen pedestrians in many cities complain about nearly getting run down by cyclists, but in New York, with its dense crowds of walkers, it's more of a danger. A city study of bike safety found that eleven pedestrians were killed in crashes with cyclists from 1996 to 2005. Of course, in that same period, more than 1,900 pedestrians were killed in accidents involving motor vehicles.

Cycling advocates have had to wage what sometimes seems like a block-by-block battle in this balkanized city of more than 8.2 million. I got a sense of that one day in March of 2007—shortly before the start of the Sadik-Kahn era—when I met Noah Budnick at his home in the Bed-Sty neighborhood of Brooklyn for a ride into Manhattan. Budnick, the deputy director of Transportation

Alternatives, was the group's reigning bike expert. Slim and tousle-haired with a shy grin, Budnick seemed all too gentle for fighting City Hall. But his quiet demeanor hides his tenacity. After suffering a brain injury in 2005 when he hit a pothole that knocked him off his bike, Budnick came back an even more determined cycling advocate. If anything, he said, it made him appreciate how vulnerable average people felt riding the streets of the city. We talked about his neighborhood, which first became crowded with cyclists when artists, hip young professionals, and other creative people began moving there in the 1980s and 1990s, fleeing the escalating housing costs in Manhattan. Many of the more adventurous found cycling a quick and cheap way to get back and forth from Manhattan—to the point, Budnick said, that "the old-timers see cycling as another sign of gentrification." We hopped on our bikes and rode on back streets into a leafy neighborhood of restored townhouses near Fort Greene Park. It is here, he said, where Transportation Alternatives joined with local activists to win a series of traffic-calming projects aimed at reducing cut-through traffic. But, he added, negotiations still continued with the neighborhood over a bike lane slated for the area. Because of the city's diversity, "you have to go slow," he said. "People say every block has its own mayor. On my block, there are two guys who think they are."

We rode into downtown Brooklyn, through a new pedestrian plaza at the intersection of Willoughby and Adams. It didn't look like that big of a deal to me—there were a few heavy-duty tables and permanently anchored chairs—but it was celebrated by activists as a hard-won victory in reclaiming public space from cars. We made our way to the Brooklyn Bridge, where cyclists gained a safer approach when the city installed concrete barriers along Tillary Street to create a protected bike lane in front of a federal courthouse. And as we pedaled over the bridge, Budnick delightedly showed me the precise moment when our view of the Chrysler Building was framed by the arches of the nearby Manhattan Bridge. "Bicycles give you a much more intimate view of the city," he said. "During my first year here, I learned so much by just riding around. I would have missed so much if I had just been on the subway." It has been a long battle, he explained, to open all of the East River bridges to bicycles, something only accomplished in the last few years. One of the toughest fights was getting the city to replace viciously angled expansion joints on the Williamsburg Bridge that were hard for cyclists to navigate. The problem was fixed in 2005, but only after reporters found out that the city had paid out $10 million in legal claims brought by injured cyclists.

Budnick and I glided down the west end of the bridge ramp, rode past City Hall and cut down Reade Street to head over to the West Side Greenway. Shorn of my need to figure out where I was going, I found it easy to follow Budnick as he skillfully moved through traffic. I began to realize that, A) Manhattan drivers often have to drive slowly because of congestion anyway, and B) when they do have clear streets, there is often plenty of room to move around a bicyclist (although it also became clear to me that being "doored" is a huge risk in the city). I was beginning to realize that even though the city often feels close to gridlock, there are many times of the day when many of the cross streets, and even some of the boulevards, are startlingly empty.

We soon reached the West Side Greenway, said to be one of the busiest bike paths in America. With the exception of a few gaps, the greenway stretches the length of Manhattan. Much of it was built after plans for a new "Westway" freeway imploded in 1985 after years of political infighting. Westway was designed to replace another highway that had collapsed in 1973. The fact that the city's traffic didn't grind to a standstill after 1973 emboldened transportation reformers who said it showed that more highways simply generated more traffic. Instead of Westway, the city built a surface boulevard that included room for the greenway along the river (ironically, some argue that the full freeway would have been better for bikes because the road would have been buried with a linear park on top). Shoehorning in a bike path along some of the world's most expensive real estate was not simple. Budnick noted how the greenway narrows near the Chelsea Piers sports and entertainment complex, which happened to be owned by Roland Betts, whose abundant political connections include a long-standing friendship with George W. Bush. At the complex and at several other points, vehicles cross the path without much in the way of traffic calming to slow them down. Two fatalities along the path in 2006 enraged the cycling community. A fifty-six-year-old physician, Dr. Carl Nacht, was killed by a police tow truck turning across the path to get to an impound yard. And twenty-two-year-old Eric Ng died when he was struck by a drunk driver who had left the Chelsea Piers and sped down the bike path in his BMW. We paused by the "ghost bike" memorial left for Ng as Budnick talked about the safety improvements he was—so far unsuccessfully—pushing the city to implement.

But despite these problems, the greenway has revolutionized bicycling in New York. As Budnick explained, it gave beginning riders—and those who simply don't like cycling next to motor vehicles—a car-free route through the world's busiest city. I met a fellow journalist who told me she rides on the sidewalks or even walks her bike from her Upper West Side apartment over to the greenway, rides down to mid-town Manhattan, and then walks a few blocks cross-town to her office. Budnick said he knows someone who rides all the way over from the Upper *East* Side to use the greenway. My most poignant experience riding the greenway came one day when I looked across the boulevard and gazed at the empty hole of Ground Zero. And then I looked back in front of me and realized I was approaching a young mother riding behind a young child—who could not have been more than three or four—wobbling along on a bike with training wheels.

Budnick and I rode the few blocks down West 26th to the Transportation Alternatives office. It was late morning now, and, once again, the street was surprisingly empty. Budnick pointed out a children's playground he admired, which had a play structure topped with a pretend version of the city's skyline. Another sight he would miss on the subway, he said. As we sat in the TA offices—which, with their unruly stacks of paper and casual air, looked like the home of a money-losing political magazine—he talked about the bike movement evolving to take on a more urban air. Ever since the passage of ISTEA, the landmark 1991 transportation law, there's been so much focus on getting federal money for things like rail-to-trail projects. But the "next evolution or focus of the movement is going to be on urban areas," he argued. It is in the cities, for the most part, where the political leadership is pushing the most dramatic plans to combat global climate change. And it is the cities that point to a way of living that doesn't depend on big suburban houses and long automobile commutes. New York City in 2007 released a greenhouse emissions survey that found the average city resident emitted 7.1 metric tons of greenhouse gasses, less than a third of the 24.5 metric tons produced by the average American. We would be much closer to solving our global-warming problem if we all lived like New Yorkers (hard as that is to imagine). And, added Budnick, "The fact is that cities, just by their nature, are more bike friendly." he said. We talked more about the environmental movement and he lamented how difficult it has been to work with the major national conservation groups. "TA has worked with the local offices of national environmental groups for years," he said. "But when you get the mail from their national headquarters and it shows a picture of a young fashionable couple in front of the backdrop of a large city standing next to a hybrid car, it makes us want to tear our hair out." They're still appealing to a suburban ethos, he said, not an urban one.

Later in the day, I met with Paul Steely White, TA's executive director. Boisterous where Budnick is quiet, White draws attention to himself, favoring interesting sartorial combinations (suit vests and blue jeans, for example) and fast, single-speed bikes. The rush hour was reaching its crescendo as we decided to ride down to one of his favorite taverns, the Great Jones Café, in Greenwich Village.

White sped off and I followed along on a not-so-dashing folding bike I had borrowed. I managed to keep him in sight as he headed down Broadway and I tried to keep my small-diameter wheels out of potholes. I remember squeezing through an impossibly small gap between a bus and a cab and dancing through lights nano-seconds before and after they turned red. I was suddenly seeing life from the perspective of a bike messenger, which involves not so much staying out of the way of cars as figuring out how to match their velocity. White grinned at me as he dismounted to walk the last block to the tavern, noting that he did draw the line at riding down the street the wrong way. Yes, he acknowledged, he's supposed to be a better role model, but running lights is part of the "unwritten social contract" in New York City. The key is to not make life difficult for pedestrians, he said.[1]

We settled in with our beers and he talked about growing up in New Orleans and in Illinois and studying environmental science at the University of Montana. He was interested in grizzly bears but he said a professor convinced him that the future of the environmental movement was in the cities. As head of the TA, White has been able to continue expanding the expertise and funding of a group that was, until the early 1990s, essentially an all-volunteer organization. In his first four years, he roughly tripled the annual budget to $1.6 million and had similar increases in staff, which totaled eighteen full-timers and five part-timers at the beginning of 2008. The group has churned out a number of provocative reports that, among other things, attacked widespread parking permit abuse by city workers and suggested that much of the auto traffic in Manhattan's central business district is unnecessary, either because drivers have good transit alternatives or because they are crossing the island to

---

1. Several months later, White slid out on an oily slick he said was left by a garbage truck and broke his hip. He said he was back on the bike almost before he was walking again but has become a more cautious rider.

Paul Steely White (left), executive director of Transportation Alternatives, rides through Central Park with Klaus Bondam, Copenhagen's mayor of technical and environmental administration.

Photo by Clarence Eckerson, Jr.

avoid heavier tolls on other routes. And sometimes Transportation Alternatives was willing to use the confrontational tactics for which their founders were noted. White hired bike activist Matthew Roth, a leader of the more militant Time's Up group that was deeply embroiled in fighting the police crackdown of Critical Mass. Roth started a new Web site, uncivilservants.org, that published photos of illegal parkers ranging from cops and teachers to politicians, and he wasn't afraid of a little inflammatory rhetoric. "This little whore of a hydrant gives it up for anyone with an NYPD placard," said one caption under a photo of two vehicles parked on both sides of a hydrant.

Unlike most other bike groups, Transportation Alternatives styles itself as a lobby that promotes transit and walking as well as cycling. But cycling "is our heart and soul," said White. "It's what drives us, what makes us so fervent about this thing. Maybe because we do it every day. It's like Gandhi, be the change you want to see in the world ... Everything we do has one common denominator, and that is giving the streets over to those who use it more productively—whether it is bicyclists, pedestrians, bus drivers, people lounging on a street corner. Yeah, we're anti-car. Cars suck." He paused, digging into one of the spicy chicken wings we had ordered. Then he said, "Sometimes we have to use cars, but that doesn't mean they have to dominate our lives. Instead it should be dominated by human interactions ... the level of car use in New York City is so inconsistent with what we want out of our city," whether in terms of health, quality of public life, or air quality. "This isn't the ravings of a lunatic anymore," he added. "You have the mayor saying managing car use is a good thing."

In fact, the ground was starting to shift inside the Bloomberg administration. After focusing on the recovery from 9/11, schools, and a shaky budget picture in his first term, Bloomberg had started turning his attention to transportation. His go-to guy, as in so much of his administration, was Deputy Mayor Dan Doctoroff, whose broad portfolio included the city's transportation network. Doctoroff, a former investment banker, also happened to be a bike commuter. Budnick and White talked about him in tones that suggested they might have a behind-the-scenes ally at the top levels of City Hall. Curious, I went to see Doctoroff, who with his crisp pinstriped suit certainly belied the stereotypes many people have about people who get to work on a bike. "I was working incredibly hard and feeling like I wasn't getting any exercise at all," Doctoroff explained as we sat in a conference room at City Hall. "I happened to live very close to the bike path in Hudson Park [part of the Westside Greenway]. In fact I could get basically all the way downtown without really having to get on the road and I figured I could kill two birds with one stone. I could both get exercise and commute and it would only take about twenty to twenty-five minutes a day." Since the start of the administration, he said, he would ride at least a couple days a week on his high-end road bike ("I like to go fast"), unless the weather was icy. Doctoroff said he also liked to ride around the city with aides on weekends to take a firsthand look at various infrastructure issues. "There's actually no way to get to know New York better than on a bike," he said. "In a car you don't see anything. In a subway, you pop up, but you don't see how the city is connected. Walking takes too long. It's great to do, but you can't cover a city the size of New York doing that."

When we talked, Doctoroff and Bloomberg were putting the finishing touches on the mayor's "PlaNYC," a sweeping initiative to sustainably handle an additional one million residents by 2030 while reducing greenhouse gas emissions by 30 percent. "We have to find ways of accommodating more people, and it isn't by cars," said Doctoroff. Their plan's centerpiece was congestion pricing, which would levy an eight dollar charge on motorists entering Manhattan below 86th Street. The idea was both to reduce traffic volumes—as happened in London—and to raise more money to beef up the city's overcrowded public transit network. The Bush administration, which also supported congestion charges as a free-market way to improve the transportation network, promised its own sweetener: some $354 million in federal money the city could use to quickly improve express bus service. To paraphrase White, the idea of congestion pricing had once been restricted to, if not the raving lunatics, at least a small fringe. The Bloomberg administration hoped it would reduce the number of cars in Manhattan by more than 6 percent, or the equivalent of 110,000 motor vehicle trips a day. They also saw it as a new source of money to expand not only bus service but the overloaded subway system as well, increasing the attractiveness of transit as an alternative to driving. Proponents hoped they could establish a kind of virtuous cycle that would cause car use to steadily dwindle in the city. By April of 2008, however, congestion pricing was dead. It was killed by Democrats in the state assembly engaged in a Byzantine political war with Bloomberg and responding to opposition from motor-vehicle commuters in the suburbs and outlying neighborhoods of the city.

But as the Bloomberg administration fought over congestion pricing, they began to also articulate a role for bikes. "We do believe that we have to shift, for a number of reasons, people from cars onto mass transit and other non-carbon-emitting modes," Doctoroff said. "Bicycling can be an important component of that. It will require an investment ... There has been a dramatic increase in the number of people commuting by bike over the last five or seven years. And we'd like to see that continue."

In fact, the city had seemed to start to get serious about expanding its bikeway network starting in September of 2006. That's when the city commissioners of transportation, health, parks, and the police released an exhaustive study of bicyclist injuries and fatalities (which TA had pushed for following a rash of cycling deaths) and concluded that a more extensive bikeway system would improve safety. The report set a goal of developing another two hundred miles of on-street bike lanes and forty miles of off-street paths by 2009, an increase of more than 50 percent over the current four hundred twenty-mile network.[2]

That was an ambitious goal for a city that had added only 13.6 miles in the previous year and had just seen its bicycle program manager, Andrew Vesselinovitch, quit in disgust, saying he was tired of waiting for Transportation Commissioner Iris Weinshall to either get serious about bikes or to lose her job. "Our efforts were so rarely encouraged, and so often delayed, that I came to the conclusion that the department is not truly committed to promoting bicycling in New York," he wrote in an op-ed in the *New York Times*. But following the safety report, Weinshall, the frequent target of criticism from the transportation reformers, became a more adamant supporter of bike lanes (and she would frequently point out that her husband,

---

2. The report also called for improving safety for commercial riders, particularly the food-delivery cyclists who are often foreign-language immigrants. In 2007, the city required employers to provide workers with helmets that they must use. Businesses using riders were also required to put up posters listing traffic safety laws for cyclists in a language they can understand.

Sen. Chuck Schumer, D-N.Y., loved to take weekend bike rides through the city). She put two new officials in charge of building the bike network: Ryan Russo, director of street management and safety; and Joshua Benson, the new manager of the bike program. The two were devoted cyclists and took the mandate for more bike lanes seriously. They challenged the idea that the city would wilt in the face of any community opposition to bike lanes.

I watched Russo and Benson one night at a boisterous community meeting in the venerable Old First Reformed Church in Brooklyn. That's where the transportation committee of Community Board 6 met to discuss the city's plans for a road diet on Ninth Street that would include bike lanes. The meeting attracted about seventy people, many of whom feared the bike lanes would make it harder to double-park in the crowded Park Slope neighborhood where parking spaces are at a premium. Benson, tall and soft-spoken, described how the road diet would slow traffic on a street that has had some serious crashes while also providing a crucial cross-Brooklyn connection for cyclists. The whole point of the expanded network, Benson explained, is so that "you can really get around the city on a bike." He was quickly challenged by Bob Levine, a local resident who had handed out fliers asking, "Do we want to solve Ninth Street's traffic problems by using bike riders as traffic calmers?" He told Benson that there are lots of times residents need to double-park to do such things as load groceries and help elderly people into cars. "That's realistic," Levine said. "That's life in the city—it isn't just about biking."

After that, it didn't take long for the meeting to turn acrimonious, with several people yelling over each other, reminding me of the dinner table scene in *Annie Hall* where everyone in Woody Allen's family talked at once. "We haven't asked to have bike lanes added to what is there," Levine said, pressing his point that it ought to be the neighborhood's say. No, responded Benson firmly, the safety concerns are real—for motorists, pedestrians, and cyclists. "That's really the reason we want to make it a better route for cyclists," he said. Several in the crowd guffawed at that, and after some more back and forth, one man stomped out of the church muttering, "They lie … This is nuts."

Paul White was there as well, along with a cadre of supporters who generally looked younger than the opponents, and he stood up to support the city. "People bike on Ninth," he said. "It's a reality and it's going to increase … Bicycling is the future for a lot of reasons." Councilman Bill de Blasio, trying to thread the needle between supporters and opponents of cycling, pressed Russo several times for a commitment the city wouldn't target double-parkers for enforcement. Russo told the councilman to talk to the police about that. Russo, wiry and intense, told the crowd that compromises needed to be made in the city because of its tight confines. "It's not like we're in San Diego where there is room for everything," he said. "These are very contested spaces." Afterwards, Russo told me that he recognized the concerns people had about the impact of bike lanes on traffic and parking. But part of it, he said, was also simply "cultural hostility" to cyclists. In the end, the transportation committee came out in favor of the bike lanes and they were installed less than four months later.

I also met Benson in his office at DOT's headquarters in lower Manhattan and he made it clear that his goal was not just to put in bike lanes where it was politically easy. "We're not going to hide two hundred miles [of new bike lanes] tucking them into corners," he said. "We're really trying to make good connections. And it's tough because everybody wants to be on these streets … It's not just the cyclists. And there is pain involved. You have to remove travel lanes sometimes and it's not always pleasant for everyone, but in the grand scheme of things it's worth the small pain that we have." New York City is expected to add another million people by 2030, he noted, "and we just have to make better use of our transportation infrastructure and by converting trips to bike is one way to do it … It's unlikely we will convert half of all New Yorkers to biking or something that extreme, but it will help use the limited space as we add more people ... We're also trying to have a more environmentally friendly transportation system and getting people away from polluting modes."

While Bloomberg was trying to sell his new congestion charge to a skeptical New York Legislature, he had another big transportation decision to make. Weinshall announced in early 2007 that she was leaving, and Doctoroff made it clear to me that the mayor was expecting something different from the new commissioner. That new person will be "much more focused" on shifting the city away from automotive travel, he said. Bloomberg's appointment, which I'm told leaned heavily on Doctoroff's advice, turned out to exceed the fondest hopes of livable-streets advocates.

Janette Sadik-Kahn had plenty of establishment credentials. Once the city's liaison to the Metropolitan Transportation Authority (which runs the subway), she was later deputy administrator of the U.S. Department of Transportation and a senior vice president at Parsons Brinckerhoff, a heavyweight engineering firm. She had broad international experience that had given her a different view of urban transportation, and she immediately made it clear she had a reformist conception of the city's public spaces.

"I sort of look at myself as the commissioner of the Department of Public Space," she told me in a telephone interview, noting that the city's six thousand miles of road constitute the biggest chunk of New York real estate. "Let's re-imagine this public realm," she added, both to provide mobility for all types of users and to create inviting plazas and other civic spaces. On her second day in the job, she cycled to work on a new bicycle, accompanied by Benson and Russo. "It's invaluable to get on a bike and see firsthand the conditions that our projects are trying to address," she told the *New York Times*. "We are really emphasizing connectivity in the bicycle lane network, because all cyclists, myself included, know that it's maddening to be coming along a lane and have it simply end and leave you off on your own on a big avenue."

Early in her tenure, she and the planning commissioner, Amanda Burden, visited Copenhagen, where Sadik-Kahn toured the city by bike with famed Danish planner Jan Gehl. He is legendary in planning circles for playing a big role in carving out pedestrian plazas and other public spaces that transformed Copenhagen's street life. While New York will never be Copenhagen, she said, she raved about the experience of riding a bicycle in a city where the car is not a priority. She quickly hired Gehl to consult with her department. Sadik-Kahn also raided the ranks of the reform community to round out what became known among transportation reformers as her "dream team." This group included Jon Orcutt, a former Transportation Alternatives executive director, who more recently had headed a regional transportation reform group, and consultant Bruce Schaller, who had authored studies for the TA. She also brought in Andrew Wiley-Schwartz of the Project for Public Spaces, a nonprofit dedicated to reclaiming public space from automobile traffic. She quickly moved on some small plaza projects and helped persuade the mayor to reduce the number of parking permits for city workers. White said he hoped that the permit reforms, combined with congestion pricing, would prod more city workers to bike and use the transit system, further increasing the constituency pushing for improvements in alternative transportation.

Sadik-Kahn gave Benson the go-ahead to experiment with a new bike lane on Ninth Avenue in lower Manhattan that was a daring departure from conventional design: a European-style cycletrack that would place cyclists between the curb and parked cars. The test project was in place by October of 2007, less than six months into her stewardship. Just seven blocks long, the project is like a mini-theme park of the possible for cycling advocates. "Riding on that is very similar to riding on a greenway," said White. "You can ride two abreast, you feel dignified; you feel safe. It's a wonderful experience. Unfortunately, it only lasts for a few blocks." The hope, White said, is that it could be replicated throughout Manhattan, something he said Gehl would like to do if he had his way. Benson said that the bikeway was designed with the knowledge that American traffic engineers often frown on this type of treatment as unsafe, chiefly because motorists have trouble seeing bikes at intersections. To deal with the intersection conflicts, Benson said, the project included separate signal phases that prevent cars making left turns (the bikeway is on the left side of the one-way boulevard) when cyclists are going straight through the intersection. That was necessary, he said, because, unlike in European bike cities, we "don't have a great culture of cyclists and motorists getting along and sharing the road." The bike lane itself is as wide as a full car lane, allowing access to street sweepers and emergency vehicles.

So far, Benson said, the new bikeway has a good safety record, and he noted that it has the added benefit of improving pedestrian safety because walkers have a shorter distance to travel to get across the vehicle lanes. The bikeway also includes a cross-hatched area next to the bike lanes that gives pedestrians a place to stand to hail taxis and the like. That's important, because pedestrian incursions were one thing that doomed Mayor Ed Koch's 1980 experiment with barrier-protected bike lanes in New York.

Koch, who had sponsored some of the first federal bike legislation as a congressman in the early 1970s, decided after a trip to China to install similar bikeways in New York. In the summer of 1980, he ordered transportation officials to install bike lanes on Fifth and Seventh avenues and Broadway, protected by stout asphalt median strips. Samuel Schwartz, a former city transportation engineer and author of the "Gridlock Sam" column in the *Daily News* (he claims to have invented the term "gridlock"), wrote that the bikeways ran through a major swath of mid-town Manhattan. But he said that within days, the complaints poured in from motorists who thought it increased congestion and pedestrians who feared getting hit by cyclists. Part of the problem was that, during a transit strike earlier that year, three pedestrians had been killed by cyclists and public sentiment wasn't exactly running in their favor. Schwartz wrote that many pedestrians regarded the new bike lanes as an extension of the sidewalk, creating more conflict with cyclists. As he told the story, the *coup de grâce* for the new lanes came when Koch and New York Governor Hugh Carey were riding in a limousine with President Jimmy Carter one chilly fall day and saw the lanes empty of cyclists. "See how Ed is wasting your money," Carey reportedly joked to the president. Within days Koch had the barriers ripped out. Steve Faust, a longtime Brooklyn bike activist, said motorists, pedestrians, and cyclists were just getting used to what was, for America, a radical experiment. "It was just beginning to work," said Faust, noting that even staunch bikeway opponent John Forester had supported keeping them in place for a year as an experiment.

Flash forward twenty-seven years and the city was much more cautious this time as it built its new cycletrack. "I have to say, it was extremely valuable for us to have that experience," said Benson. "It's a pretty intense treatment and I don't think that this treatment would be appropriate for just any street in the city." However, he added, "It works very well on a wide avenue like Ninth where you have intense traffic that is very intimidating to cyclists ... You know, we see mothers riding with their young children on Ninth Avenue and you never would have seen that in the past." He said it was certainly possible that cyclists could someday ride through Manhattan's central business district on a protected bike lane. "I think you're going to see them primarily on the larger streets," he said, "where we need to really interfere in the way the street is functioning to make it a very different experience for cyclists." Sadik-Kahn talked about creating a "luxurious experience for the biker that recognizes their role in the transportation network." She said she hoped to at least double the number of cyclists in the city and described how she wanted to rid urban cycling of the image of something done only by a radical fringe. "I enjoy biking but as my son would tell you, I'm hardly radical," she said. "We really want to change the paradigm of how cyclists are looked at" by promoting cycling as a "fun, sexy" way to get around the city.

With her broad smile and constant presence at ribbon cuttings for new plazas and charity rides for cyclists, Sadik-Kahn cut quite a different image than past transportation commissioners, who tended to make the news talking about gridlock, potholes, and pedestrian safety. White said he thought Sadik-Kahn promoted cycling both for its own values and as a symbol of how the streetscape needs to become "more green, more efficient, and more humane." He described Sadik-Kahn as engaged in kind of a race, to see how far she could go before being reined in by Bloomberg, or before he leaves office. In mid-2008, several months after our conversation, the city unveiled a plan to extend the Ninth Avenue cycletrack by another ten blocks and to build a similar northbound twin on Eighth Avenue. Later in the year, Sadik-Kahn's department unveiled a stunning remake of Broadway between Times Square and Herald Square that involved converting two travel lanes to plazas and protected bikeways. By late summer, New Yorkers were sitting at outdoor café tables that had once been automobile-jammed streets.

In the meantime, the bike program was also pursuing other innovations. In dozens of intersections around the city, the department began installing bike boxes. Those boxes hold cars back from the intersection while allowing cyclists to filter to the front of the line. While bike boxes are common in Europe, they've been rare in America. The other city installing several of them, Portland, was doing it primarily for safety reasons. Benson said the intent in New York is to allow cyclists to easily make turns onto intersecting streets that also have bike lanes, a problem given the city's frequent use of one-way streets (imagine trying to turn from a bike lane on the far right of a three-lane avenue to go left onto a cross-street and you get an idea of the purpose of bike boxes). The city also began installing shared-lane markings—or "sharrows"—on streets too narrow for bike lanes, making it clear that cyclists are allowed to be in the middle of the lane and should not be passed by motor vehicles. And on bike lanes next to curbs where no parking is allowed, the city began painting the lanes an almost neon shade of green to make it clear cars shouldn't park in them.

Budnick said he was also impressed that the city was doing a better job of choosing which routes to put bike lanes on. For example, cyclists had pushed for years to get bike lanes along one major stretch of Bedford Avenue in Brooklyn north of Dean. But it had been bogged down in New York's fierce neighborhood politics, including the Hasidic community, which had complained that the bike lanes would bring immodest lycra-clad cyclists through their neighborhood.

Bike advocates like White still have plenty to push the city on. Now that they've seen the Ninth Avenue bikeway, they're talking about not just racking up the bike lane miles, but having more protected ones. It's not just about quantity, but quality, said White, conjuring up an image of a cyclist being able to bike in a protected lane from Central Park to Battery Park. And cycling advocates have been quick to point out instances when they thought the Bloomberg administration was still encouraging more auto traffic, such as the subsidies it gave for the construction of additional parking garages at the new Yankees stadium.

Advocates also saw bike parking as a huge problem in a city where many commercial buildings still ban bikes—and where bike theft is epidemic. In PlaNYC, Bloomberg said large commercial buildings should be required to accommodate bikes, but this proposal has faced opposition from the real estate industry and at this writing has not been enacted. The city did get more aggressive about outdoor parking. It reached a deal with a Spanish company, Cemusa, to supply bus shelters, some of which would include bike racks, and other street furniture at no cost to the city. In exchange the company would be able to sell advertising. And the city also took out five auto parking spots at the Bedford Avenue subway stop in Williamsburg to provide bike parking at a station that had become a popular bike-transit link.

Sadik-Kahn said she was working with musician David Byrne—who has become an artistic champion of urban cycling—to help boost cycling's status in New York. Byrne helped judge a city contest to design new bike racks and was inspired to build his own whimsical bike racks for different neighborhoods, such as in the shape of a dollar sign for Wall Street. The city is giving away thousands of free helmets, Sadik-Kahn noted, with a cross-hatched stenciled design she hoped would become trendy. As Sadik-Kahn talked, it at once became clear to me how far cycling can go in a city when it gets the right champion. To understand that, let's make a slight diversion to America's Second City: Chicago.

Chicago was once the center of the American bicycle industry and has many of the same attributes that make New York such a target of opportunity for cyclists: flat topography, a good street-grid network, and the density to make biking competitive for many trips. Chicago also happens to have a tradition of strong mayors, exemplified by the incumbent, Mayor Richard Daley, who has now been in office longer than his father, once seen as the epitome of the big-city boss. The younger Daley also happens to be an avid recreational cyclist, and under the tutelage of bike advocate Randy Neufeld, who ran the Chicagoland Bike Federation for nearly two decades, he has come to see the value of utilitarian cycling. "There is no question that his personal attention to this has opened a lot of doors," said Neufeld, who has stepped away from the leadership of the group to work on such issues as traffic safety. The bike federation has forged a close working relationship with the city, doing bike planning under contract and detailing staffers to work inside the transportation department. "Our attitude is, 'let's become the entrenched bureaucracy,'" said Neufeld. "The city [government] isn't what we have to change—it's the culture, and it's the city we're trying to enlist in that change."

In Chicago, it is the mayor's picture that is plastered on bike maps and a group of young people who work for the city to encourage cycling are known as Mayor Daley's Bicycling Ambassadors. In turn the mayor used his fund-raising juice to get McDonald's to put up $5 million for the naming rights for a state-of-the-art bicycle station—which features secure parking, showers, rental bikes, and repairs—in Millennium Park, a new green space and cultural center between the lakeshore and downtown. "The mayor's vision is very simple: he wants to make Chicago the most bicycle-friendly city in the United States," said Ben Gomberg, the city's bike coordinator. "The approach came from the mayor—and you can see this throughout his administration—define best practices throughout the world and what the best practices are that would work in Chicago." The city's new bike plan, largely drafted by the Bike Federation, sets the goal of bikes making 5 percent of trips of less than five miles by 2015. In total, it calls for a five-hundred-mile network of bikeways. But what's really striking about the plan is that it sets a series of performance standards the city should regularly meet, ranging from fixing five to ten dangerous intersections every year to reaching two hundred fifty thousand Chicagoans annually with bike safety and encouragement programs. Before I visited Chicago in June of 2007, I had heard plenty of stories about the hazards of biking among the city's aggressive motorists. And I did get honked at more than I do in Portland. But I also found an expanding network of bike lanes and a growing number of cyclists, particularly on the north side. One night, during rush hour, I positioned myself on Milwaukie Avenue, one of the main bicycling routes heading north out of downtown. Bikes consisted of more than 40 percent of the outbound traffic for the hour I was there.

Even before Sadik-Kahn came on the scene, biking has also been gaining in popularity in New York. The city regularly counts cyclists along seven key commute routes and found that traffic had climbed from around 5,500 cyclists a day in the late 1990s to some 9,300 a day in 2007. Just one year later, ridership jumped by another 35 percent, probably at least in part because of rising gas prices. But Sadik-Kahn and local bike advocates also took it as evidence that the city's infrastructure improvements were also bearing fruit. Transportation Alternatives estimated that some 130,000 cyclists were on the city streets on any given day. That's not an overwhelming number in a city of 8.2 million, but they're becoming a more visible presence, and there are signs that biking is crossing from the fringe to the mainstream. The *New York Times*, which regularly shoots fashion as it appears on the street, in 2008 featured several stylishly dressed women (who were not all that young either) out running errands on bikes with big baskets. The *New York Observer*, which chronicles Manhattan's glitterati, ran a large piece in September of 2007 about the "beautiful bicycle girls of New York." The story begins this way:

On a recent sunny Saturday afternoon, Vikki Eichmann was striding through the Union Square farmers' market, one hand steering a sea-green, 1970s Schwinn Breeze bicycle and the other tossing a curtain of silky brown hair over her bony shoulder. She was wearing a strapless plum-colored sundress and $400 Cole Haan knee-high boots. "They're perfect because they're sturdy and I don't get scratches or bruises from the bike or anything," Ms. Eichmann said, stopping to pick through a crate of peaches. "Plus they just plain look cute on a bike."

Indeed, I had noticed this on my own rides around New York. Amid the chaos of Manhattan traffic, I would see a stylish woman— usually without a helmet—pedaling serenely up one of the avenues, almost as if there was an invisible shield between her and the traffic. I met Kim Kalesti, forty-nine, one evening at Time's Up. Kalesti, a jazz singer with the sense of style that implies, said that she's fallen in love with bicycling in the city. Unlike the bike messengers, though, she takes her time. "It's better to be a little patient," she said.

"That two minutes hanging out behind a truck [instead of trying to squeeze by it] can be worth your life." She later sent me a picture of her carrying a music stand on her bike while she's garbed in a short white dress and gold high heels. For cycling advocates, the number of women cyclists is not unimportant. The great biking cities of the world, such as Copenhagen and Amsterdam, have no gender gap when it comes to bicycling. But in the U.S., where conditions are more dangerous, men predominate in most cities. They're willing, on average, to take more risks. And if a woman feels safe enough to ride on the street in her high heels carrying a music stand, that's a good sign for a city's friendliness to bicycles. On another day, I rode up the Bowery following a woman in some kind of fake fur brown coat, with big Jackie O sunglasses and her red hair streaming behind her as she rode a neon purple cruiser with a big wire basket. We halted at Delancey Street for a stoplight and watched as a fixie rider maneuvered through the intersection, balancing on two wheels without moving before he could dart through a gap in the traffic. Then the light changed and we continued our relaxed ride. As it happened, I was on my way to Clearly First, a boutique on the Upper East Side that got a small write-up in the *Times* for selling designer bikes to an upscale clientele. I thought a visit to the store might give me a handle on the new bicycling zeitgeist.

At first, I didn't see any bikes at Clearly First, which turned out to specialize in Scandinavian design and sold everything from watches to furniture. A couple of workers were fussing with a window display but one promised to get a manager. Justin Argenti, stylish in New York black pants, sports coat, and shirt with an open collar, eyed my frayed pants and plebian jacket warily as I sought to convince him I was a legitimate journalist. He showed me a $1,500 Biomega cycle tucked away in a corner that he said was impossible to steal (the boutique's Web site says the lock is integral to the frame and the bike becomes useless if it is cut). And then he took me around a corner to show me two handsome Skeppshult bicycles from Sweden with a classic European utilitarian design. I could envision riding one down a tree-shaded lane to the *boulangerie.* "These are obviously much more country and conservative than the other," Argenti explained, "although just as interesting in design and quality." So, I asked, do people ride these bikes in the city? Is it part of a new interest in bicycling? Argenti shrugged. "These are bikes for people who enjoy design—form vs. function, these kinds of things," he said. He pointed to the Skeppshults. The men's version is $2,100 and the women's is $1,795. "It's a very country bike," he said with finality. "It's going to appeal to a person who has it for their country home—their second or third home."

I rode back downtown, cutting through Central Park—now increasingly car-free thanks to lobbying by bike advocates—as I was passed by several lycra-clad riders on featherweight road bikes. Near Columbus Circle, I passed a clutch of pedicabs waiting for customers. While they're popular with tourists, the city council, over the mayor's veto, passed a law at the behest of the taxi industry to restrict their numbers. Confident of the streets now, I headed for Times Square, swallowed up by the sensation of the crowds, the neon, and the nearly gridlocked traffic. Somehow, I got spit out the other end in one piece and it seemed like I was just getting my bearings when I passed Madison Square Garden. Making my way through America's greatest city had never seemed easier.

7

Overcoming the
Safety Barriers

I never knew bicycle bells could sound so mournful. Like a funeral dirge, the sound echoed off the buildings as I joined several hundred cyclists for a memorial ride up one of Portland's busiest boulevards, West Burnside Street.

We were marking a cycling death that had shocked even the most hardened riders. On a balmy Thursday afternoon, as the autumn leaves crunched underneath, nineteen-year-old Tracey Sparling rode toward the Pacific Northwest College of Art. She was one of the many young creative people who gravitated to Portland and embraced cycling as a fun, inexpensive way to travel around town. She had grown up in Salem, Oregon, and gone to school back east but, homesick for Oregon, had returned. She was in the bike lane on SW Fourteenth Avenue, stopped for a red light. Seconds later, when the light changed, she was crushed under the wheels of a cement truck turning right. The bad news didn't end there. Less than two weeks later, an experienced cyclocross racer and bike store employee, Brett Jarolimek, thirty-one, was killed when he collided with a right-turning garbage truck at the bottom of a steep hill.

The deaths caused an outpouring of emotion and discussion about bike safety that I had never before seen in Portland. On one of the local cyclist listservs, cyclists expressed anger about the deaths and the inattention of drivers. But they also swapped links about safe bicycling guides and discussed how to do a better job of teaching people to safely cycle around the city. The local news media carried several stories analyzing what kind of bikeway improvements would make cycling safer. Transportation Commissioner Sam Adams quickly announced a plan to install European-style bike boxes at fourteen problematical intersections with high cycling volumes; these would allow cyclists to filter to the front of the intersection, hopefully reducing the danger that they would be hit by a right-turning vehicle. And when another cyclist was injured at the same intersection where Jarolimek had been killed, the city put up a barricade to prevent cars from turning right across the bike lane. Before the memorial ride for Sparling, Scott Bricker, executive director of the Bicycle Transportation Association, held his one-year-old daughter in his arms and told participants that, statistically, the greatest danger to his daughter's life for the next thirty-four years would come from traffic—whether she ever rode a bicycle or not. And, he added, "the more cyclists ride, research shows, the safer we will be."

In many ways, those two horrible tragedies and their immediate aftermath captured the safety issues swirling around cycling in the United States. Survey after survey shows that safety fears are the biggest factor keeping people off of bikes. As long ago as 1996, the U.S. surgeon general, in a landmark report on physical activity, said that 53 percent of people who had cycled in the previous year said they would commute to work by bike if they could do so on "safe, separated designated paths." Even if there's a certain amount of telling pollsters what they want to hear, it also tells you that millions of additional people would like to make cycling a part of their daily life if they felt safe. This fear of traffic is not just an inchoate worry: riding in the U.S. is far more dangerous than in countries such as the Netherlands and Denmark where the road authorities treat the bicycle as a serious form of transportation. And in some ways it is a terrible self-fulfilling prophecy: so many Americans regard bicycling on the road as so intrinsically dangerous that they almost think cyclists have it coming if they are injured or killed. And the more people are discouraged from riding, the more that attitude persists.

However, Portland has advanced far enough as a bike town that I didn't hear any serious discussion about trying to remove cyclists from the road, although there were the usual complaints about the bad behavior of the many cyclists who ignore traffic laws. Instead, there was at least the beginning of a public discussion about facility improvements and about providing more education for both cyclists and motorists. And finally, in Bricker's comments, I saw what many cyclists hope for the future in American cities: that there will indeed be safety in numbers for cyclists. There is research that demonstrates exactly this, and I've seen it play out on the streets of Portland, where ridership has climbed while the number of crashes has stayed flat. (These two deaths, coming so quickly upon each other, may well have been an anomaly, as awful as they were. While there were seven bike fatalities in Portland in 2007, the city didn't have a single one in 2006 after ranging between one and five deaths a year in the previous decade.)

However, in many American cities we are now in that awkward period where utilitarian cycling has become visible but still not mainstream. There is a modest flow of money for bicycling improvements, but certainly nothing that rivals the resources that go into improving and building roads for cars or, for that matter, transit. And even within the cycling community, there is heated argument about whether and how streets should be designed to better accommodate bicycling. At its most elemental, the issue is whether to push hard for the sweeping kinds of street changes seen in many European cities, where bikes are often given their own protected lanes, special traffic signals, and even special routes that allow them to speed through inner city areas more quickly than cars. I recall standing on a sidewalk with one cycling advocate who pointed to the street and said, "Motorists have their space, pedestrians have their space on the sidewalk, and cyclists need their space too." Others regard it as foolish and potentially dangerous to try to provide cyclists with separate facilities. Inevitably, they say, cyclists will need to interact with cars and bikeways need to be sparingly and judiciously planned. And they say that cyclists must above all learn the precepts of vehicular cycling to ride safely.

There is no doubt that unsafe riding causes many cyclist injuries and deaths. A 1996 study by the University of North Carolina Highway Safety Research Center (which has conducted much of the research on bike safety) found that as many as a third of all bike accidents involved simply riding against the flow of traffic. In addition, although many riders think they are safer on the sidewalk, it can actually be more dangerous because they can be hit by drivers in both intersections and driveways who don't expect to encounter anyone moving faster than walking speed. A study of 803 cyclist crashes in the Orlando area in 2003 and 2004 found that nearly two-thirds involved riding on the sidewalk or another unsafe choice by the cyclist. And, just as with motor vehicles, alcohol is often a factor. In recent years, nearly a quarter of those killed bicycling had blood-alcohol levels of at least .08 percent, the legal limit for drivers in most states. Many of the people killed cycling are the marginalized, such as people who are homeless or poor immigrants.

David Glowacz, education director for the Chicagoland Bicycle Federation, is the author of a book on safe bicycling tips and has written a curriculum for bicycle safety instructors. We sat on his porch one June afternoon in a leafy Chicago neighborhood and, ironically enough, one of the first things we saw was a cyclist riding the wrong direction on his one-way street. "I get scared for them, some of the things they do," he said of his fellow cyclists. "Sometimes I'll jump out in the street and say, 'I wish you wouldn't do what you just did.'" The problem, he said, is that few cyclists have had any training. They are picking it up as they go, and that doesn't always include following the traffic laws—or even knowing that they should follow these rules. Glowacz spends much of his time teaching cyclists to ride with traffic, to stay far enough left of parked cars to avoid being "doored" by a motorist getting out of a vehicle, and to be careful of right-turning vehicles suddenly moving into their line of travel. "Those are the big three," he said. What about stoplights? I asked. Glowacz smiled, remembering his own learning curve. "I know when I stopped running red lights, I stopped having so many close calls," he said.

Bike safety instructors do typically teach adhering to the traffic laws. But Glowacz was being honest about the fact that few cyclists follow them to the letter. And in my experience, nothing drives motorists crazier about cycling than what they see as the widespread evasion of traffic laws by cyclists. It's hard to have a sensible discussion with the motoring majority about how to change their behavior when they can point to the countless cyclists who blow through red lights, ride the wrong way, and hop up and down curbs. That's why we probably can't go much further in a discussion about bike safety without dealing with this issue first.

To begin with, most cyclists aren't taught how to ride safely in traffic. Instead, they learn by experience, and they are navigating in an environment where many drivers—and sometimes even police officers—don't recognize their right to be on the street. In that situation, it's not surprising that they will invent their own rules of the road. Even John Forester, who is generally quite scathing of the riding behavior of most cyclists, says drivers are to blame in one sense: they've failed to see cyclists as legitimate users of the road, so why be surprised when they don't act that way? "When motorists complain about these damned bicyclists," growled Forester, "I say, 'It's your own damned fault, because you have insisted for forty years that bicyclists stay out of your way.'"

Sometimes cyclists surprise motorists with actions that are necessary for their own safety. For example, few drivers know that it isn't safe for cyclists to hug the far right of a lane next to parked cars because of the danger of being hit by an opening car door. And even when there are no parked cars, debris often collects near the curb that is hazardous to cyclists. It's also the rare rider who comes to a complete halt for every stop sign, simply because of the physics of being on a bike. It is hard to explain this to non-riders, but the loss of kinetic energy for a bike is roughly akin to a driver being forced to jump in and out of his or her car at every stop sign.

That's one reason why countries like the Netherlands often use yield markings in place of stop signs and traffic circles instead of traffic signals. Joel Fajans, a physics professor at the University of California at Berkeley, has calculated that a cyclist who rolls through a stop sign at just 5 mph uses 25 percent less energy to get back up to 10 mph than a cyclist who comes to a full stop. Fajans expanded on this by testing two routes in Berkeley: one was along a low-traffic street recommended for bikes that had twenty-one stop signs and a traffic light over the course of about two and one-quarter miles. Near it was a busy four-lane street with eight traffic signals and no stop signs. Fajans found that by obeying the traffic rules he could travel on the busy street—Sacramento—at an average speed of 14.2 mph without straining. But on the side street—California—his average speed was 10.9 miles at the same level of exertion. Fajans noted that this may not sound like much of a difference, but in percentage terms it is the equivalent to a motorist driving 45 instead of 60 on a highway.

In fact, cyclists take their cues from their environment and their technology, as do motorists. Cyclists (even including safe riders like Glowacz and Forester) feel they have enough visibility to go slowly through stop signs if they don't see any car traffic, just as motorists feel they can safely exceed the speed limit by at least a few miles per hour. The truth is that there are the strict rules of the road in the statute books, and there are the actual social rules that we abide by on the streets. Motorists have become accustomed to social rules that allow them to speed—at least a little bit—with no expectation of getting a ticket, or even thinking they are doing anything wrong. And most drivers also fail to halt completely at stop signs if the traffic is clear. I happen to live near a complicated intersection where traffic is coming from six directions—and each has a stop sign. Sometimes, when walking our dog, I like to stand near the intersection, and watch the behavior of motorists. (Since the dog is happy to sniff in the bushes for quite a while, I can just stand there and look inconspicuous.) I've never yet seen one motorist come to a complete stop if there is no cross traffic. (The only way you can tell for sure is by looking at the hubcaps, because the car itself appears to stop because it has lost so much speed.)

Because motor vehicles so dominate the road, we accept car-based social standards as right and proper. A friend once gave me a long lecture about how cyclists routinely flouted the law, but when she was later ticketed for driving in excess of 100 mph, she said she simply didn't realize how fast she was going. When the Virginia Legislature passed a law placing steep traffic fines for going more than 20 mph over the speed limit, more than 177,000 people signed a petition calling for its repeal. News stories quoted outraged citizens complaining about how they could be hit with fines of as much as $2,500 for a "simple" error. "These fines are draconian and take the enjoyment out of one of my favorite hobbies—driving fast," one Virginian wrote on a blog.

Idaho—which does not have much of a reputation for bicycle friendliness—is actually the one state that has sought to reshape its traffic laws to recognize the difficulty cyclists have with stop signs. Since 1982, the state has allowed cyclists to treat stop signs as yield signs. They are required to slow but they only have to stop "if required for safety." In 2005, the legislature also allowed cyclists to go through red lights if it was safe, but only after first stopping and yielding to other traffic. Mark McNeese, the state's bicycle and pedestrian coordinator, said the 1982 change slipped through the legislature with no debate as part of a larger bill and has not appeared to have any impact on safety. "Why should it?" he asked rhetorically. "Nothing changed except for the law. This is the way cyclists ride." Lawmakers changed the stoplight law in part because most traffic signals weren't sensitive enough to be triggered by a bicycle, and there was no interest in retrofitting them. That change also hasn't produced any change in the injury or fatality rate, he said.

Of course, many Idaho motorists are unfamiliar with the unusual law and frequently complain about lawless cyclists. And there's no doubt that some cyclists can be flamboyant in their lawbreaking. In some ways, nothing has changed since the late 1800s when reckless cyclists became known as "scorchers" for their dangerous riding. (New York Police Commissioner Theodore Roosevelt even established a squad of bike-mounted cops to hunt down scorchers in what sounds like a cycling version of the movie, *The Fast and the Furious*.) Young males continue to make up a large share of cyclists, and they are naturally going to gravitate to riskier behavior, just as they do behind the wheel of a car. When I see a young man—as I did once—riding with no hands the wrong way down a one-way street, all I can think is, it's better for the rest of us that he's on a bike than behind the wheel of a ten-year-old SUV with sketchy brakes.

Certainly cyclists can increase their safety dramatically by being judicious. William Moritz at the University of Washington surveyed two thousand members of the League of American Bicyclists for a 1996 study and found that, while falls were relatively common, these well-trained cyclists could expect to ride for eleven years without having a crash of any consequence. Another now quite old study, from 1975, calculated that experienced cyclists had one-fifth the crash rate of college students. "If you could train everybody to ride completely safely and legally, think how great that would be," said Amanda Eichstadt, president of the bicycling league and a strong proponent of cycling education. The league in recent years finally reached one thousand certified instructors. That, however, is not a large number in a country of three hundred million, and only a small percentage of riders seek out any formal instruction. I confess I was one of those who learned to ride as a youngster and never thought I needed to do more until I began researching this book. Now I know that some of my most personally valuable time was spent with skilled riders, learning how to ride safely in traffic. I spent a particularly rewarding day with John Allen, author of *Bicycling Street Smarts*, on the back of his tandem; we started in Cambridge, Massachusetts, and made a loop tour through Boston.

Allen said his style of riding "was put on its head" after he read Forester's *Effective Cycling* book in the late 1970s. Allen remembered merging from a right turn lane out into the middle of the straight-through traffic on a bridge and how smoothly it went. "Not only did it work, it gave me a tremendous feeling of empowerment," he recalled. Allen said he once was hit by a drunk driver on a rural road, but he's navigated Boston and the suburbs for decades now without trouble. Vehicular cycling is "several times as safe as people who ride the other way," he insisted. I noticed as we rode that Allen placed himself a bit closer to the middle of the road than I would but that cars still didn't have much problem getting by us. In many ways, Allen explained, vehicular cyclists are communicating with drivers what they are going to do by how they position their bike in the lane. Once in the city, we easily maneuvered around the swirling traffic patterns around Boston Commons and had a pleasant tour of the downtown. Still, I noticed that we did have a few epithets thrown at us from drivers. Allen shrugged them off, later explaining that because he follows the law, he has developed the confidence that he is in the right.

One thing that just about everyone in the cycling community agrees on is that it would be valuable to have cycling education taught in schools (a subject I take up in Chapter 9). But unless and until that becomes widespread, bicycling remains a folk form of transportation often resistant to hard and fast rules. On any day, cyclists on the road can include adventurous ten-year-olds venturing outside their neighborhoods for the first time, adults who have lost their driver's license because of drunk driving, immigrant delivery riders who don't speak English, bike messengers who court danger, lycra-clad venture capitalists out for a lunchtime ride … and me, heading off to a press conference.

What is hard to do is to answer a simple question: just how dangerous is cycling compared to being in an automobile? Virtually all of the cycling safety experts say direct comparisons are impossible because nobody has collected good data on how many miles U.S. cyclists ride every year. And while we know how many cyclists die in crashes every year, injuries are greatly under-reported. One study of hospital admissions found that only 48 percent of the cyclists treated at hospitals in an eight-state region were listed in crash-data reports. However, on a per-mile basis, by my calculations, it does appear that cycling is more dangerous than being in a motor vehicle. I started with the 2006 National Highway Traffic Safety Administration data showing that 42,642 people were killed that year in auto accidents, which is 1.42 fatalities per 100 million vehicle miles traveled. NHTSA also reported that 773 people died while cycling that year.

I then took a survey from the National Sporting Goods Association, which estimated that nearly thirty-six million Americans aged seven or older rode at least six times in 2006. Using that estimate, I could calculate how far those thirty-six million cyclists would have to ride to achieve a lower per-mile fatality rate than for motorists. The answer? An average of more than fifteen hundred miles a year.

I'd love it if 12 percent of the population rode an average of four miles every day, but the real cycling mileage in America has to be much lower. And that means the per-mile fatality rate for cyclists is almost certainly higher than for motorists. Rutgers Professor John Pucher and Lewis Dijkstra did try to estimate cyclist mileage in a

2003 study that compared bicycle and pedestrian safety in the U.S. with Germany and the Netherlands. They took U.S. estimates of bike mileage from commute data and extrapolated them to arrive at a rough per-mile injury and fatality rate. They concluded that the per-mile fatality rate for cyclists was about ten times as high as for motorists. (If my calculations are at all accurate, that seems too high.[1])

Still, that is not the end of the story. Comparing car and bike mileage to arrive at safety rates is not necessarily valid. Motorists can obviously cover much greater distances than cyclists in the same time period. Cyclists are generally much more likely to choose closer destinations than people who drive. If my wife and I are going to ride our bikes to a restaurant, we'll choose among a smaller range of establishments than if we're going to drive. So how many miles you travel makes a difference. Think of it this way. Say that Janice on average crashes her car once every sixty thousand miles while Amy is in a crash every fifty thousand miles. You might think Janice is a safer driver. But if Janice drives twenty thousand miles a year and Amy only ten thousand miles a year, that means Janice crashes every three years and Amy has just one crash in five years. If I decide to spend the morning on a bike ride with friends, I'll probably travel thirty to forty miles over the course of two to three hours (including stops). Or I could have spent that time driving as much as two hundred miles.

---

1. Here's why Pucher and Dykstra's estimate may be too high. Based on my calculations, the average cyclist would have to travel less than 150 miles a year for cycling to be ten times as dangerous on a per-mile basis. I think that average is too low. Also, the Outdoor Industry Association does its own study of bicycling that suggests a much higher number of Americans cycle at least occasionally. Bike industry analysts who I have talked to think the sporting goods association number is better. But it would not surprise me if it falls between the two. Even if you assume much higher levels of cycling, the per-mile fatality rate for cyclists still looks higher than that for motorists.

For that reason, some cycling pundits prefer to use per-hour exposure comparisons, feeling it more accurately captures the true risk. Am I safer if I spend an hour on a bike, or an hour in a car? They've been spurred on by a curious piece of data that seems to have gained an eternal life on the internet. In 1993, *Design News*, a specialty publication that focuses heavily on the automobile industry, wrote an article debunking that staple of Hollywood chase scenes: the car that explodes in flames upon impact. Actually, the article said, motor vehicles almost never explode even in the most violent collisions. Accompanying the article was a chart by Failure Risk Associates that said the risk of dying from an exploding fuel tank is vastly lower than a number of other activities on the basis of per-hour exposure. According to the chart, the most dangerous activity was skydiving, which makes some sense. While very few Americans die skydiving—sixty to seventy a year—it's high on a per-hour exposure basis because skydivers are not so numerous and spend so little time in the air.

Cyclists seized on the chart because it said the fatality rate for passenger cars—0.47 fatalities per million hours—was higher than for cyclists, at 0.26 fatalities per million hours. Those figures have been cited on countless cyclist Web sites and included in at least one book, *The Art of Urban Cycling*. For a risk-averse cyclist like me, it's a comforting thought. However, the chart leaves more questions than answers. Failure Analysis Associates is now part of a larger firm, Exponent, which would not provide me with any of the underlying data. There's no way to know how the firm quantified the number of hours cyclists rode. Other bike safety researchers I've talked to said they simply have not seen that kind of information. "The true figure is out there," sighed Bill Hunter, a respected University of North Carolina bike safety researcher, "and none of us can get a perfect grasp on it."

Since the chart was designed to show the rarity of gas tank explosions, I wonder how extensively the firm researched the myriad of other activities they included. Did they take some rough estimates from a ridership survey, like I did above, and regard it as adequate? Bear in mind they were not trying to compare the risk of driving and cycling; they were trying to compare driving, cycling, and other activities with the danger of exploding gas tanks.

For all of that, it does make sense that bikes fare better on a per-hour basis than a per-mile basis. Malcolm Wardlaw, a traffic researcher from Glasgow, in a 2001 paper, said his review of statistics found that cycling was roughly similar to motor-vehicle safety using an hourly measurement in the Netherlands, Germany, Sweden, and Switzerland. Those are all countries with better cycling *and* driving safety records than in the U.S., however, so it's not clear they apply to this country.

However, these European statistics do demonstrate why a less car-centered lifestyle contributes to safety. William Lucy, a University of Virginia planning professor, has started something of a cottage industry comparing homicide and motor-vehicle death rates in urban and suburban areas. He has found that people on the fringes of suburbia in Virginia are more at danger of a violent death from these two causes than are people in the high-crime cities of Richmond and Washington, D.C. Alan Durning, who runs the Sightline Institute in Seattle, performed the same analysis in his region and found that the city was safer than the suburbs. The reason, of course, is that people in the suburbs drive so much more, often on what were once country roads that now feature plenty of swift-moving traffic and hazardous curves.

I've talked to countless numbers of people over the years who say they moved as far out of the city as they could to provide their children with a safer environment. But, oblivious as most people are to the dangers of driving, they never think about the greater risks to which they may be putting their family. Todd Litman of the Victoria Transportation Policy Institute found that states with higher rural populations invariably have higher per capita death rates from driving. "You know all those people who moved way out in the suburbs to find a safe place to raise their children?" he asked.

"Boy, are they are wrong."[2] In fact, more than in most countries, Americans seem to have an ability to dismiss the country's poor road safety record.

The U.S. was once considered a world leader in traffic safety. Now, in the developed world, you largely have to go to the old states of the Soviet Union to find roads that kill a higher percentage of the population. In contrast, most European countries tackle road safety with the zeal that we reserve for preventing airline crashes. The Netherlands, for example, has a per capita road fatality rate a third of the U.S. rate. Australia, which once had a similar per capita death rate on the roads as America, has now cut it to about half of the U.S. rate, thanks in part to the quicker adoption of photo radar and the targeting of hazardous road sections for improvements. In America, we spend more on dental research than traffic safety research. Because we are so wedded to our cars and to our freedom on the road, we tend to resist any restrictions. In my state, the legislature cut the number of state troopers—primarily responsible for enforcing traffic laws on Oregon's highways—in half over twenty years because of repeated budget crises, without much objection from the public. Yet the public revolted and passed tougher prison sentences when they thought the state was getting too lenient on criminals.

At the same time, we don't even like to own up to the full toll of automotive mayhem, which is the equivalent of two jumbo jetliners crashing every week and killing everyone aboard. Traffic engineers, the automotive industry, and government officials "love to measure risk per million miles traveled because it makes them look very successful," said Litman. "But the per capita rate of deaths has hardly

---

2. Even the auto industry equates more driving with more death. *The New York Times* has reported that, in one court case challenging emission controls, the industry says more fuel-efficient cars "could be dangerous" because they are cheaper to operate and could lead people to drive more. More tellingly, preliminary data show that fatalities dropped in 2008 as gas prices rose and people drove less.

changed at all. We have failed to [really tackle the problem] because they don't want to recognize that increases in vehicle miles increases risk and reducing it is a safety strategy."

"It is not homicide or HIV, it is a traffic crash that is going to cause you to die," added Terecia Wilson, director of safety for the South Carolina Department of Transportation. "The average Joe Public is not aware of that." Instead, most people seem determined not to think about the problem. In a series of papers the AAA Safety Foundation commissioned on America's traffic safety culture—or lack thereof—several experts repeatedly noted that American drivers seem determined to shift the blame to the bad behavior of other drivers.

In one survey, only 6 percent of drivers conceded that they could possibly be at fault if they were in a traffic crash. And 72 percent of drivers said they were above average (shades of Garrison Keillor's mythical Lake Wobegon!). In one study that examined 321 crashes, only 20 percent of the drivers conceded blame. In the stress-filled world of the American road, we're quick to claim our territorial rights and to find that the enemy is not ourselves, but the barbarians in the next lane. Is it any wonder that most motorists are quick to fix on the obvious traffic sins they see committed by cyclists and to want to end the conversation right there?

Bike activists are much less likely to be oblivious to the risks. There's something about cycling next to the warm metal of a two-ton vehicle that focuses the mind. Charles Komanoff, a New York City economist and former director of Transportation Alternatives, perfectly describes how many experienced riders feel. He has been cycling in Manhattan for decades and says he finds that he no longer has as many close calls. "I don't know if it's me that has changed or the environment that has changed," he explained as he sat in his comfortably cluttered office in lower Manhattan. "I just don't have as many scary moments." But then he paused and added, "Every now or then I will have one and it will just send a shiver into me and makes me realize just how perilous the whole enterprise can be."

Komanoff and a small circle of bike activists have tried—so far with only limited success—to ignite a "traffic justice movement" that would focus on improving the safety of not only vulnerable walkers and cyclists, but of all other road users as well. "We don't create whole system safety here like they do in Europe," he said. "It's really foreign to Americans ... Driving is so ubiquitous here. It's so automatic, it's so ingrained in the culture, people so identify with their cars, they get extraordinarily attached to driving and it becomes really difficult to have a rational discourse that might call into question certain aspects of that attachment." Komanoff and other leaders of the movement would like the country to be much more aggressive about enforcing speed limits using the latest technology, such as photo radar. They want to design—and retrofit—roads to slow the speed of cars. And they'd like to shift much more responsibility to drivers in crashes involving vulnerable users. In a speech at the Pro-Bike/Pro-Walk conference in 2006, Komanoff told about seeing a sign in the Adirondacks warning drivers that deaf children were present:

We've all seen such signs countless times. But this time, it occurred to me that Deaf Child Area embodies what we're fighting to overturn: the presumption that the driver's sounding of his horn, or just the mere sound of the engine or of the car moving through space, requires the child in the street or person on the road to get out of the way—or else. Isn't it the driver's responsibility to avoid the child, not the reverse? Don't we want all children to be treated by all drivers all the time as if they are deaf? Shouldn't every street with kids around be a Deaf Child Area?

Komanoff also talks about bringing new technology to bear. Vehicles now carry electronics that could be deployed like cockpit flight recorders to give crash investigators information about such things as braking action and how fast a driver was going. "I think it is a real wedge to get inside the beast," he said. It could provide the same kind of quantifiable data used to combat drunk driving, the one traffic offense that American society has come to regard as unacceptable.

While Komanoff got a positive reception from cycling advocates, he and other traffic justice advocates haven't been able to raise the money to get their movement off the ground. Instead, it's been left to traffic safety activists at the local level where, once again, cyclists are often in the forefront. Randy Neufeld, who built the Chicagoland Bicycle Federation into one of the country's major local bike advocacy groups, stepped down from the executive director's position in part to concentrate on a traffic safety initiative he started. "That's my passion these days, the traffic crashes," he said. "The issue is, how do you re-establish the social compact on the road?"

Neufeld, working with the city, established an 8.9-square-mile zone on the North Side of Chicago where he is trying to inculcate a new safety culture. "We're looking for techniques that actually change behavior," he said, such as trying to get people to sign written safe-driving pledges and then to advertise that fact on bumper stickers. And he got a public service spot made. It's in the form of a satirical ad for "Bob Fuller Roadside Memorials" that suggests an inattentive driver can soothe her conscience over killing a pedestrian by ordering a customized roadside marker. Neufeld's belief is that changing the road culture could go a long way toward making the streets safer for cyclists. "Our goal is to get down speeds, like the 30 km zones they have" in residential areas in Europe, he said. "The idea is a child can sit in the middle of a street and play with a doll and the parents are not going to worry about them."

Cyclists have also been in the forefront of seeking to toughen penalties for motorists who injure or kill pedestrians or riders because of inattentiveness or aggressive driving. Far too often, Neufeld and others say, drivers are able to avoid much in the way of consequences for the way they handle what can be a lethal weapon. The grim joke I've heard from many cycling and pedestrian advocates is that the only form of legalized murder in the U.S. occurs on the streets. A case in Illinois illustrates the point—and how it has begun to lead to change.

On September 2, 2006, Matthew Wilhelm, twenty-five, a newly minted engineer working for Caterpillar in Peoria, was cycling on a road shoulder when he was struck from behind by a car driven by Jennifer Stark, nineteen, who was downloading ringtones for her cell phone when she veered off the road. Wilhelm died four days later of head injuries from the crash. Stark was fined $1,000 for improper lane usage, put on unsupervised probation, and ordered to attend traffic school. The case caused an uproar. The local prosecutor, Julia Rietz, said that Stark's actions didn't meet the standard for recklessness that would allow authorities to charge her with reckless driving or reckless homicide. But Rietz joined with Wilhelm's parents in trying to create a new crime—of negligent vehicular homicide—that would cover cases like this.

"There's no disincentive or deterrent in Illinois, and you can kill somebody and if you didn't do it with wanton or willful intent, you're going to get off," Chuck Wilhelm, Matthew's father, told me. The bill passed in the House but stalled in the Senate. "We're trying to figure out how to build grassroots support" to try again in the next session of the legislature, said Wilhelm after the bill failed. He recalled how "one state senator told me that he eats while driving and that means he could be subject to a misdemeanor and I said, 'Well, yeah.'" They didn't come away entirely empty-handed. The legislature created a distracted-driver task force and moved to make it easier for the state to revoke the licenses of negligent drivers. Chuck and Gloria Wilhelm have become community activists, visiting classrooms to talk about their loss and to stress the dangers of driving while being distracted, particularly by using a cell phone.

In Oregon, lawmakers passed a bill that would allow authorities to levy a fine of as much as $12,500 and a year's license revocation for drivers who killed or injured a vulnerable road user due to carelessness. The bill gained momentum after a well-publicized case involving a woman with a suspended license who struck and killed a recreational cyclist as he waited to make a left-hand turn on a rural road. Still, I talked with a number of prosecutors and cycling experts who say that jurors in car-bike cases tend to sympathize with drivers because they find it easier to put themselves in the motorist's shoes. Joshua Marquis, a district attorney from Oregon who was a vice president for the National District Attorneys Association, said one of the few vehicular accident cases he lost involved a cyclist. "The idea that a car is automatically a weapon doesn't fly legally," he said. Added Ed Barsotti of the League of Illinois Bicyclists: "Cycling is viewed by many people who don't bike as being inherently dangerous. It's like, yes, you have a right to be on the road but there is an implied risk you're taking."

Andy Clarke, who heads the League of American Bicyclists, said there is a deeper reality for why society is slow to crack down on miscreant drivers. "We think it is a real hardship to take away someone's license," he said. "How are they going to survive without being able to drive? How they are going to get to work? How are they going to visit their friends?"[3]

So far, it seems the best strategy cyclists have found to change the behavior of drivers is to increase their numbers on the streets. Peter Jacobsen, a Sacramento public health consultant who now works with a water agency, has become widely quoted in bike safety circles after he authored a 2003 study that showed cyclists and walkers gained safety in numbers. Jacobsen said he began his research after he worked on a bicycle plan for the City of Pasadena. One of the

---

3. One argument for beefing up the system of bikeways is that it makes it easier for judges to remove the licenses of dangerous drivers. In Portland, for example, most people can now safely get to work either by using transit, by bicycling, or by a combination of the two. In addition, those recovering from drug addiction and alcoholism are particularly encouraged to exercise. So, for example, drunk drivers could help themselves and society if they got out from behind the wheel and got on a bike.

council members asked him if the city was dangerous to cycle in, and Jacobsen began looking up statistics. He found more cycling crashes in Pasadena than in many other cities—but there were also a lot more cyclists. Jacobsen eventually studied sixty-eight California cities and concluded that increases in biking and walking produce much smaller increases in the numbers of fatalities and injuries. He also found European data that suggested the safety-in-numbers theory applied there as well. "Basically what I'm saying is that there is a strong response from the motorist," Jacobsen explained. "If the motorist expects to see someone walking or bicycling, he will behave accordingly." Other researchers, particularly in Europe, had noticed the same thing. In a way it is common sense. If you regularly encounter a potential hazard while driving—whether it's a particularly bad pothole on your neighborhood street or a group of kids who use the same crosswalk every day at the same time to get to school—you are going to pay more attention to it. Fred Wegman, who runs the Netherlands' traffic safety research institute, said he prefers to call it "awareness in numbers" because there can still be unsafe conditions that need to be addressed.

Jacobsen's findings dovetailed with what cycling advocates wanted to hear. If they could increase the number of cyclists, they could make progress in overcoming their biggest obstacle. They argued that the issue was not so much about what made the current cyclists out on the road safe—although that was important too—but what was the best way to attract the numbers of cyclists that would bring enhanced safety along with them. (At its extreme, of course, this means no cars at all and everyone on bikes, on foot, or in transit. As Jacobsen noted, virtually no one gets hurts in traffic crashes in canal-laced Venice.) This gave advocates another argument to make as they pushed for bike lanes, bike paths, and other bikeways. Charlie Gandy, the longtime bike advocate from Texas, noted that a bike lane doesn't solve many of the toughest safety problems, such as cyclist-car conflicts at intersections. But, he said, "It does provide an invitation to ride a bike." A 2003 study by Jennifer Dill and Theresa Carr at Portland State University found that cities with the most miles of bikeways also had the highest ridership. To some extent, it may have been that the cities with the most riders were able to demand facilities. But the data reinforced the notion in bike advocate circles that increasing bikeways will spur a virtuous cycle: more riders demand more facilities, which bring more riders who demand more facilities, etc. However, not everyone buys this argument. John Allen said he's skeptical of the "safety in numbers" theory and argued that it is being used to sell cities on facilities that could be hazardous. "Bicycling is supposed to be made safer by installing dangerous facilities, because safety automatically increases when there are more bicyclists," he said derisively. "I call it the 'Pied Piper of Hamelin' approach to bicycling advocacy."

Despite such critics, bike lanes have indeed become increasingly common in the last ten years in cities around the country. They gained favor largely because of their popularity with cyclists, not because they were demonstrably safer than having wide lanes next to the curb, which is the approach that John Forester and his followers preferred. Hunter, the University of North Carolina researcher, and his colleagues videotaped cyclists riding in both bike lanes and wide curb lanes for an influential 1999 study. They concluded that both worked about equally well but that bike lanes were much more popular among cyclists.

"Bicyclists like to think that if they are in their own space motorists won't intrude on them," explained Hunter. I nodded in agreement at this, because that's exactly how it feels to me— emotionally at least—in a bike lane. I am more comfortable riding on busy streets that have bike lanes because I instinctively feel that motorists will respect my right to be there. Several studies have given at least some indication that bike lanes have increased safety. Davis, Eugene, and Corvallis all documented lower bike crash levels along streets after bike lanes were installed. New York City released a 2006 safety report that found that just one of the 225 cyclist deaths over the previous decade had been in a bike lane. "Clearly, riding in bike lanes is safer," said Iris Weinshall, then the city's transportation commissioner. In Cambridge, Massachusetts, researchers found that more cyclists felt safer riding further away from parked cars after a bike lane was installed on a busy commercial street. Still, Jane Stutts, a retired safety researcher from the University of North Carolina, said that, like so much about bike safety, it is hard to draw simple conclusions about bike lanes. "About the best you can do is show they increase bike traffic without increasing crashes," she said.

At the same time, bike lanes can also be a false invitation of sorts. "In some ways it is a set-up," said Glowacz, noting that much or all of a bike lane can be inside the door zone of a parked car, and that riders can be particularly vulnerable at intersections. In fact, those two fatal crashes in Portland both involved "right hooks," when drivers crossed into the path of riders in bike lanes who were going straight. That's one of the most common types of bike crashes, and one of the big reasons why Forester and many other vehicular cyclists dislike bike lanes. Left turns from bike lanes can also be a problem if cyclists aren't able to move from the right to the proper position in the left of the lane (and vice versa if bike lanes are on the left side of a one-way street, as sometimes is the case). Motorists are also sometimes befuddled by bike lanes. Are they supposed to enter the bike lane to make a right, or wait until the intersection and then turn? State laws disagree on that point.

As traffic engineers and bike planners get more experience with bike lanes, they've also experimented with improvements. In Washington, D.C., I rode on a street near Pennsylvania Avenue with a bike lane moved further away from parked cars so that it was clearly out of the door zone. In Portland, the city has widened bike lanes where possible to make it easier for two to ride abreast. And, as I mentioned earlier, the city is looking at bike boxes to help solve the right-hook problem. In New York, some bike lanes have been painted green to make them more visible to motorists. Chicago is considering slightly raised bike lanes to reduce motor vehicle incursions.

It's clear that bike lanes have now taken on a momentum of their own. Dan Burden and other livable street advocates often recommend them as part of road diets aimed at shrinking the number and/or width of travel lanes to reduce traffic speeds. Burden and others also say bike lanes benefit pedestrians by moving cars further away from sidewalks and provide extra space for stopped emergency vehicles. Cities also like the fact that bike lanes are relatively cheap, since they are largely just paint on the road. And bike advocates like the fact they attract more riders, at least if they are in a location where there is already some cycling demand. For example, Bozeman, Montana, installed a bike lane on a busy street that provided a good connection to downtown and Montana State University in spring 2005. The city counted bike traffic for a week before the lanes were added and then at the same time of year in 2006. They found that the average number of cyclists a day jumped from 62 to 153 despite the fact that the bike lane was less than optimal because it didn't continue all of the way to the university.

Bike lanes, of course, are far from being the only engineering solution for cyclists. Off-street paths—which usually allow both walkers and cyclists—typically attract the most cyclists, particularly those who are unskilled. The Rails-to-Trails Conservancy, which started in 1986, counted more than 13,500 miles of trails by 2007, with double that mileage in some form of development. While most of that mileage is in largely recreational settings, the conservancy is focusing more on creating "active transportation" trails that would be attractive to bike commuters. In Madison, Wisconsin, which is crisscrossed by railroad lines, a network of trails on many of the abandoned lines serves as the backbone of one of the country's most extensive bikeway systems. In Manhattan, the West Side Greenway has transformed cycling in the city by providing a car-free route for virtually the entire length of the island. A well-designed trail can almost be like an interstate highway for bikes. The problem is that trails can be relatively expensive and often don't take cyclists where they want to go. Planners can often use rail beds and green spaces along waterfronts, but it's extremely difficult to push trails through much of the urban landscape.

Trails are also not devoid of their own safety problems (which I take seriously since my mother was once very seriously injured cycling on a trail with a bad slope on a turn). Some studies indicate cyclists have more crashes on trails than on roads, although the great majority of these are not serious. In addition, paths often intersect with roads and riders suddenly darting across a street can catch drivers unaware. Many are too narrow and are poorly maintained. Once, on a ride with several officials from Oregon and Washington, we investigated a trail in Vancouver, Washington, that had repeated bone-jarring up-thrust chunks of asphalt caused by tree roots (local officials said they planned to resurface the trail). Sheila Lyons, the bicycle and pedestrian coordinator for the Oregon Department of Transportation, was gritting her teeth as she rode next to me. She said she has fought more than once with local trail builders who want to skimp on the trail surface or narrow the width because they are on a tight budget or because they want to get more miles built. Many trails have also turned into occasional battlegrounds between pedestrians and cyclists. The eleven-mile Minuteman Trail in suburban Boston is one of the busiest in the country and has had so many conflicts among different kinds of users that the local police have coined the term "bikeway rage," according to the *Boston Globe*. I have seen conflicts on trails several times. When I was riding along the Lakeshore trail in Chicago, I could only cringe as lycra-clad road bikers sped past photo-snapping tourists, wobbly kids on bikes, and rollerbladers swaying from side to side.

Bike boulevards are also increasingly winning favor among bike planners. They typically work best in areas where there is a good grid system of streets, a feature unfortunately not found in many newer cities and suburbs where self-contained subdivisions with numerous cul de sacs are the norm. The best bike boulevards are low-traffic streets that discourage all but neighborhood auto travel while providing good through routes for cyclists. I frequently ride on Southeast Ankeny Street in Portland. It has an almost unobtrusive raised median (with small gaps for cyclists) in the middle of one busy cross street, preventing cars from continuing on the bike boulevard. In addition, the stop signs are turned to face the side streets so that cyclists on Ankeny can ride along unimpeded. In Portland, at least, these bike boulevards have proved less controversial than bike lanes, perhaps because they are not as visible to drivers, who tend to never see them unless they live in the neighborhood. And they also don't seem to raise the hackles of hard-core vehicular cyclists as do bike lanes. Allen, for instance, said he thinks they may provide a safe place for less-experienced cyclists to ride. City crash data also show that the boulevards have a good safety record, despite high volumes of use on some of them. I've seen similar kinds of streets that work well in the central parts of Amsterdam, but they are rare in the U.S., in part because merchants fear they will lose business if motor-vehicle traffic is curtailed on their street.

The big question is whether cyclists can, in a sense, have it all. Can they find separation from cars while also still getting everywhere they want to go? Many bike advocates believe the answer is plain from the experience of Amsterdam and other major bike cities in Europe, which provide bikeways called cycletracks on many busy roads. Cycletracks typically are one-way paths dedicated to bikes that are physically separated from the rest of the street. A drawing of the public right of way would look like this: sidewalk, cycletrack, curb, parked cars, main roadway and then the same repeated on the other side. I lurk on the listserv of the Association of Pedestrian and Bicycle Professionals, and on many days there is a fairly routine exchange of information on subjects as mundane as nonslip concrete coatings. But the conversation quickly turns as heated as a political blog the week before an election when the subject of developing cycletracks in the U.S. is brought up. Cycletracks—as well as side paths, which also allow pedestrians—are denounced by many U.S. bike planners as unsafe, especially so in American traffic conditions. They note that most bike-car conflicts occur at intersections, where the two modes have to co-exist even if they are separated in the middle of the block. In addition, American roads are much more likely to be punctuated by driveways, alleyways, and other mid-block entrances to the road that cause conflicts.

Traffic engineers have raised enough concerns that the American Association of State Highway and Transportation Officials has long recommended against cycletracks and side paths in its highway design manual, which is generally followed by road designers. Richard Moeur, a traffic engineer for Arizona's Department of Transportation who frequently works on bicycling issues, told me that Netherlands-style bikeways don't work here because "there's a completely different culture and driving environment." He talked about how traffic engineers tried to reduce the high crash rate of a side path in Flagstaff that paralleled Route 66. "We couldn't find any driver control system that would stop the crashes," he said. Forester and many other vehicular cyclists also vehemently oppose cycletracks and side paths, saying they are more dangerous and force riders to go at slower speeds than they could on the regular street. Many critics also say they think the better safety record in European countries may be in spite of cycletracks, not because of them. "Part of the reason that cycletracks work reasonably well there, and there is some debate about that, is because you have so many cyclists," said Mighk Wilson, the bicycle and pedestrian coordinator for the Orlando region. Take away the large volumes of riders, he added, and cycletracks start to resemble the largely empty sidewalks he sees all over his sprawling metropolitan area. And his data show that cycling on those sidewalks is more dangerous than on the road.

But many bike advocates say that providing separated bikeways is the only way to persuade large numbers of Americans to bike—and that their very numbers will help increase safety. Pucher, the Rutgers researcher, travels the country with charts showing that high ridership numbers are only achieved in cities where cyclists are protected from fast-moving traffic. "The most important approach to making cycling safe and convenient in Dutch, Danish, and German cities," Pucher wrote in one paper, "is the provision of separate cycling facilities along heavily traveled roads and at intersections, combined with extensive traffic calming of residential neighborhoods."

Many of the rhetorical fires over cycletracks on the APBP listserv were sparked by Anne Lusk, a researcher at the Harvard University School of Public Health, who has pushed for the separated bikeways with dogmatic intensity. An intense, vigorous woman in her late fifties with silver-blond hair that falls to her shoulders, Lusk greeted me when I came for a visit and then bounded up the two flights of stairs to her office without pausing to consider taking the elevator. Settled in her office, she wasted no time dismissing the concerns of cycletrack critics. When you get down to it, she insisted, it's the strong, experienced vehicular cyclists who are happy with the current system. That's because, she added, they are more worried about being forced off the main road than about attracting large new numbers of riders. The current system primarily serves a "population that is white, that already bicycles, that is already healthy," she said. "You can't improve the population of white males that is already skinny." Lusk argued that women are generally more risk-averse and don't want to cycle without some separation from traffic. She also has insisted that modern cycletrack designs can work in America under the right conditions. She took me for a drive along Route 9 near her home in Brookline, pointing out that the busy four-lane highway would be ideal for a cycletrack because it did not have a lot of intersections and driveways. "We could do nothing and not have the cycletrack and nobody would die," she said. "But you have nobody cycling and nobody getting physical activity." She added, with a trace of anger in her voice, that nobody tells traffic engineers to stop building new roads because some motorists will inevitably die on them.

Lusk first got involved in cycling issues in 1981 when she was hired to do a feasibility study for a bike path in Stowe, Vermont. She got the path built, became passionate about the trail movement, and promoted the idea of inner-city greenways. She went back to school to get a Ph.D in architecture and became a visiting scientist at Harvard. Although a serious enough cyclist to have once biked from Boston to Washington, D.C., Lusk said she hadn't been on a bike for about four years. "It's too dangerous," she said of riding around the city. Instead, most days she walks the nearly two miles to work from her home in Brookline. In her zeal to promote cycletracks, she has not only made enemies of the vehicular cyclists but alienated some of her own allies. "In her own ways, she is as doctrinaire" as the Foresterites, said Bill Wilkinson. But however unlikely a Netherlands-style cycletrack system may seem in the U.S., many activists have come to see Lusk as correct in seeing it as the only way to make cycling a significant force in transportation.

"I think separated cycle paths are what is next for the U.S.," said Noah Budnick, deputy director of Transportation Alternatives in New York, as he pointed to their increasing popularity in such disparate cities as Montreal, Bogota, and Melbourne. For all of the complaints about translating cycletracks to America, he added, "Our traffic engineers are very smart people even if we don't always agree with them. They are experts at tweaking what is happening on every inch of our streets. Engineers like to solve problems and I have no doubt they can figure this out." When he said that, New York City traffic engineers were still balking at merely putting in bike lanes. But when a reform-minded transportation planner, Janette Sadik-Kahn, took over a year later at the city's Department of Transportation, one of the first things she did was to install a cycletrack on Ninth Avenue in lower Manhattan. (I discuss it in more detail in Chapter 6.) Cycletracks are also popping up in other cities. The Massachusetts Institute of Technology, with Cambridge's approval, has built one on Vasser Street, which runs through campus, and plans to extend it to a dormitory a mile away. Indianapolis is building a two-way cycletrack (and lots of experts on the APBP listserv are not happy about that either) that will connect several inner-city neighborhoods and commercial districts.

Whatever roadway designs work, said Peter Jacobsen, the Sacramento public health consultant, the main issue is what increases cycling's numbers. "That's good for the health of the community, it's good for the air quality, it's good for traffic congestion, it's good for keeping money in the local economy," he said. "You know, if safety was our societal goal, we'd definitely get rid of automobiles—we'd throw them all in the Grand Canyon. ... I mean this is a huge health burden, all these automobiles. It's 2 percent of all deaths. You have a one in fifty chance of dying in a car crash.[4] That's huge. I work for the water industry ... we deliver a one in a million risk of cancer. That's what we treat drinking water to. And then we have a one in fifty chance of dying in a car crash?"

In fact, many cycling advocates gradually get to the point where they want to revamp the entire road system, not just figure out how to integrate cyclists into the current one. In this country, "we speak safety but vote for capacity," said Michael Ronkin, a long-time bicycle and pedestrian coordinator for the state of Oregon who is now an influential consultant. The designs of the best European cities can be replicated in America, he said, if traffic engineers, politicians and citizens are willing to make tough choices. "It's the political will to restrict driving and dedicate more room to bicycling and walking," he said. "It's that simple." Ronkin and many other biking and walking advocates say the biggest issue is not so much bikeways, but the overall design of cities. The more sprawl wins out over more compact development, they say, the harder it will be to develop true alternatives to driving.

Jacobsen has also been a participant in another debate over bike safety that may strike observers as counter-intuitive. He has argued against helmet laws on the grounds that they discourage cycling

---

4. Jacobsen defends the methodology he used to arrive at a one in fifty calculation. However, other studies I've seen range between one in sixty and one in ninety in calculating the lifetime risks of dying in a car crash.

by building the impression that it is a risky activity (and in fact, mandatory helmet laws in parts of Australia, New Zealand, and Canada did seem to reduce cycling). And he has argued, as have many others, that risk compensation comes into play: just as drivers in cars with seatbelts and airbags may feel it is safer to go faster, people wearing helmets may be less cautious.

Personally, I almost always wear a helmet while riding (although I didn't in the Netherlands and I recently felt safe riding around on the bike paths at the Sunriver resort in Central Oregon sans helmet). I have fallen a couple of times, and my arms, leg, and torso absorbed most of the shock. But each time it ended with my head slamming into the asphalt—and I didn't feel a thing thanks to my helmet. Promoting helmet use has been a mantra of the American public health establishment, and statistics show that the vast majority of cycling deaths involved riders who weren't wearing a helmet. From 1994 to 2005, the percentage of fatalities involving cyclists who didn't use a helmet ranged from a high of 97 percent in 1994 to a low of 83 percent in 2004. New York City's 2006 study looked at 122 fatalities where helmet use had been recorded. Only four of those killed had been wearing a helmet. But that New York study also noted that more than a fourth of those who died did not have head injuries. So the lack of helmet use could also be associated with other dangerous riding. I certainly saw this in New York where many food-delivery cyclists did not wear helmets and rode against traffic.

Still, all too often in this country, news coverage of cyclist deaths has tended to focus only on whether the rider wore a helmet and not on other problems that may have caused the crash. And it's clear from the experience of the Netherlands, Denmark, and other European countries with high cycling rates that helmet use is far from being the last word in safety. Fred Wegman, who runs the Netherland's traffic safety research institute, said that safety regulators would like people to wear helmets. But there is little public or official support for doing that, he said, "because we are afraid it will reduce" bicycling. And the Netherlands has been able to achieve dramatic gains in safety (as I discuss in Chapter 2) though virtually no one wears a helmet. The same is true for Denmark, which at one time had some of the most dismal traffic safety statistics in Europe.

One of the most colorful studies of the safety of bicycle helmets was conducted by Ian Walker, a researcher in Cambridge, England, who electronically measured how close drivers came when they passed as he cycled. He found that drivers gave him more leeway when he wasn't wearing a helmet—and even more space when he wore a long blonde wig so he looked like a woman. The point, of course, is that cycling safety sometimes has a lot to do with the actions of the motorists around the rider. I have now cycled in several cities where bikes are a common sight, and there's no question that motorists drive differently as a result. In the meantime, if I'm riding in a really dangerous city, maybe the best thing I can do is to keep wearing my helmet, but add a blonde wig.

8

Health and the Bicycle

"Elvis would have needed to cycle 160.74 miles at 17 mph to burn off his 65,000-calorie daily intake. Conclusion: What killed Elvis was his chronic lack of cycling."

—from "Number Freaking," by Gary Rimmer

Fortunately I have never had Elvis-sized food issues. But I am a pretty typical American male. I was a beanpole-skinny teenager who gained the "freshman ten" when I went off to college and discovered that nobody in my dorm's cafeteria stopped me if I wanted to eat three grilled cheese sandwiches. Then I joined the pound-a-year plan, gaining weight slowly enough that I hardly noticed it except that by my mid-thirties I realized that I was looking a little paunchy in photos. And then something happened in my mid to late forties after I started bicycling around town regularly instead of driving or taking the bus. Gradually, after decades of slowly gaining weight, I was slowly losing weight. I didn't even notice until I saw a chart of my weight on my doctor's computer that had suddenly gained a down slope. I *was* feeling fitter. And my wife noticed the muscle in my legs, which was pleasing.

And then I had what I called my "Super Size Me" experience, named for the documentary about the guy who ate only at McDonald's for a month. Mine, however, lasted eight months. During this time I gave up my daily bicycle round trip of about ten miles for a super-sized, fifty-mile commute from Portland to Salem covering the Oregon Legislature. I could drive it in just over an hour each way if the traffic was free-flowing (which it often wasn't). I still planned to get exercise. I joined the athletic booster club at Willamette University across the street from the Capitol so I could use the school's pool at lunch. Of course, I didn't make it to the pool every day. Meetings would run long. I would have a lunch appointment. Or there would be, as there always is in daily journalism, the inconvenient crisis. Like the time I heard, just as I was walking out the door with my swim gear, that a man was holding a knife to his throat on the floor of the state senate and threatening to kill himself. When I did make it to the pool, I could barely stand to swim for twenty minutes before I'd get bored and convince myself I just had to get back to the office immediately. And I actually like to swim.

The first thing I noticed during my super-sized commute was that after a few months I felt grumpy when I arrived home in the evening. I no longer bounded up the steps, invigorated by my ride. I trudged. As the session wore on, I found myself *arriving* at work in a sour mood. Then I discovered that I had gained three or four pounds in about as many months. I was back on the old pound-a-year plan, with a vengeance. I decided to stop snacking in the afternoon, which I had depended on for a burst of energy, or at least as a mood elevator. I had mixed success with that. Well, the politicians solved my problem by finally wrapping up the session. Within six weeks of getting back on my bike, I had returned to my pre-session weight. And here's the thing: I didn't do anything special. I just went back to my old commute, which gave me about an hour of exercise every day that I didn't even think of as exercise. My ride wouldn't do much with Elvis' 65,000-calorie problem, but it did seem to burn off that afternoon snack.

As I reflect on my own experience, I realize why the health community has now firmly adopted the view that the only way to get Americans to exercise regularly is to figure out how it can be incorporated into their daily lives. The experts don't even call it exercise any more. They talk about being physically active.

CHAPTER 8: Health and the Bicycle

This simple insight has given cycling powerful allies in the health community. As late as the early 1990s, when public health experts thought about bicycling, they tended to think in terms of getting riders to wear helmets. But now many are seeing the health virtues of getting people out of their cars, at least for short trips. As a result, bike and walking advocates have been rebranding their cause as "active transportation," which manages to come off as non-threatening to your average couch-bound American while carrying a nice touch of gravitas as well. Of course, the health experts are just recognizing what devoted transportation cyclists have always known, which is if you're on a quick ride to the store to pick up a carton of milk, you're not really paying attention to the exercise part. You're focused on the traffic, the sights, the (hopefully) fresh air, and the sheer joy of movement. It's kind of like the same trick your mind plays when you hike to the far end of the shopping mall and back in pursuit of the perfect gift for mom. You are thinking of the hunting and gathering, not the half-mile or so you've walked.

Unfortunately, walking to the far end of a shopping center is about as much exercise as too many people are getting in modern America, which seems to be on an extended "Super Size Me" experiment. Despite being bombarded with pro-exercise messages for decades, just under half of Americans don't meet the fairly easy minimum standard—thirty minutes of at least "moderate intensity" activity five days a week or 20 minutes of vigorous effort at least three days a week—recommended by the surgeon general. I think most people are quite aware that they will feel and look better if they exercise. We watch enough sports on TV to get that. However, our culture doesn't value the importance of exercise as highly as watching TV (which occupies roughly half of the leisure time of the average American) or shaving a few minutes off a routine trip to the store by driving instead of walking or biking. In part, the problem may be that most people have only a dim idea of how important exercise is to warding off a list of diseases that seems to get longer every year as more research is done. Here, drawn from several studies, are a few of the grim statistics for the physically inactive majority: a 30 to 50 percent increase in coronary heart disease, a 30 percent increase in hypertension, and a 20 to 50 percent increase in strokes. There's a 30 to 40 percent increase in the risk of colon cancer and a 20 to 30 percent increase in the risk of breast cancer. Inactivity also increases the likelihood of type 2 diabetes, and some studies suggest that exercise can help delay the onset of Alzheimer's and ease the symptoms of Parkinson's disease in men. In addition, men in their fifties are more likely to have erectile dysfunction if they don't exercise.

Andrew Dannenberg, a physician and top environmental-health official at the Centers for Disease Control, said that one of the most remarkable things about exercise is its impact not just on physical health, but on mental health as well. "Depression is both treated by and prevented by physical activity," he said. "It's phenomenal. There aren't many things that can do both prevention and treatment."

There is, of course, a strong link between most of the diseases I just listed and the obesity epidemic, which was called the "terror within" by Surgeon General Richard Carmona in 2006. "Unless we do something about it, the magnitude of the dilemma will dwarf 9/11 or any other terrorist attempt," he said. In 1991, only four states had adult obesity rates over 15 percent and none were over 20 percent. By 2007, the rate for the entire country had reached 34 percent and only one state, Colorado, was under 20 percent. In addition, another third of adults were overweight, according to the Centers for Disease Control. Obesity has become the country's second-largest cause of preventable death after smoking. It was cited by one 2004 study as being responsible for 12 percent of the increase in health care costs.

Experts argue over the complex stew of factors responsible for obesity. Clearly, a key factor has been the rise of cheap processed food laden with fat and sugar. In part, it may be the steady accumulation of labor-saving devices in our lives, from automatic garage door openers to electric can openers. Some even point to lower rates of smoking, which can help suppress appetites. But one thing is clear: although Americans keep searching for the magic diet—or so I'm led to believe by the magazines at the supermarket checkout counter—study after study makes it clear that weight loss can't be achieved by diet alone. A 2007 University of California, Los Angeles, report that looked at the utter failure of diet-only regimes said the real key to slimming down appears to be not the cleverness of the food plan, but the amount of physical activity. "Studies consistently find that people who reported the most exercise also reported the most weight loss," the UCLA researchers reported. There's simply no replacement for exercise. Even when people remain overweight, they show gains in health when they exercise.

These health concerns grew in the 1990s as physical activity levels stayed essentially flat and people continued to drive more than ever, with per capita vehicle miles climbing 13 percent over the decade. In 1996, the surgeon general issued a landmark report on physical activity that essentially concluded that efforts to get people to exercise more were increasingly swamped by the sedentary nature of modern life. "The major barrier to physical activity is the age in which we live," the report said. It pointed to cycling as one alternative to short car trips and cited surveys suggesting interest in bicycling to work, with 53 percent of those who had cycled in the last year saying they would commute by bike if they could do so on "safe, separated designated paths." As I made clear in the last chapter, we're far from meeting that standard (which advocates of vehicular cycling would even scoff at as a goal). Still, this was an important landmark for cycling advocates. They had been talking about the downsides of America's sprawling suburbs for years, but this was new terrain for the public health community.

Until the 1990s, "This kind of stuff was barely on the agenda of people like me," explained James Sallis, a psychologist at the University of California, San Diego. He is now one of the most influential health researchers on the impact of America's development patterns on physical activity. I met Sallis at his office in the lively university district north of San Diego's downtown. For three days, I had been driving and bicycling—mostly the former, unfortunately—to a series of interviews in Southern California and it was a pleasure to stumble into his neighborhood, an appealing mix of restaurants, shops, condos, and crowded sidewalks where I actually had to search to find a place to lock my bike that hadn't already been claimed by another cyclist. This little oasis of walking and biking in automobile-dominated Southern California was chosen deliberately by Sallis, the program director of Active Living Research, which is funded by the powerful Robert Wood Johnson Foundation. The foundation, one of the largest in America, became famous as a nemesis of the tobacco industry by spending millions on local initiatives to enact bans on smoking in public places. In the 1990s, they decided to tackle the design of American communities and how that affects health.

Sallis, a short, cheerful man whose office overflows with stacks of studies and computer printouts, had become interested in the 1980s in what it took to motivate people to exercise. As a devotee of behaviorist B. F. Skinner he was more inclined to look at outside stimuli than to assume it was all a matter of an individual's inner motivations. He was particularly struck by one program he worked on to help college students develop long-term fitness routines. The students seemed to be well motivated, but their gains all too often dissipated once they fanned out into the workforce and suburbia. "I was frustrated and thinking, 'We have to do things better,'" he recalled. People have the right instincts, but they find themselves too busy, and too reliant on getting around by car, to be very active. "Trying to get a person to exercise is like trying to teach them to swim in a river," he said. "As long as they are holding onto a pole or something, it is okay. But as soon as you let them go, they are swept away by the current."

In 1988, Sallis and two colleagues published a paper laying out a rudimentary case for the connection between community design and physical activity. He was also among a group of advisors who helped the Robert Wood Johnson Foundation shape its move into active living. Over the next decade, the charity spent $80 million on research, advocacy, partnerships, and grants to local groups to help work on fitness-friendly communities. Bike advocates were among the beneficiaries of the foundation's work, and they relished the help of a powerful new ally. As Bill Wilkinson put it: "The best thing that has happened to bicycling advocacy in thirty years is having the public health community come in with concerns about obesity and starting to do research that says the nature of the built environment has dramatic health impacts." These health issues, and the obesity crisis in particular, came along at a propitious time for the bicycling movement, when gas was cheap and few policymakers thought much about the threat of peak oil or climate change.

The Robert Wood Johnson Foundation became a big figure in the "active transportation" world. In Albuquerque, the foundation worked with smart-growth advocates to lobby for more sidewalks and other improvements to encourage walking. They also tested a "prescription trails" program that would give health-care providers specific route information they could use to provide patients with detailed walking regimes. In the Bronx, the charity helped fund efforts by grassroots activists to develop the South Bronx Greenway. In Portland, the foundation helped activists in the low-income Lents neighborhood to improve and promote the Springwater Corridor Trail, one of the city's key off-street bike routes. All told, the foundation established partnerships in twenty-five cities and worked with a variety of national groups. Perhaps more importantly, the foundation helped raise the visibility of the debate about the impact of community design and public health. Researchers built a stronger case that people were doing more walking and bicycling in denser neighborhoods and that they tended to weigh less. By the turn of the century, the news media began popularizing the issue and asking whether suburban life made people fat.

⫯⭗

One of the most influential researchers studying the link between health and urban design and transportation is Lawrence Frank, a planner and engineer at the University of British Columbia, who has frequently worked with Sallis. His voluminous work includes guiding a massive research project of Atlanta's sprawling population. The project, dubbed SMARTRAQ, began in 1998 when the region faced a cutoff of federal highway money because it violated air quality standards. Frank and his fellow researchers found a strong link between neighborhood design and physical activity. In neighborhoods with good walking environments—as defined by such things as sidewalks and nearby destinations—twice as many people reported getting moderate amounts of exercise compared to those in far-flung suburbs. Frank reported that for each additional hour spent in a car each day, the odds of obesity increased by 6 percent. It is easy to see why time spent in a car can affect fitness, looking at some of the eye-popping numbers in SMARTRAQ. Between 1982 and 1997, Atlanta added 1.3 million people by urbanizing about one acre of land for every two new residents. In that period of time, the average miles driven per day doubled, to thirty-four miles. Residents in the region's outer counties were spending an average of seventy-two minutes a day in a car, often in congested stop-and-go driving. In 2004, Frank and two physicians, Howard Frumkin and Richard Jackson (who at the time was also California's state public health officer), published the book, *Urban Sprawl and Public Health*, which focused heavily on the dangers of designing communities solely for automobile travel. "Ironically, the pedestrian fatality rate is slowly declining nationally, probably because fewer and fewer people are walking," they wrote. "If this is a public health victory, it is one we purchase at the steep price of widespread physical inactivity. We need community designs that seduce people into traveling on foot and by bicycle."

Not everyone was ready to blame America's health problems on community design. Urban geographer Susan Hanson, a professor at Clark College in Worcester, Massachusetts and a devoted recreational cyclist herself, chaired a committee formed by the Transportation Research Board that concluded in 2005 that people in communities less favorable to biking and walking indeed seemed to exercise less. But the panel said that more physically active people may simply choose to live in communities where it is easier and more inviting to walk and cycle. "There could be an impact on exercise," she said, "but we don't know it." Hanson noted that even in her own neighborhood—which is a model of grid streets and a lively mixture of uses—motor-vehicle use has clearly become more intense. At a nearby elementary school, she noted, parents now line up in their cars to drop off and pick up their kids. In her own family, Hanson said, she walks to work but her husband has to drive an hour to his job. "Multiply that by millions of families," she said, and you get an idea of how difficult it is to reduce motor-vehicle travel. I can relate to that. My wife and I choose to live in the city, giving me the pleasure of a bike commute of not quite five miles. Karen, however, is a nineteen-mile drive from her suburban job. "In general, the health people really wanted to believe it's the environment," said Hanson, "because they've tried everything else and they can't get people to exercise."

When I talked to Frank, the UBC planner and researcher, in mid-2007, he argued that the case for a link between health and land use had become even stronger. Besides, he noted, "It's intuitive that if you have nowhere to walk and there is no way to walk to anything, people are going to drive everywhere." In his latest research, Frank has been questioning the value of new highway construction, noting that he was working on new research in Seattle that found more road capacity would lead to declines in transit and walking. It's a new twist on the old "induced demand" argument made by highway critics who say that building new roads leads to more sprawling development that makes the roads as clogged as ever. As it happens, the Seattle region had a big vote in November of 2007 on a massive program to fund both new highway capacity and transit. The Cascade Bicycle Club (as well as the Sierra Club) broke with other transit advocates and urged a no vote on the measure, saying that the new roads would make the region even more dependent on the automobile. They joined with other opponents who objected to the amount of money spent on transit and to large tax increases, and the voters decisively turned the transportation package down.

Although traditional suburban developments continue to be the most prevalent new housing, Frank said his Atlanta research disclosed the beginning of a desire for more walkable neighborhoods. In a survey of fifteen hundred Atlantans, sizable percentages expressed a desire to walk to at least some retail destinations and said they would be willing to trade larger lot sizes for shorter commutes. And a majority said they would trade cul de sac subdivisions for a denser grid system that would make it more possible to walk and cycle to local schools and other locations. Frank noted that since the 2002 survey, several "New Urbanist" housing developments—featuring a mixture of housing types and retail services—have come on the market in Atlanta and done well. In cities around the country, old "streetcar" neighborhoods with their grid networks have become newly chic and there's a booming market for downtown condos. Even after the meltdown of sub-prime mortgages in 2007 sent housing into a downspin, the biggest declines came in the suburban fringes.

Seattle, with all of its traffic congestion, is an instructive example. For years, the city's central business district turned into a ghost town outside of business hours. Now there is so much condominium development that officials have discussed limiting downtown residential construction to preserve enough room for office space. While these downtown condo dwellers are walking and using transit more, there's no particular indication they are cycling in large numbers. But local cycling advocates are banking on the hope that the higher residential density encourages more lively streetscapes that—with the right bikeway development—will make cycling more popular. And the Cascade Bicycle Club played an important role in that by helping shape a city transportation tax passed in 2006 that provided $27 million for bicycle projects.

Besides exploring the link between the shape of communities and physical activity, researchers also started looking at how biking and walking infrastructure can—in a sense—produce economic savings. One study found that four new cycling and walking trails in Lincoln, Nebraska, generated enough new physical activity that the costs of construction and maintenance were dwarfed by the savings in medical costs. Of course, no health insurer is handing out "savings" in health care costs to the developers of bikeways, but it does give cycling advocates a strong argument to present to policymakers.

In Europe, where the tradeoff between health care and other public costs is more explicit because of national health care plans, these sorts of studies have had a bigger impact. Denmark used the City of Odense to test out various cycling programs, and a study found that savings in health care costs and sick leave were more than 50 percent greater than the investments in cycling. Since then, the government has continued to devote additional spending—and road space—to cyclists. Denmark now rivals the Netherlands in its use of the bicycle as a form of transportation. European health experts have also been influenced by a Finnish study that recruited previously sedentary adults to walk and bike to work, and found that both produced pronounced improvements in cardiovascular fitness but that the greatest gains were among those who cycled.

There is also evidence that the all-too-real safety risks facing cyclists are outweighed by the gains in their personal health. Cycling advocates often cite Mayer Hillman's study for the British Medical Association—"Cycling Towards Health and Safety," published in 1993—that concluded that regular cycling added twenty years of life for every year lost to fatal crashes (you have to think of this statistic as a ratio, not that the average person will gain two decades of life by cycling). The *British Medical Journal,* citing Hillman a decade later, archly suggested in an editorial that physicians should present a better example to their patients by cycling for short trips. "Doctors have bought the motor myth as hard as anyone," the journal said, "and it is time for change." As it happens, I have had more than one doctor tell me I would be wiser to get my exercise at the gym or in the pool than in rush-hour traffic. But I suppose if we strictly assessed our risks, we'd also all be taking public transit to work, which is statistically much safer than driving and usually involves some walking as well.

The health benefits of cycling have also become a major part of the case for cycling made by John Pucher, who has emerged as one of the most prominent supporters in academia of a more prominent role for the bicycle in urban transportation. Pucher, a professor at the Alan M. Voorhees Transportation Center at Rutgers University, spent most of his career researching public transit. But after a mid-1980s sabbatical in Muenster, Germany, Pucher was struck by the broad cross-section of residents who cycled in that city. He then turned his attention to figuring out what elements produced high rates of cycling in cities like Muenster (which borrowed many of its traffic schemes from the Dutch), and whether these could be replicated in the U.S.

I caught up with Pucher in Washington, D.C., in March of 2007 at the National Bike Summit, the annual gathering organized by the League of American Bicyclists. Pucher, an effusive man in his late fifties with an elfish grin, makes no pretense of being the detached academic. He calls himself "car-free John" and is an unabashed booster of alternative transportation. During a luncheon address at the summit, he cheerfully went over his allotted time bombarding his audience with a mixture of photos and charts to make his case. "The more auto dependent the country, the higher the obesity," he declared as he displayed a chart that unfavorably compared the obesity rates in the U.S., Canada, and the United Kingdom with countries more dependent on transit, walking, and cycling. The other possibility, he joked, was that speaking English makes you fat. To make his point that almost anyone could cycle if given safe facilities, he showed a photo of nuns on bikes in Muenster, in their full religious garb. "You see those nuns cycling and you think, 'I can do that too,'" he proclaimed. And he argued that the extra time people spend walking and cycling is offset by the gains in their healthy lifespans. "It just doesn't take huge increases in physical activity to give you health benefits. You don't have to cycle two hundred miles or run the marathon to get health benefits," he said. "Getting someone to cycle two or three miles a day is great for their physical health."

I talked with Pucher afterwards, and he described Americans' heavy reliance on the car almost in terms of disease. "It is an addiction," he said. "It is such a strong habit [among so many people] that they don't even think of doing it another way." He said he even sees it in his own family. He talked about a brother and sister-in-law who own five cars and think nothing of driving to the end of the driveway to pick up the mail. "When I tell audiences this I think they will say, 'No way, this can't be.' But everyone says, 'Yeah, I know somebody like that.'" Pucher argued that heavy auto users—and that's about how he puts it—are risking more than their own waistline. Besides the risk of auto crashes, he pointed to a German study that found an unusually high percentage of people having heart attacks had spent time in traffic congestion on the day they were stricken. In fact, the study, published in the *New England Journal of Medicine*, concluded that the risk of a heart attack tripled for those who had been in their car in the previous hour. And several studies have confirmed what seems to me to be obvious: that the uncertainty and anxiety of clogged commutes raises stress levels in drivers.

It can also be stressful cycling on busy streets with traffic. But I've been struck by the sheer number of health testimonials I have heard in the cycling world, particularly from people who were indifferent athletes when they were young. Deb Hubsmith, the Marin County bike activist, was repeatedly hospitalized for asthma, both as a child and an adult. But, after she wrecked her car and a friend insisted she couldn't be a real environmentalist and a car owner, she decided to go without. She began traveling around her hilly county on two wheels. "At first when I started biking I couldn't make it up any major hill without having an asthma attack," she said, but gradually the attacks tapered off. "I could feel myself getting healthier," she said. "It's really helped to strengthen my lungs." She said she hasn't been hospitalized for years, and every time I see Hubsmith I think of when I first met her. It was 2005, and she came rushing into her office at the Marin County Bicycle Coalition, a dimunitive presence with a bundle of energy who talked so fast she made my tape recorder scream in agony. We parted ways and a while later I was sitting in a park in Fairfax eating a sandwich. I saw Hubsmith come cruising around the corner, merging onto a busy street in front of the park. She was the lone cyclist among plenty of cars. And she was smiling.

Donna Marie Bryan of Portland is a more recent convert to bicycle transportation. In early 2005, at the age of thirty-two, she had surgery to remove a tumor that, while benign, threatened her with brain injury. Bryan, who had initially been treated with large doses of steroids, found that her weight—already problematical— had ballooned both before and after the surgery. Because of the dizzy spells that were part of her recovery from surgery, she stopped driving and began getting around Portland on the bus and by walking. Three months after her operation, inspired by a housemate who seemed to effortlessly bike to school, shopping, and work, Bryan (who was now past her dizzy spells) started thinking she could do the same. "I remember how much I enjoyed riding a bike when I was younger," she said.

Bryan bought a new bike and vowed she would ride the three and a half miles to work at least twice a week. After a week or two of adjustment, she was hooked. In the next year, she hardly skipped a day. As her strength improved, she found she could ride to work quicker than by taking the bus. And after an initial weight gain while she built muscle mass, she has dropped fifty pounds. "I'm never going to be a skinny little waif," she said. "I am just not built that way." But she's pleased at her energy level when she arrives at work and her blood pressure has dropped enough so that she no longer needs to consider taking medication. Going to the doctor now is an ego builder. "I'm like the highlight of their day. The positive feedback I get is the kind that is usually reserved for rescuing a baby from a burning building," she said. "I don't think they see it very often that people follow their advice" to get more exercise, she added. Bryan no longer owns a car and has come to rely on her bike for almost all of her transportation. Recently, she and her brother jointly bought a bike trailer, which she uses to haul such heavy loads as kitty litter. She has decidedly moved from the sedentary majority to the active minority. "I get really bored doing exercise for exercise's sake," she said. "I could never follow through on a gym routine. I don't believe human beings evolved to take part in repetitive exercise for no purpose."

Of course, cycling is not without its own risks, chiefly because of road dangers, as I detailed in the last chapter. There is one other health-related hazard that transportation cyclists need to consider: bad air quality. Busy roads are toxic air corridors, with pollution levels that can be much higher than a few hundred yards away. An Amsterdam study found that people living near busy streets are exposed to two times as much particulate matter, nitrogen oxides, and carbon monoxide. Similarly, a Harvard School of Public Health study concluded that there is a 500-foot to 1,500-foot zone around heavily trafficked streets with significantly higher pollution levels. And even motor vehicles provide little or no protection from this toxic airstream. A report from the Center for Technology Assessment found twenty-three studies showing higher pollution levels in cars than in monitoring stations along the side of the road. California's Air Resources Board, which used a van filled with monitoring equipment, also found high pollution levels inside the vehicle. When the van moved to the less-congested carpool lane, the levels dropped somewhat. "If you can just imagine a river of air flowing through the line of traffic—and being pushed along as well—that is where the emissions are the highest," said Thomas Scheffelin, an engineer with the air resources board.

This means drivers of motor vehicles are often exposed to worse air pollution than they may be led to believe by measurements of overall air quality. Researchers believe these high pollution levels may be one factor in the previously mentioned German study about driving and heart attacks. The question for cyclists is what kind of risk they are putting themselves in when they ride on busy streets—which in many cities is often a necessity.

A Dublin study found cyclists were exposed to higher levels of particulate matter, probably, the researchers concluded, because they were frequently sharing the lane with diesel buses, a prime cause of particulate pollution. In addition, depending on how deeply cyclists are breathing, the study said they may also be absorbing greater quantities of benzene, which can cause cancer, and of other pollutants implicated in respiratory and heart problems. "We encourage people not to exercise near a busy highway," said Janice Nolen, an official at the American Lung Association.

Scheffelin, who rides his bike to work in Sacramento, said he doesn't think that most commuting cyclists are breathing particularly heavily when they are traveling in stop-and-go traffic. "Sometimes I'm at a stoplight on a downtown street and I'm thinking what am I breathing? And actually I'm breathing what I'd be breathing if I was sitting in a car," he said. And just being in a bike lane and in the open, instead of the enclosed space of a motor vehicle, might even slightly minimize the exposure, he added. Still, it is a dilemma. Cyclists are the only zero emitters in the roadway, but that may not spare them from the worst exposure to air pollution. In many cases, at least, cyclists do have a greater ability than motorists to avoid busy streets, either by taking trails or side roads. That's one reason I avoid arterials if I have a decent alternative, and I try not to spend much time behind trucks and buses.

In the end, the larger issue is whether society considers health issues like obesity when we're building our communities and transportation infrastructure. Cyclists have certainly made our society's ill health an important part of their pitch for bike-friendly communities. To me, it seems like another front in the long cultural war over just how much power to give the public health community. Are we furthering the Nanny State or simply creating healthier communities? Many Americans thought Ralph Nader's auto safety crusades in the 1960s were over-reaching, as did smokers who believed no one had the right to tell them whether they could light up in a restaurant or in their office (let alone a bar, the last and slowly disappearing bastion of indoor smoking). Americans by and large have become accustomed to seatbelts and smoke-free restaurants. But each new attempt to influence behavior—whether it is banning sodas in schools or raising taxes on alcohol or tobacco—raises new concerns that we're trampling on our traditions of rugged individualism.

I thought of this as I read a remarkable book, *Prescription for a Healthy Nation,* by two physicians, Tom Farley and Deborah Cohen. They argue that America's fixation with the accessibility and cost of its expensive health-care system obscures the real issue: that we've all too often forgotten that "health care" often does little to provide real health. The authors say that medicine is limited in its ability to heal chronic disease. Instead, they say that more than 40 percent of early deaths can be attributed to such underlying factors as smoking, diet, physical activity, alcohol use, and vehicle crashes (in fact, they rely heavily on an influential 1993 paper co-authored by Michael McGinnis, who later, as a top official at the Robert Wood Johnson Foundation, played an important role in developing the charity's active living programs). Most people, of course, know they should eat better, get more exercise, and not smoke. But programs to encourage individuals to change their behavior have only a limited impact, Farley and Cohen write. We're social creatures and we tend to mimic behavior we see around us. "Every collection of people shapes an average, acceptable, 'normal' behavior," Farley and Cohen wrote. "The discrimination people experience when they are different can sometimes be severe, but more often it is simply the social threat of being viewed as 'weird.' On the other hand, people who stay within the social norm feel comfortable and supported. It's tough to swallow, but we usually behave more like herds of sheep than lone wolves."

To really change behavior, they said, you have to change society, which is exactly what anti-smoking campaigners did by making cigarettes less available (through higher taxes, restrictions on vending machines, and tougher bars on youth smoking), less visible (through a ban on television advertising), and harder to use (through indoor smoking bans). I certainly relate to this as a cyclist. I'm pretty conventional in most of my life, and sometimes I feel like the hardest part about using my bike to get around town is the comments I get from people who think I'm just plain weird for doing so.

Just as we made society less welcoming for smokers, Farley and Cohen say we have to think similarly about re-engineering America so it does not encourage sedentary behavior. "We have to put walking and bicycling back into our daily lives and temper our addiction to cars," they said. "For starters, we can require that when developers build neighborhoods they put in sidewalks and bike paths, and we can direct federal and state highway funds to building them on existing streets." More than that, these communities should be organized so that these sidewalks and bike paths go somewhere useful, they say. This, of course, is exactly what gets some people complaining about the rise of the Nanny State. If people want to ride their bikes, I remember one conservative transportation pundit telling me, they will. There's nothing stopping them. He did, however, neglect to mention the safety concerns most Americans have about riding in traffic that have turned many of our streets into an automotive monoculture. But Farley and Cohen say it makes little sense to simply chalk up our individual failings as a lack of personal responsibility without looking at the larger forces at work. Should we give up treating drinking water and assume that people should instead take individual responsibility for boiling their water? Should we assume they will be physically active when their local streets are designed solely for the automobile?

In Europe, there's much more of a tradition of coming down on the side of community responsibility, which is one of the reasons why many cities on the continent have been willing to more severely restrict auto traffic in favor of biking and walking. But so far, most Americans aren't ready to question the health implications of the way we design our communities. I remember watching Al Gore try to gingerly raise the issue of sprawl early in his 2000 presidential campaign. He appeared at a New Urbanist development near Portland and talked about how communities like these would give people a chance to get more exercise and shorten their commute so they would have more time to spend with their families.[1] Gore quickly dropped the issue as a political non-starter, and I notice he hasn't talked about it much in his Nobel Prize-winning effort to combat climate change. Still, the issue of community design and health has taken root among many planners and health professionals

---

1. It's also worth noting that Democratic Sen. Barack Obama of Illinois in 2008 became the first major presidential candidate that I'm aware of to explicitly mention bicycling as a legitimate transportation alternative. Both he and his primary rival, New York Sen. Hillary Clinton, said they supported more compact growth and wanted to boost funding for mass transit. And before Obama ran for president, the Active Living Network named Obama one of its top ten heroes for sponsoring legislation to encourage healthy community design.

in a way that could give cyclists powerful new ammunition in their push for bike-friendly streets. And the more that average people see cyclists on their streets and the more they see the beneficial health effects, the more it will start to shape a different community norm. To paraphrase Farley and Cohen, cycling to work and the store will be more accepted when cyclists are seen as herds of sheep instead of lone wolves.

9

Bringing Kids Back to Bikes

It was a fine spring morning and the neighborhood around Sacramento Elementary School was filled with large packs of children walking to school. For anyone of my generation, growing up in the 1960s, it was an ordinary sight. Except on this day, there is an undeniable air of excitement around Sacramento school, which is on the eastern edge of Portland. The kids were amped up, chattering and waving to friends on the other side of the street. Parents and teachers bustled alongside, taking pictures and keeping an alert eye at intersections. At the school itself, festive banners and snacks awaited the walkers, as well as a smaller number of cyclists. The special occasion was Earth Day, which the school was celebrating with its annual walk and bike to school day. Britt Christiaansen, a fifth-grade teacher, smiled as she arrived at the school and saw only four or five cars waiting in line to drop off kids. "This is how I like to see the parking lot," she said. "Usually it's packed."

Indeed, something has happened since I was in elementary school and children were expected to walk and bike to school if they could, and the sight of a kid skipping along, lunchbox in hand, was as American as anything Norman Rockwell could paint. A government travel study in 1969 found that 87 percent of all kids who lived within a mile of school walked or biked. In fact, 42 percent of all schoolkids did, and most of the rest took a school bus. That changed over the ensuing decades as traffic became more intense, parents became more fearful, the neighborhood school became less common, and two- and three-car households became ubiquitous. By 2001, only about 15 percent of kids were getting to school under their own power. And, depending on what survey data you used, as few as one-third of students who lived within a mile of school walked or biked. Some suburban schools are so ringed with busy arterials that parents don't even want their children to walk across the street.

The changing nature of the commute to school is just one marker of a radical change in childhood. In just one or two generations, we've moved from a time when kids by and large freely roamed their neighborhood, and even beyond, to a point where many parents are reluctant to let kids out of their sight. The freewheeling exploration of the neighborhood creek, which I remember so well from my childhood, has been replaced by the elaborate backyard play set or, more likely, marathon video game sessions. Impromptu games of street football have given way to organized youth soccer. Some of the changes have been good. For all of our fretting about schools, achievement levels are up and I'd argue that the average kid is a lot more sophisticated about the broader world than we were forty years ago. But we're also paying a price in physical health. The percentage of overweight children has tripled since the mid-1970s. The number of cases of type 2 diabetes, once almost never found in children, has skyrocketed and increasing percentages of young people get little exercise. According to the Centers for Disease Control, nearly half of young people aged twelve to twenty-one said they don't get regular vigorous exercise. If you're not going to be physically active when you're the most capable of it, when are you?

For bicycle advocates, this poses a big dilemma: they fear that if young people don't ride, cycling is in danger of eventually withering away. Surveys show that people who cycled in their younger years are much more likely to ride as adults. Beyond that, not having kids walk and ride to school seems to violate everything that so many bike advocates held dear about their own upbringing. Again and again, as I talked to the people in the bike world, they would tell me stories of being a free-range child.

"I grew up in Princeton," Bill Wilkinson of the National Center for Bicycling and Walking told me. "I had the run of the community, from the age of nine years on … I could go anyplace. My only admonition was, be home by dinner." Charles Komanoff, the former Transportation Alternatives director in New York City, told me about growing up on Long Island, in Long Beach City. "There was kind of a social compact that if a car was coming down the street, if the car was half a block away, the car would slow down until the play was over and then we'd happily get out of the way … We never, never had an incident. This went on for years." Recently, he said, he was in his old neighborhood. There were no kids in sight.

Being of the right age, the stories resonate with me. At my elementary school, the big deal was to be on traffic patrol, which was drilled to a paramilitary sheen that is now hard to imagine. But there's no longer a children's traffic patrol; the road in front of the school was judged too dangerous for kids to handle traffic duties. And besides, most kids are chauffeured to the front of the school by car, avoiding the crosswalks altogether. Somewhere in the last twenty years, long lines of cars appeared in front of my old elementary school at the end of the day. Recently, my sister told me a story about our childhood that I had never heard before. She had been friends with a girl down the street who was an only child and coddled by her mother, who drove her three-quarters of a mile to elementary school almost every day. My mother fumed at that, thinking that the girl needed not only to get more exercise but also not to expect other people to do so much for her. I nodded when I heard that, remembering how my mom often refused to drive me downtown when I was a teen (but too young to drive on my own). "Take the bus," she would say. Is there any parent today who says that to their fourteen-year-old? Hara Estroff Marano, an editor at *Psychology Today* and author of *A Nation of Wimps*, argues that over-protective parents are harming the psychological development of their children. "In the hothouse that childrearing has become," she writes, "parents not only got the definition of success exactly backwards, many of their attempts to encourage achievement (like removing play) actually wind up undermining their children's success and short-circuiting necessary brain development."

椖

There are other reasons, as one influential report put it, for "Why Johnny Can't Walk to School" any more. That report by the Historic Trust for Preservation talked about how historic neighborhood schools were increasingly being replaced by large campuses often found on the edges of cities. That's where land is cheaper and there's room for the sprawling athletic fields that are so popular with taxpayers. According to the National Center for Education Statistics, the number of public schools declined from about two hundred thousand in 1940 to about ninety-seven thousand in 2005, during a time the population more than doubled. As we've consolidated in the name of efficiency, kids are simply not as close to school as they used to be. In 1969, when the government began compiling statistics on travel to school, almost half of all students lived within a mile of school. By 2001, fewer than 25 percent were that close.

A 1999 survey of parents by the CDC found that 55 percent listed distance as the major barrier preventing their child from walking or biking to school. That was followed by traffic danger (40 percent), adverse weather (24 percent), and fear of crime (18 percent). In my discussions with school officials, bike advocates, and parents, I suspect that the fear their child could be harmed by a predator is a bigger factor. No matter how rare they are (and they are extremely rare[1]), brutal child kidnappings and murders now reverberate

---

1. The odds of a child being abducted are about one in one million, according to a Cox News Service story that compared the risks of

through our media-saturated culture. When I started reading up on this topic, I realized that I still vividly remember the 1993 murder of Polly Klaas, who was kidnapped from a slumber party in Petaluma, California. Getting struck by lightning is statistically more likely, but those tragedies don't stick in my mind. Child sexual abuse may not be any more prevalent than it was when I was young, but we're a lot more aware of it today (and it's more likely to be reported to authorities). Somewhere we reached a cultural tipping point. As one mom, Rashana Strong, told me as we walked with her son to Sacramento School, "with the crime rate and all the funky things, you always worry about your child ...You are always afraid your child is going to be the one" to be hurt.

Ironically, the more parents drove their kids to school, the more dangerous it did become to walk or bike. There was no longer the safety in numbers, either when it came to a predator or to simply capturing the attention of motorists so that they would drive more carefully. The zones around schools became so clogged with cars that they became the most common danger. The Washington Department of Transportation found that half of the children hit by cars in school zones were hit by motorists driving another child to school. In some suburbs, officials estimate that more than a fifth of morning rush-hour traffic consists of kids being driven to school. I have certainly noticed—during my periods of long auto commutes—how much lighter traffic is on days when there is no school. With more cars on the street in general, walking and biking often feels more perilous, particularly in suburban or rural locations where little attention has been paid to providing sidewalks or any other roadway accommodation to anyone who is not a motorist.

While many adults of my generation have fond memories of walking and riding to school, it is easy for society to dismiss these feelings as just nostalgia. Schools, under constant pressure to

---

different activities. The risk of dying playing youth football is one in 78,260.

increase academic standards, have had a lot more to worry about than how kids are getting to school. In fact, many schools have been cutting recess time and physical education. With the rise of two-income families, dropping the kids off at school during the morning commute has seemed the most efficient thing to do. And many parents say the drive to school gives them some of the best quality time they have with their kids, away from all the demands of running a household. I can relate to that as well. When my kids were teens I loved to chauffeur them and their friends to events. If I shut up and let them talk, I learned more about what they were really up to in fifteen minutes than in hours at home.

But cycling advocates, who are nothing if not passionate, have been trying to reverse this trend for years. For one thing they have found that it is a good mom-and-apple-pie issue to promote biking and walking since it touches on the fond childhood memories of so many adults. It also ties in with the concerns of the public health community. As James Sallis, the San Diego active living researcher, pointed out, there isn't much that can be done once people become obese, but you can make huge gains in the long run if you change the behavior of people when they are still young. And there's also a growing body of evidence that children who get regular exercise do better academically. As my wife, a middle-school math teacher, could tell you, every teacher would rather have a classroom full of kids who have had a chance to burn off some of their nervous energy.

More prosaically, for many bike advocacy groups, teaching bike and pedestrian safety to kids is a reliable revenue stream. Several of the large bike groups—including the Chicagoland Bicycle Federation and the Bicycle Transportation Alliance in Portland—have become contractors for schools and local governments. These activities help support the rest of the organization. But most importantly, this work is about growing the bicycle and pedestrian advocates of tomorrow. For the long-range health of the movement, you need to reach the kids.

That's what Deb Hubsmith and Wendi Kallins thought. The two Marin County women played a major role in creating and selling the Safe Routes to School program, which is now spreading rapidly to schools around the country and has become one of the federal government's major programs to support cycling. After funding a pilot program early in the decade, the 2005 transportation bill contained $600 million to take Safe Routes to School to every state. Kallins and Hubsmith were both environmental activists who first started working together on a program to teach children about how their transportation choices affected the environment and society. Kallins, then forty-four, said she had been inspired by a workshop she attended with Dan Burden, the "walkability" guru who was also one of the founding fathers of the modern bike advocacy movement. It made her think, she said, "wouldn't it be great if we could teach our kids not just driver's education, but transportation education." Hubsmith, then twenty-eight, was just learning to live without a car. "I always was averse to transportation experts driving around in SUVs and other gasoline-powered cars to tell people how they could become more environmentally conscious," said Hubsmith, "and I wanted to find a way to go around to schools that would be completely pollution free."

The problem was that she also needed to be able to haul about seventy pounds worth of pamphlets, a slide projector, and carousel (this still being pre-Power Point days). Hubsmith rigged up an electric bicycle with a trailer. For power, she used boat batteries that were recharged by solar panels. Hubsmith and her solar-powered bike attracted plenty of attention. She liked to tell kids about how she had lusted after a car when she was young, started saving early, and bought an MG sports car when she was seventeen. "I learned that MG stands for Maximum Grief because my car kept breaking down," she said. Within a year and a half, she was broke and cured of her car-lust (although it would be another decade before she finally gave up car ownership). However, the two activists could not attract the funding to create a permanent program. Sure, some kid might remember years later about the woman on the solar-powered bike who said you didn't have to drive everywhere, but would it really create lasting change?

Kallins did some more research, and she learned about programs to teach children in Europe how to walk and bike safely. She said they first started in Denmark in the 1970s when the country had a high child-pedestrian fatality rate. The concept spread to the Netherlands, Britain, Australia, Canada, and other countries. Kallins received a large box full of materials on a program from British Columbia that she used to write a grant request to the Marin County Foundation, a major local charity. She also attracted the interest of Anne Seeley, who worked for the California Department of Health and was looking for ways to promote physical activity among children. They weren't the only ones converging on this idea. Chicago had started an annual walk and bike to school day at about this time and Transportation Alternatives had launched its own safe routes program in New York City. Most importantly, Rep. Jim Oberstar, D-Minn., and the biggest bicycle advocate on Capitol Hill, was casting about for some sort of program to get kids on bikes. Oberstar said years later that he had been appalled by a briefing he had received from Rich Killingsworth, then a key CDC public health official, about the rise in childhood obesity and diabetes, and Oberstar tied it in part to the fact that three-quarters of trips that kids took were by car. "I thought, 'My God, we've got a whole generation of mobility-challenged children,'" said Oberstar. "I went for a long ride and pedaled as far as I could," he added, thinking that there had to be some way to get kids back to walking and biking to school. He began reaching out to his friends in the bike community and it wasn't long before he discovered Hubsmith, who was then running the Marin County Bike Coalition. Hubsmith, Marin County bike manufacturer Joe Breeze (who was also a famous mountain bike pioneer), and Patrick Seidler, president of WTB, a bike parts company based in Marin, arranged to meet with

Oberstar at the 2000 Sea Otter Classic, a bike festival in Monterey County, California.

Hubsmith and Oberstar hit it off, and they began plotting how to take the safe routes concept national. He managed to get federal funding for pilot programs in Marin County and in Arlington, Massachusetts. After these programs demonstrated some success in getting more kids to walk and bike to school, Oberstar, now the ranking Democrat on the House Transportation Committee, inserted the $600 million for a national safe routes program in the 2005 bill. (That was the year that Oberstar also obtained another $100 million for a pilot program to demonstrate how four counties could boost the mode share of bicycling. Not surprisingly, Marin County was chosen to be one of the pilots.)

To get a sense of how the program operates, I spent a day with Frances Barbour, one of the safe routes teachers in Marin County. Like almost everyone I've met connected to the program, she seems to have her own quirky story of learning the transportation value of the bike. She grew up in a well-to-do family in Washington, D.C., and became an avid cyclist in college. "I learned all the things you can do on a bike, even riding to church in high heels and a long dress," she said. "Instead of gaining fifteen pounds" in her freshman year, "I lost weight." She returned to D.C. where she continued to ride her bike to work, even when she got a job for a nonprofit involved in international affairs. "It was considered a liability that I bike-commuted," she said, "so I went to great lengths to hide it … to the extent of putting hot rollers under my bike helmet." Now living in one of the most expensive suburbs in America, Barbour joked that she is the right person to "mainstream this program into Marin culture" by talking to people at "my church (Episcopalian), the yacht club, and the tennis club."

The safe routes program has become deeply embedded in Marin County, where taxpayers included money for it in a 2004 ballot measure that boosted the sales tax to provide additional transportation funding. While it is overseen by the local transportation authority, the Marin County Bike Coalition actually runs the program and employs Barbour and the other teachers. On this particular winter day, she was teaching pedestrian safety to a group of second graders at Pleasant Valley School in Novato. The kids had already been exposed to the program and when she begins by asking the class what they know about safe routes to school, several reply in unison, "wear a helmet."

Barbour asked whether there are times when it is not good to drive. Another chorus as several replied, "Yeah!" Why not? she asked. "Because it's wasting energy," one girl replied. "I think my mom says it helps the trees or something," added another. Yes, Barbour responded, pollution from cars can hurt trees. "We say we are part of the pollution solution," she added. And there's another side to it, she said. What about health? "Our bodies are made to move," she explained. How much exercise should you get every day?

They batted that one around for a while until, with prodding from Barbour, they settled upon an hour of exercise a day. You feel better, sharper, when you do, she said. "You actually do better in school." Still, Barbour wasn't through piling on reasons for avoiding a drive to school. Why, for example, might you want to consider biking two miles to school when you get older, she asked. They're stumped. She then explained how it would help reduce traffic and congestion, because about one in five cars on the road are bringing kids to school. Finally, she concluded, "my favorite reason is missing." After a pause, she asked, "Who likes to walk, who likes to bike with friends?" Several raise their hands. "It's fun," concluded Barbour. "That's my favorite reason. "You get to see the world around … you get to see the birds and smell the flowers around you." With that, the class moved on to a discussion of how to safely cross streets, with the main point being that children have to learn how to make safe decisions. Later, she told me that adults instinctively make the decisions on whether it is safe or not to cross the street when they are with their children. Barbour said she has to make a conscious decision to hang back when she is with her own son, to let him learn how to deal with traffic. "If we don't give them the skills to make these kinds of decisions," she said, "what kind of society are we giving them?"

These were all noble sentiments, although the safe routes program has irritated some conservatives who didn't like to see the schools promoting what they saw as anti-car environmental correctness. But the hard task of changing a culture became apparent to me the moment I stepped outside the classroom at the end of the school day. The driveway out front was full and the line of cars stretched far down the street. "It's an uphill climb," sighed Barbour as she observed the idling vehicles. As I talked with parents, it soon became clear that many were affected by two scary incidents several months before. According to an account in the *Marin Independent Journal*, a man had sprayed a girl with an aerosol can and attempted to sexually assault her before she escaped. And there was a report of an attempted kidnap in a park of a twelve-year-old girl. "Given what happened early this year," said one young mother, "I don't want them to walk without me being present."

Kallins, who continued to run the Marin County program, downplayed the two incidents, saying that both girls did the right thing by running away after being approached by the two men. "The thing about stranger danger is that it is very overblown," she said. "If you talk to the experts, you don't want to lock your kids up—you want to give them the skills to handle it."

Still, she acknowledged, the incidents had a huge negative effect on the safe routes program at that school. One of the main ways that safe routes tries to overcome such parental worries is by organizing "walking school buses," which essentially involve parent volunteers who agree to walk a morning route that kids can join. Kallins said the walking school buses also improve communities overall by providing more "eyes on the street," to use the phrase of urbanist Jane Jacobs, who noted that communities were safer and more vibrant when more people are out and about. The walking school bus has proved to be particularly popular in suburban and upscale urban communities where there are a lot of adult volunteers. Robert Ping, of the Safe Routes to School National Partnership, noted that it's harder to find volunteers for many inner-city schools. Often, these schools already have large numbers of children walking, but they can face serious traffic safety and neighborhood crime problems. Some volunteers also help kids ride bikes to school, although they tend to be fewer in number.

Nationally, safe routes advocates say one of their big goals is to reverse the trend toward larger schools built on the outskirts of communities. "School siting is the eight-hundred-pound gorilla nobody is talking about," Ping said. If schools aren't within relatively close distances, there's not much advocates can do to encourage walking and bicycling, he noted. They've had some success in getting states to drop laws requiring that new schools meet minimum size requirements. At the urging of the Environmental Protection Agency, the Council of Educational Facility Planners International has changed its guidelines to encourage school leaders to be flexible in deciding how much acreage they need for a school. Ping argued that communities can preserve neighborhood schools and reduce their costs by doing such things as using a nearby park for some of their athletic facilities. What's tougher, Ping admitted, is to figure out a way to get school districts to consider the traffic impacts of school siting. The problem is that schools can save money by building on the outskirts of a community, but they don't have to pay for the additional demand they put on the road system.

In addition to education and encouragement, the safe routes program emphasizes two other "E's": engineering and enforcement. Much of the money is directed toward safety improvements in school zones and on routes that children are likely to take. Kallins showed me photos of some of the work funded through safe routes. In Fairfax, for example, officials installed sidewalks on a street where kids walking to school were forced to veer into the street when there was no room along the edge. That caused some fuss because a few parking spaces were eliminated as a result. "People love safe routes to school until it affects their parking," she noted drily. In a largely Hispanic neighborhood in San Rafael, traffic engineers have installed raised crosswalks and bulbouts at corners to reduce traffic speeds and improve safety. More than half the kids already walk to school, Kallins said. "It's not a matter of engaging them" to walk or bike, she said. "It's a matter of making it safe for them." Following the lead of Dan Burden, who encourages communities to do "walkable audits" to figure out the barriers to walking, the safe routes program seeks to enlist educators, parents, police, and traffic engineers to work together to map out promising routes to school and figure out where improvements need to be made.

The Marin program has had its promising successes but some failures as well. Kallins said the program has averaged about a 13 percent shift away from solo car trips to school. But the rate varies widely for individual schools, from a high of 27 percent to some schools where the program has made no dent at all and car trips have actually increased. Some schools have had major increases in cycling, but safe routes advocates say their biggest successes have come in increasing the number of walkers. Cycling is more complicated, involving not only parking and theft issues but a wider range of traffic issues as well.

Still, on my visits to Sacramento School, I have been struck by the enthusiasm there is for biking when kids get a chance to try it. Portland's Bicycle Transportation Alliance, which also runs a pioneering safe routes program, has a fleet of bikes that it takes to schools to give hands-on instructions to kids. After participating in the walk and bike to school day, I returned to the school later in the spring to watch some of the bike education classes.

Sacramento is an interesting school, located far enough on Portland's east side that it feels more suburban than urban. There's little sign of Portland hip here, with few trendy restaurants and not many people on bikes. Instead, the neighborhood has a 1960s feel to it, dominated by modest ranch houses, with cheap apartment complexes on the edges. It's old-fashioned in the sense that almost the entire student body lives within a mile and a half of school. But it's also economically and ethnically diverse, with the 430 students coming from homes where fourteen different languages are spoken. Despite the short distances, only about a quarter of the students regularly walk, school officials estimate, and just a handful bicycle regularly.

The principal, Stevie Blakely, welcomed the safe routes program, thinking it would help knit together the neighborhood if more kids were biking and walking to school. "If we could get more adults out walking with their kids, other parents would not be so apprehensive about their kids walking to school on their own," she said. With people living so close, "there isn't any reason to drive except I think there is a fear factor," she added. "That way they watch the kids get out of the car and go into the building … The huge issue for them is safety."

Blakely said she knows many of her students need to be more active—"Don't you feel better in the morning if you get some exercise?" she asked rhetorically—and she said she worries that they spend too much time inside. "I'm really concerned about kids using their imagination. Back in the day, we had to make up things … Now it's just an onslaught of video and TV—it's passive." In talking to parents, I also got a sense that driving was also just a habit, reinforced by the culture. Lori Jeremiah, an educational assistant who also has a nine-year-old at the school, sheepishly acknowledged that she only lived about a quarter-mile from school but that she and her son drove almost every day. "Every minute counts in the morning," she said, explaining that it was hard to get her son going. Vanessa Inman, a parent listening in, added that she did walk every day. But she said that she saw a lot of people driving crazy and she could understand why parents could worry about walking. "There are perverts out there," agreed Jeremiah, seemingly relieved to find another reason to drive. "It's scary. That's my big concern." One parent also told me that walking is fine, "except when it is cold and rainy."

Anna Scalera, who ran the BTA safe routes program until May of 2007, said it often doesn't take much in the way of inclement weather to discourage parents. "The kids aren't the ones who mind the rain," said Scalera. "It's mostly the adults who are the wimps when it comes to the weather."

I watched a couple of fifth-grade classes practice on an asphalt playground as they spent several days preparing for the culmination of the program: an afternoon ride around the neighborhood. I was pleasantly surprised that in each class, only a couple of kids didn't get on a bike; one was a girl who had worn open-toed sandals despite having been told to wear enclosed shoes and another was an autistic boy who chose not to ride. "I think the kids appreciate the break," said Brett Davidson, one of the teachers. "It doesn't feel like school to them. Hey, I get antsy in the classroom, too."

Jaye Marolla, the bicycle education instructor, ran them through a series of drills, including proper signaling, positioning themselves on the roadway, and how to make right and left turns. The kids seemed to throw themselves into the task with determination. "Sometimes I'm shocked they have so much fun learning core skills," Marolla said. She also mixed things up by holding a competition to see who could ride the slowest from one end of the playground to the other without having their feet touch the ground. I returned for the big neighborhood ride a few days later. The kids grabbed their bikes, lined up for a safety check, and were off. I fell in toward the end of the group with a boy who was clearly a deft rider but was having trouble with a balky derailleur. We finally got that problem fixed, and he zoomed ahead with a smile on his face. Another boy grinned as he veered off the street to bump over some paving stones in a rock garden. It made me think of my old Sting-Ray. When we approached one end of the neighborhood, I heard several of the kids talking about the approach of a steep street that they called "dead man's hill." "We should ride down it," one boy said. "That would be cool." "No way," said a girl, riding next to him. We turned before the hill. There would be nothing scary on this ride.

I lagged behind with an overweight girl who was wondering when we would get back to school. "My butt hurts," she complained. We caught up with the rest of the group at a park across the street from the school. Except for the girl riding next to me, spirits seemed high. Sid Tyler, another BTA instructor, popped a wheelie and rode that for a while, to much appreciation from the kids. "Cycling is one of the things you can do your entire life," he said. "If you like this, this is something you can do your entire lives."

After we returned to school and got the bikes squared away, I sat out front and watched the end of the school day. It was like a choreographed drill. One woman drove up in a minivan and hopped out of the driver's seat as her daughter ran toward her. The woman slid back the rear door, the girl hopped up in the rear seat and the mom buckled her in. They were on their way seconds later. It certainly looked convenient, but I found myself thinking that the girl seemed old enough to open the door and put on her own seatbelt. If we're so intent on doing these little things for our kids in the name of efficiency, how interested will we be in prodding them to get around on their own like my mom used to do with me?

Well, I have one idea—and it helps bicycling too. As part of the safe routes program (or sometimes separately from it), many schools have started bike clubs. They fill the need of providing an adult-guided afternoon activity after school that is both physically active and wholesome. They also offer kids an updated version of what my free-range childhood gave me: a sense of how the community fits together and how you can move about in it. Lastly, they provide the kind of bike experience that will both help kids become safer riders and make them more likely to ride as adults. I saw how this worked when I spent a few afternoons hanging out with Gregg Lavender, a thirty-five-year-old BTA instructor who used to be a classroom teacher in the San Francisco Bay Area and is a big champion of education and bikes. "I'd like to see thirty-five bikes at every school as standard equipment," he said. "You could use them for field trips. If you want to learn about water quality, why don't you go to the river and get a sample? Instead of just reading about the history of a city, why don't you go to some of those places? You don't need a school bus." One day, I met him at Sunnyside Environmental School in Southeast Portland. There were only four kids participating that day—Lavender says he is used to much larger groups—but they did excitedly tell me about a bike trip that he had led them on down to the Hawthorne Bridge, which provides the most popular bike route into downtown. "It was so awesome," said one girl, "we went on the esplanade," the path that runs along the river. "And it didn't take very long, either." As we rode slowly through the neighborhood, diligently coming to a complete halt at each stop sign and red light, I noticed how carefully drivers maneuvered around our small group. We were like a moving traffic-calming device. We rode along the SE Lincoln Street bike boulevard and we stopped at the intersection with busy SE Thirty-Ninth Avenue to study what Lavender called an "exceptional intersection." It was designed to allow bikes to continue traveling on Lincoln while forcing cars to turn onto Thirty-ninth. He told the kids how he'd love to live in a city without cars. "That's what they're trying to do in London," said one boy, who has heard about congestion pricing from his parents. Lavender nodded and said, "I think everyone would be healthier and happier."

As we rode along, it started to rain, lightly at first and then hard. Lavender moved the group under an awning and we sat there eating energy bars and doing route-finding exercises on a bike map until the rain passed. That provided one valuable lesson. I've noticed that many adults think any day with rain is unsuitable for riding, but I've found that there are a lot of dry times in all but the wettest days (and I live in a region where the rain is so common we call it liquid sunshine). After about fifteen minutes, we set off for a nearby park, where we flung a Frisbee around and then made our way back to school. One of the girls, who had finally figured out how to smoothly brake as she approached an intersection, was pumped. "That was great," she said. Lavender smiled. "She only learned how to ride a bike two weeks ago," he said with evident pride.

There are several other kinds of bike programs for kids. In New York City, Recycle-A-Bicycle trains youths how to fix up donated bikes, either for their own use or for sale. Many of the youths now work as on-the-spot mechanics at the big organized rides and find they can earn big tips keeping cyclists on the road. The Community Cycling Center in Portland receives about five thousand donated bikes a year that it uses to fund a number of programs, including several for youths. One of their most popular is a holiday bike giveaway for needy kids aged four to nine. "Every year, we help kids get their first bike," said Alison Hill Graves, the cycling center spokeswoman. Trips For Kids started in Marin County as a way to introduce disadvantaged kids to mountain bicycling and now has forty chapters around the country. Not surprisingly, the founder, Marilyn Price, is a favorite of the mountain biking industry.

As urban bicycling becomes more popular among adults in cities like Portland, youths also pick up the habit on their own. I joined a group of teens one morning for their daily bicycle commute to Cleveland High School in the Southeast part of the city where cycling is particularly popular. They gather at the home of Lee Rosch, fifteen, a sophomore. "My friend Keegan (Heron) was the one who got it started," said Rosch. "He made a decision when he was about fourteen that he was going to do something to improve the earth and he was going to bike, and we just jumped on the bandwagon." Rosch's parents, Ned Rosch and Maxine Fookson, said they're both bike commuters themselves. Heron was out of town that morning, but seven other teens showed up and we started out for the two and a half-mile journey to school, with other teens joining in on the way. At one point three girls joined the group, which definitely lifted the spirits of the male riders.

Rosch said one of the selling points he uses to attract new riders is that bicycling is as fast as driving, which is important with teens who aren't wild about getting up early for school in the first place. In fact, the ride seemed over almost before it started, with the kids quickly locking up their bikes and rushing in to beat the starting bell. I counted thirty-four bikes parked outside, a small fraction of the hundreds of cars driven to the fifteen-hundred-student school. But Principal Paul Cook said he's noticed an increase in bicyclists in recent years. "They look at biking as helping to save the environment," he said, adding that what he appreciates is that the cyclists seem to be more awake and alert when they come through the door in the morning. "You see the kids coming out of the cars and buses and they are definitely not as awake as you'd expect," he said.

There are some signs that driving isn't quite as popular—or at least as achievable—for teens. The percentage of teens aged sixteen and seventeen licensed to drive has dropped from about 52 percent in 1992 to just under 41 percent in 2005. Part of it is probably due to tougher licensing requirements that many states have adopted. But driving has also become more expensive and, in many metropolitan areas, more difficult than it once was. If bicycling continues to gain in stylishness among young adults, it may also find a more receptive audience among teens. And if you win over status-obsessed teens, you've begun to change the world.

Epilogue

Susan Zielinski was speaking at one of those wonkish transportation seminars at New York University when she threw everyone a curve by suddenly putting up a slide of a woman's legs in sexy fishnet stockings. It was her attention-getting way of illustrating the future of urban transportation. The idea, she explained, is that people will have an interlocking network of transportation choices that resembles a dense grid. Okay, you might say. But why the eroticism? That's all part of it, she said. "The idea is to be a positive, sexy way forward—not a sacrifice."

Zielinski, a cheerful blonde woman who runs a transportation think tank at the University of Michigan, has been giving speeches like this around the world promoting what she calls the "new mobility." She sees urbanites shedding their private cars for a range of electronically linked transportation choices that allow people to seamlessly move through the city. Someone may bike or walk a mile or so from their home to a rail or bus rapid-transit stop, timing their journey to arrive just when their cell phone tells them the next train or bus is arriving. Our future commuter will then electronically reserve a shared bike downtown—like the ones that now blanket Paris—for the final half-mile ride to the office. And maybe, it being a Friday, our commuter will also reserve, Zielinski said with a twinkle in her eye, a "natural-gas Maserati for your hot date."

As Zielinski noted, we're moving into an urban age. More than half of the world's population now lives in cities, for the first time in human history. And it just may be that there isn't the room or the resources for everyone to drive like late-twentieth-century Americans—including in America itself, where we're worried about four-dollars-a-gallon gas, obesity, epidemic congestion, and evidence that our auto-centric lifestyle is a primary cause of global warming. But Zielinski doesn't like to dwell on the negative. She wants to talk about a new urban lifestyle, where people trade in the hassles of private car ownership for the ability to use different transportation tools depending on their immediate needs. Look at it as the difference between owning a set of encyclopedias and quickly looking up the information you need on the internet. "It's not a sacrifice," she insisted, using that word again. "It is how we move into a better way of living." To hear her talk, even riding the bus (known in some cities as the "loser cruiser") can be more fun if it's marketed right, with clever ads like, "Please ensure you have the correct partner before exiting the bus." There's that sex thing again.

"We think about cars and mobility, meaning that there is growth, there is forward movement," she said. "But actually what we should be thinking is how much of what people want to do and need to do is getting done. Well, a way to think about it is in Europe you can get five good meetings done in a day. In Australia, maybe three, and in Atlanta, maybe two, because you've gone way, way farther and way, way faster but you haven't been in an accessible place that allows a lot to happen. You've spent a lot of time sitting in traffic. What kind of life is that? Really what we are aiming at is access, not mobility."

Zielinski began thinking about these things bicycling around Toronto as a master's student in environmental studies. "I sort of got into transportation accidentally by just being a cyclist," she told me in a subsequent conversation. "And then I started to see what a key role transportation plays in shaping cities and making or breaking them, and I was seeing that from a bicycle seat." Bikes "are so underrated in how huge a role they can play in transforming a place," she said. "And it is not just about transportation. It's about transforming the life of the city. And it's even about affecting safety—the whole idea of eyes on the street, people being around. The notion is that people then participate in the city, they're in touch with it more, they begin to care about it more." It got her thinking about creating transit systems that are as elegant as a bike, that give off the same glow as someone who has been riding instead of stewing in her car in a traffic jam.

Am I getting too fanciful here? Perhaps. Zielinski will admit that she sees only glimpses of the urban transportation systems she envisions, in places like densely packed Hong Kong, where commuters can use cell phones and debit cards to move seamlessly among different transportation modes, or in Paris, where twenty thousand bikes are scattered around the city for use at the swipe of an electronic card. But it's not an implausible vision, and it illustrates the point I have made throughout this book: that cyclists are weaving their way not only into the urban fabric but into the debate about how we are creating the transportation network of our future. It's a debate invisible to most Americans, who live in suburban environments essentially created for an automotive monoculture. That may not change anytime soon. But the inner cities, after years of decline after World War II, are coming back, reinventing themselves as lifestyle and creative centers. The single-family home located in a residential subdivision, so long the dominant housing type, is giving way to a broader mix of housing, from townhouses to high-rise condos. In this dense urban environment, the bicycle becomes a competitive form of transportation—if it can be safe, attractive, and socially acceptable. Considering how marginalized the bike once was in America, it is remarkable how several cities, from Portland to New York, are making that happen.

Suburbs may not be as attractive a target for cyclists, and builders are still throwing up plenty of developments that make livable-streets advocates tear their hair out. But things are changing there as well. Bike trails are attractive amenities that find their way into real-estate advertising. And in suburb after suburb, local officials are working to create lively commercial districts and walkable neighborhoods that replicate the feel of a small-town atmosphere that so many Americans feel they've lost. One day I tagged along with Dan Burden—the pioneering biking and walking advocate—as he met with officials and residents in the San Diego suburb of La Mesa. Once a distinctive small town of its own, it has been swallowed up by suburbia and is now bisected by three freeways that leave the landscape as balkanized as Cold War Berlin.

Burden's chore was to help the city figure out how to help knit La Mesa back together by creating pleasant walking and biking routes on the freeway overpasses and underpasses. That's no easy task since nobody had worried much about people on foot or on two wheels when these highways were built. So we spent a day looking at maps and trekking over goat trails that some poor walkers had etched in the hillsides next to the freeway underpasses. And then my big surprise came at the end of the day, when I talked with Gregory Humora, the city's public works director. Intense and earnest, Humora told me that his not-very-rich city had the density to support a more lively street life. Many people are close enough to walk downtown, although few do. And then suddenly, he added, "You know whose fault it is? It's the cars, it's the manufacturers' fault. People will drive as fast as they feel safe," he said, and with all of the soundproofing and horsepower and improvements, they feel they can go faster. "These roads were designed for 1960s autos. What we're left with is old road technology and new auto technology. Now they don't think they're driving fast, they don't think they're speeding." In other words, after years of going on automatic pilot, allowing automotive technology and strip commercial development to change the feel of the streets, people are starting to figure out what it takes to once again achieve a lively sense of community on their streets.

Of course, it is increasingly looking as if we won't have any choice but to change. After having lived through the 1970s doom and gloom, I've learned to be humble about predictions. But it's getting harder to argue that global climate change is not a real threat and that plenty of cheap oil is waiting to be found. I can see the political consensus developing behind a cap-and-trade system for carbon emissions that will raise the cost of energy and drive alternative forms of transportation. Each time there's a spike in gas prices, I see more cyclists out on the streets, more stories in the mainstream news media about how to be a bike commuter. In 2008, for the first time in more than twenty years, Americans actually drove fewer miles than the year before.

As I've been working on this book, I've seen an almost parallel story play out on the national transportation scene. After years of providing the money for our huge national freeway network, the highway trust fund is running out of money. Transportation officials have become obsessed with figuring out a new way to finance the road system. The problem is that there is no political consensus. Voters were skeptical about raising gas taxes even before oil prices jumped, feeling they are already overburdened by taxes and wondering if new road construction will solve their congestion problems (as it so often hasn't). And there seems little public support for road pricing, a favorite policy idea of the Bush administration, as well as of many theorists from both the political right and the environmental community. Ironically, it could be a win for cycling in either case. If we continue to be gridlocked (both literally and metaphorically) on transportation, bicycling is there as an alternative for an increasing number of people. At the same time, cyclists are now positioned, in many cases, to insist that when new construction occurs, there will have to be accommodations for bicycling and walking. I thought of this one day when I was visiting with the City of Seattle's Peter Lagerwey, one of the country's pioneering bike and pedestrian experts. After all these years, he said, he finds himself watching a pitched battle in the city over what to do with the aging Alaskan Way viaduct that runs above the waterfront—but everyone agrees that whatever the solution, it will have to accommodate bikes and pedestrians. "Isn't it an interesting world where the bike part is the non-controversial part and the car part is the part they can't agree on?" he said with a smile.

However, when it comes to building complete bikeway networks, cycling advocates are still often scrapping for the leavings of transportation budgets. As important as ISTEA was in opening the federal highway fund to bicycling and pedestrian projects, this money is often the first to go in tight times. In recent years, many states have turned to cutting those funds first because of the shortfall in the highway fund. An important new source of money for bicycling improvements could come if advocates figure out a way to pay for new bikeways under a cap-and-trade system. If a city could show that building a bike trail, for instance, will reduce driving a certain amount, it could receive money from carbon credits. Similarly, Rep. Earl Blumenauer, the Portland Democrat who heads the Congressional Bike Caucus and now serves on the tax committee, successfully pushed to extend commuting tax breaks to bicyclists (currently, motorists and transit riders who work for many employers can deduct some parking and fare expenses). While that may not seem like much of a factor for cyclists, it could help spur the growth of high-quality bike-parking facilities that would help make it easier to commute by bike and reduce the problem of theft. Finally, a bike-sharing program like Velib' in Paris could help mainstream bicycling in American cities. "To have a lot of bikes on the street, you need to *put* a lot of bikes on the street," said Paul DeMaio, an Arlington, Virginia, bike consultant who has studied bike-share programs.

For all of that, we still have a long way to go before any American city rivals the cycling levels of Amsterdam (although the prospect does cause Paul Steely White, the executive director of Transportation Alternatives, to wonder only half-jokingly what it would be like if 20 percent of New Yorkers cycled to work. Now, hardly anyone bikes who doesn't love it. Would you suddenly see people glumly riding to work with the same morose expression they have sitting in a traffic jam?) But I've seen in Portland how just an approximate 5 percent share for biking—more than five times the national average—has changed the city. And I see how learning to ride my bike in the city has changed my life. I still have a car and I still appreciate its utility. But I don't worry about high gas prices, road congestion, or the lack of parking downtown. My car has become just another tool that I often don't need. Cars no longer have status in my mind. Once you spend most of your time on a bike, the difference between a Toyota Corolla and a BMW seems insignificant.[1]

My life has changed in a lot of ways since I've started thinking hard about transportation, in ways both minor and profound. When I do drive, I no longer worry about parking close to my destination. Now, I'm happy to get out of the car and briskly walk a few blocks. I would rather spend my time stretching my legs than fretting over whether I can find the closest possible parking space. More importantly, driving a mile to the store for a quart of milk seems to me as much overkill as using a high-powered nail gun to hang a picture.

I hope that notion will become more widespread. Too often, the idea of utilitarian biking has been presented in the media as a choice between having a car and not. In fact, even most bike advocates I've met own a car, even if they sometimes do so sheepishly. For most people, the realistic choice is whether they can replace some vehicle trips with the bike—and there is a lot of potential given that half of car trips are under five miles in length. A bike really is the right tool for some jobs, and that definition of when it is the "right tool" will vary widely. For some urbanites, it's become the only transportation tool they need to own, and they rent everything else, whether it's a bus ride or a car. For some families, depending on a bike to get to work could mean the difference between whether they need to

---

1. The auto industry frets about consumers falling out of love with cars. Carlos Ghosn, who runs both Renault and Nissan, said in 2006 that people have become more entranced by their electronic gadgets than the latest automotive models. "The auto industry is in competition for the attention and affection in the minds of consumers," he said at the New York Auto Show.

own two cars or one. Given that the average annual cost of owning and operating a new car topped $8,000 in 2008, according to the American Automobile Association, a working family can save more by shedding a vehicle than any politician will ever give them in a tax cut.

As I look at the future, even the definition of a bike is being stretched. One day I visited Bill Stites, a small custom bike builder who works out of a warehouse in Southeast Portland. Stites has been focusing on cargo bikes, and he's become more convinced that they could be practical for most people with just a "light assist" from an electrical motor. His thought is that they could be great vehicles for going to the store and bringing home a family-sized load of groceries. "I realized," he explained, "that there is a lot of room between the forty-pound bike and the two-thousand-pound car."

If he's right, the city streets could become a lot more interesting, filled with some mixture of vehicles looking like they've come out of a low-budget sci-fi movie. Cities have been reinventing themselves for thousands of years. Humans are social animals and most of us want to cluster together in some fashion. And to me that's one of the great things about the bike. It provides a vehicle that enhances the city's streetscapes instead of degrading them; houses sell for less if they're on arterials, but they hold their value just fine on bike boulevards. And bikes can be a lovely way to experience the city. I thought of that one night when I was at a party for bike videographer Clarence Eckerson, Jr. in the Red Hook neighborhood of Brooklyn. I was getting ready to walk back to my guest house at the same time that two cyclists were leaving. As I chatted with them, I noticed that one just happened to have the exact same bike (a Specialized Sirrus) that I use for my commute back in Portland. I watched as they rode off into the warm night air, chatting companionably as they glided down the quiet street. And at that moment, I couldn't think of anything I more wanted to do than to be on that bike—my bike!—enjoying that same moment.

Acknowledgements

As a daily-newspaper reporter, I am used to hearing far more from people than I ever have space to put into print. I often feel bad when people complain that they talked to me for an hour and I used only one quote from them. Unfortunately, writing at book-length didn't entirely solve this problem. In the course of my research, I barged into the lives of many people who gave me their time and valuable insights but for one reason or another received only slight mention in my narrative. I want to begin by thanking several of them.

Michael Ronkin, a consultant and retired bicycle and pedestrian coordinator for the state of Oregon, was one of the first people I approached and was generous with his time and knowledge. Scott Bricker of the Bicycle Transportation Association, Linda Ginenthal of Portland's Transportation Options program, and Jennifer Dill, an associate professor of urban studies and planning at Portland State University were important resources. Also, my appreciation to Karen Frost, the BTA's first executive director; Peter Lagerwey of the City of Seattle; Cara Seiderman at the City of Cambridge, Massachusetts; Arthur Ross at the City of Madison, Wisconsin; Rob Sadowsky and Keith Holt at the Chicagoland Bicycle Federation; Andy Thornley at the San Francisco Bicycle Coalition; Ben Gomberg, the City of Chicago's bicycle coordinator; Tim Blumenthal, executive director of Bikes Belong; longtime New York City bike activist Steven Faust; Jim Sebastian, Washington, D.C.'s bicycle and pedestrian coordinator; John Fegan, longtime bicycle and pedestrian program manager at the Federal Highway Administration before his 2007 retirement; Payton Chung at the Congress for the New Urbanism; Chuck Ayers and David Hiller at the Cascade Bicycle Club; Marianne Fowler of the Rails-to-Trails Conservancy; Paul Schimek, a Boston bike advocate; Tim Bustos, former Davis, California, bicycle coordinator; Mary Crass at the European Conference of Ministers of Transport; Karen Overton, former executive director of Recycle-A-Bicycle in New York City; Clarence Eckerson, Jr. at StreetFilms in New York City; Peter Tannen, former San Francisco bicycle coordinator; Greg Raisman and Mark Lear at the Portland Office of Transportation; and Jay Graves, owner of the Bike Gallery stores in the Portland area. I also found two internet sites particularly invaluable: Bikeportland.org and streetsblog.org. In addition, I learned something of value almost every day from the Listserv of the Association of Pedestrian and Bicycle Professionals.

Of course, my thanks also go to the many people I did quote extensively. In addition, Peter Koonce, a transportation engineer at Kittleson & Associates lent his expertise to review some of my chapters. Paul Jellema kindly reviewed my Netherlands chapter. They are not to blame for my errors. Nor is anyone else who helped on this project.

Special thanks to Cathleen Carlisle, Lou Peck, Ethan Rarick, Arthur Ross and Jeanette Deloya, Dan and Beth Bootzin, Joe and Jayne Mapes, John and Tracey Gilbert, and Ron and Mary Chisholm for their encouragement and for hosting me during my travels. Also, I thank Alex Bootzin and his late wife Martha. I miss her greatly. Gihon Jordan, who died in August of 2008 after a long battle with cancer, graciously hosted me in his Philadelphia home in 2007 and shared with me his wise perspective on cities, bicycles, and transportation in general.

My colleagues at *The Oregonian* have been a great source of support, even as I was thinking about bikes instead of Oregon politics. The editors granted me a leave to work on this book and encouraged me to write several bicycling stories for the paper. I should note that some of the passages of this book originally appeared in similar form in the newspaper.

My thanks to Mary Braun of the Oregon State University Press for believing in this project and helping me make it a reality. Jo Alexander edited the manuscript with a deft hand.

Close friends Ed Jones and Jenny Cooke were a constant source of support and cheerfully learned far more than they ever wanted to about bicycle transportation over many wonderful meals.

My wife Karen and our children Katie and James were also remarkably cheerful about putting up with my absences—physical and otherwise—during the long process of writing this book. Karen swooped in more than once to save me from calamity and I will never be able to thank her enough.

Selected Bibliography

A Heavy Load: The Combined Housing and Transportation Burdens of Working Families. Washington, D.C.: Center for Housing Policy, 2006.

Allen, John S. *Bicycling Street Smarts;* Cambridge, MA: Rubel BikeMaps, 2001.

Alvord, Katie. *Divorce your Car!* Gabriola Island, B.C.: New Society Publishers, 2000.

Appleyard, Bruce. "Planning Safe Routes to School." *Planning*, May 2003.

Appleyard, Donald. *Livable Streets;* Berkeley: University of California Press, 1981.

Arterburn, David E., et al. "Impact of morbid obesity on medical expenditures in adults." *International Journal of Obesity*, March 2005.

Balaker, Ted, and Sam Staley. *The Road More Traveled.* Lanham, MD: Rowman & Littlefield, 2006.

Barnouw, A.J. *The Making of Modern Holland.* New York: W.W. Norton & Co., 1944.

Beatley, Timothy, and Kristy Manning. *The Ecology of Place: Planning for Environment, Economy, and Community.* Washington, D.C.: Island Press, 1997.

Beaumont, Constance, and Elizabeth G. Pianca. *Why Johnny Can't Walk to School.* Washington, D.C.: National Trust for Historic Preservation, 2002.

Bicycle Transportation for Energy Conservation. Washington, D.C.: U.S. Department of Transportation, 1980.

Bicycle Safety-Related Research Synthesis. Washington, D.C.: Federal Highway Administration, 1995.

Bicyclist Fatalities and Serious Injuries in New York City. A Joint Report from the New York City Departments of Health and Mental Hygiene, Parks and Recreation, Transportation and the New York City Police Department, 2006.

Brant, John. *Dying Breaths.* Men's Health, 2007. Located at http://www.menshealth.com/cda/article.do?site=MensHealth&channel=health&category=other.diseases.ailments&conitem=6dd09e134d1fb010VgnVCM2000 00cee793cd____&page=2

Bremner, Charles. "The Tram comes to Paris." *Times* of London, Dec. 16, 2006.

Buehler, Theodore J. *Fifty Years of Bicycle Policy in Davis, Calif.* Institute of Transportation Studies, University of California at Davis, 2007.

Buis, Jeroen, and Roelof Wittink. *The Economic Significance of Cycling.* The Hague: Interface for Cycling Expertise and Habitat Platform Foundation, 2000.

Burden, Dan. "Bikepacking Across Alaska and Canada." *National Geographic*, May 1973.

Burden, Dan, and Peter Lagerwey. *Road Diets: Fixing the Big Roads.* Orlando, FL: Walkable Communities, Inc.: March, 1999.

Carlsson, Chris, editor. *Critical Mass, Bicycling's Defiant Celebration;* Oakland, CA: AK Press, 2002.

Colijn, Helen. *Of Dutch Ways.* New York: Dillon Press, 1980.

Continuous and Integral: The Cycling Policies of Groningen and Other European Cycling Cities. Rotterdam: Fietsberaad, 2007.

Copenhagen, City of Cyclists. City of Copenhagen, 2006.

Cortright, Joe. *Portland's Green Dividend.* CEOs for Cities, 2007. At http://www.ceosforcities.org/pubs_projects

Culley, Travis Hugh. *The Immortal Class.* New York: Random House, 2001.

Carnall, Douglas. "Cycling and Health Promotion. A safer, slower urban road environment is the key." *British Medical Journal,* April 1, 2000.

Cycling in the Netherlands. The Hague: Ministry of Transport, Public Works and Water Management, 2007.

Delucchi, Mark A. *The Annualized Social Cost of Motor-Vehicle Use in the U.S., 1990-1991.* Institute of Transportation Studies, University of California at Davis, 1997.

Demers, Marie. *Walk for your Life!* Ridgefield, CT: Vital Life Publishing, 2006.

Dill, Jennifer, and Theresa Carr. "Bicycle Commuting and Facilities in Major U.S. Cities: If you Build them, Commuters Will Use them—Another Look." Presented at the Association of Collegiate Schools of Planning 44th Annual Conference, Baltimore, MD. Nov. 21-24, 2002.

Does the Built Environment Influence Physical Activity? Washington, D.C.: Transportation Research Board, 2005.

Driven to Spend: The Impact of Sprawl on Household Transportation Expenses. Chicago, IL: Surface Transportation Policy Project, Center for Neighborhood Technology, 2005.

Duckwall, Jane. "Former Oregonian likes that we have fewer bicyclists." *Charlotte Observer,* Feb. 19, 2006.

Durning, Alan. *The Car and the City.* Seattle: Northwest Environment Watch, 1996.

Durning, Alan. *"The Year of Living Car-Lessly Experiment."* Seattle, WA: Sightline Institute, 2006-07.

Durning, Alan. *Bicycle Neglect.* Seattle, WA: The Sightline Institute, 2007.

Enhancing America's Communities: A Guide to Transportation Enhancements. Washington, D.C.: National Transportation Enhancements Clearinghouse, U.S. Department of Transportation, and Rails-to-Trails Conservancy, 2007.

European Road Statistics 2007. Brussels: European Union Road Federation.

Evaluation of Odense, Denmark's National Cycle City. [English summary] Odense Municipality, 2004.

Ewing, Reid. "Can the Physical Environment Determine Physical Activity Levels?" *Exercise and Sport Sciences Reviews,* Vol. 22, No. 2, pp. 69-75, 2005.

Fajans, Joel, and Melanie Curry. "Why Bicyclists Hate Stop Signs." *ACCESS,* the official magazine of the University of California Transportation Center, Spring 2001.

Farley, Tom, and Deborah A Cohen. *Prescription for a Healthy Nation.* Boston, MA: Beacon Press, 2005.

Federal Highway Administration University Course on Bicycle and Pedestrian Education. Washington, D.C.: Federal Highway Administration, 2006.

Fitch, Mike. *Growing Pains: Thirty Years in the History of Davis.* City of Davis, 1998. Published online at http://www.city.davis.ca.us/cdd/cultural/30years/about.cfm

Flint, Anthony. *This Land.* Baltimore, MD: Johns Hopkins University Press, 2006.

Forester, John. *Effective Cycling.* Cambridge, MA: The MIT Press, 1993.

Forester, John. "The Bicycle Transportation Controversy." *Transportation Quarterly,* Spring 2001.

Frank, Lawrence, James Sallis, et al. "Many Pathways from Land Use to Health." *Journal of the American Planning Association,* Winter 2006.

Free Parking, Congested Streets. New York: Schaller Consulting, prepared for Transportation Alternatives, 2007.

Frumkin, Howard, Lawrence Frank, and Richard Jackson. *Urban Sprawl and Public Health.* Washington, D.C.: Island Press, 2004.

Garreau, Joel. *Edge City.* New York: Doubleday, 1991.

Glowacz, Dave. *Urban Bikers' Tricks & Tips.* Chicago: Wordspace Press, 2004.

Green, Ashbel. "Pressure builds as more bicyclists and motorists dispute right of way." *The Oregonian,* Jan. 17, 2006.

Grove, Noel. "Bicycles Are Back—and Booming!" *National Geographic,* May 1973.

Guide to Complete Streets Campaign. Washington, D.C.: Thunderhead Alliance for Biking and Walking, 2005.

Hays, Elizabeth. "City bike boss rips brass and pedals off." *New York Daily News,* July 11, 2006.

Herlihy, David V. *Bicycle.* New Haven, CT: Yale University Press, 2004.

Higgins, Paul A.T. "Exercise-based transportation reduces oil dependence, carbon emissions and obesity." *Environmental Conservation* 32 (3), 2005: 197-202.

Hiles, Jeffrey A. *Listening to Bike Lanes: Moving Beyond the Feud.* Published online at http://www.wright.edu/~jeffrey.hiles/essays/listening/. 1996.

Hillman, Mayer. *Cycling Towards Health and Safety.* Oxford, UK: Oxford University Press, 1992.

Holtz Kay, Jane. *Asphalt Nation.* Berkeley: University of California Press, 1997.

Hunter, William, et al. *Pedestrian and Bicycle Crash Types of the Early 1990s.* Washington, D.C.: Federal Highway Administration, 1996.

Hunter, William W., Richard Stewart, and Jane C. Stutts. "Study of Bicycle Lanes versus Wide Curb Lanes." *Transportation Research Record* 1674.

Huttenmoser, Marco, and Marie Meierhofer. "Children and Their Living Surroundings: Empirical Investigations into the Significance of Living Surroundings for the Everyday Life and Development of Children." *Children's Environments,* December 1995.

Jacobsen, Peter L. "Safety in numbers: more walkers and bicyclists, safer walking and bicycling." *Injury Prevention,* 2003.

Jensen, Soren Underlein, Claus Rosenkilde, and Niels Jensen. *Road safety and perceived risk of cycle facilities in Copenhagen.* City of Copenhagen, 2007.

Kalis, Aginus. *Cycling and health policies.* Presentation at Velo Mondial, an international bicycle conference held in Amsterdam in 2000.

Klem, Mary L, Rema R. Wing, et al. "A descriptive study of individuals successful at long-term maintenance of substantial weight loss." *The American Journal of Clinical Nutrition,* 1997.

Koeppel, Dan. "Invisible Riders." *Bicycling,* December 2005.

Hurst, Robert. *The Art of Urban Cycling.* Guilford, CT: The Globe Pequot Press, 2004.

Improving Traffic Safety Culture in the United States. Washington, D.C.: AAA Foundation for Traffic Safety, 2007.

In-Car Air Pollution: The Hidden Threat to Automobile Drivers. Washington, D.C.: International Center for Technology Assessment, 2000.

Leinberger, Christopher B. *The Option of Urbanism.* Washington, D.C.: Island Press, 2008.

Lewis, Tom. *Divided Highways.* New York: Viking, 1997.

Lowe, Marcia D. *The Bicycle: Vehicle for a Small Planet.* Worldwatch Paper 90. September 1989.

Lucy, William H. "Watch Out: It's Dangerous in Exurbia." *Planning,* Nov. 1, 2000.

Madden, Stephen. "Our Cyclist-In-Chief." *Bicycling,* November, 2005.

Mak, Geert. *Amsterdam.* Cambridge, MA: Harvard University Press, 2000.

Mann, Traci A., et al. "Medicare's Search for Effective Obesity Treatments. Diets Are Not the Answer." *American Psychologist,* April 2007.

Mapes, Jeff. "Cyclists will have streets to call their own." *The Oregonian,* June 16, 2006.

Mapes, Jeff. "It's all about The Bike. A curious spokehead searches out why our Rose City is the most bike-friendly big city in the U.S." *The Oregonian,* Sept. 25, 2005.

Mapes, Jeff. "Mia Birk: Return to help Portland bikers is 'pure joy.'" *The Oregonian,* Aug. 6, 2007.

Mapes, Jeff. "Pedaling toward nirvana." *The Oregonian,* Dec. 1, 2005.

Marks, N., et al. *The Happy Planet Index.* London: New Economics Foundation, 2006.

Maynard, Micheline. "Nissan Chief Says Rebates Need to Stop." *The New York Times,* April 13, 2006.

Modal Shift in the Boulder Valley. City of Boulder, Colorado, 2004.

Mionske, Bob. *Bicycling & The Law.* Boulder, CO: Velo Press, 2007.

Moritz, William E. "Adult Bicyclists in the United States.". *Transportation Research Record* 1636.

The National Bicycling and Walking Study: Transportation Choices for a Changing America. Washington, D.C.: Federal Highway Administration, 1994.

National Policies to Promote Cycling. Paris, France: European Conference of Ministers of Transport (now International Transport Forum), 2004.

Oja, P., et al. "Daily walking and cycling to work: their utility as health-enhancing physical activity." *Patient Education and Counseling,* April 1998.

Oregon Bicycle and Pedestrian Plan. Salem: Oregon Department of Transportation, 1995.

Orenstein, Marla R., et al. *Safe Routes to School Safety & Mobility Analysis.* Report to the California Legislature, 2007.

Orlando Area Bicyclist Crash Study: A Role-Based Approach to Crash Countermeasures. Metroplan Orlando, 2003-04.

Outdoor Recreation Participation Study. Boulder, CO: Outdoor Industry Association, 2006.

Parisi, David, and Brett Hondorp. "Transportation Professionals Get Involved with Safe Routes to School." *ITE Journal,* March 2005.

Passenger Transport in the Netherlands. The Hague: Ministry of Transport, Public Works and Water Management, 2004.

Peters, Annette, et al. "Exposure to Traffic and the Onset of Myocardial Infarction." *New England Journal of Medicine,* Oct. 21, 2004.

Physical activity and health: A report of the Surgeon General. Washington, D.C.: Department of Health and Human Services, 1996.

Plantinga, Andrew J., and Stephanie Bernell. "The Association Between Urban Sprawl and Obesity: Is it a Two-Way Street?" *Journal of Regional Science,* December 2007.

Pucher, John, and Lewis Dikstra. "Promoting Safe Walking and Cycling to Improve Public Health: Lessons from the Netherlands and Germany." *American Journal of Public Health,* 2003.

Pucher, John, and Ralph Buehler. *Cycling for Everyone: Lessons from Europe.* Paper prepared for 2007 annual meeting of the Transportation Research Board.

Reagan, Gillian. "The Spokes-Models." *The New York Observer,* Sept. 4, 2007.

Rimmer, Gary. *Number Freaking: How to Change The World With Delightfully Surreal Statistics.* New York, N.Y.: The Disinformation Company Ltd., 2006.

Road Safety in the Netherlands. The Hague: Ministry of Transport, Public Works and Water Management, 2007.

Rodes, Charles. *Measuring Concentrations of Selected Air Pollutants Inside California Vehicles.* Sacramento, CA: Air Resources Board, 1998.

Ryan, John C. *Seven Wonders.* San Francisco: Sierra Club Books, 1999.

Safe Routes to School Program Evaluation 2003-2004. Department of Public Works, County of Marin. 2004.

Schenk, Mary. "Wilhelms push legislators for distracted driving measure." *The News-Gazette,* Champaign, IL, Nov. 30, 2006.

Schenk, Mary. "Woman is sentenced for bicyclist's death." *The News-Gazette,* Champaign, IL, Dec. 1, 2006.

Schimek, Paul. *The Dilemmas of Bicycle Planning.* MIT Department of Urban Studies and Planning, and Volpe National Transportation Systems Center, Cambridge, MA. Revised 1999.

Schulz, Matthias. "European Cities Do Away with Traffic Signs." *Spiegel* Online (http://www.spiegel.de/international/); Nov. 16, 2006.

Schwartz, Samuel I. "Rolling Thunder." *The New York Times,* Nov. 6, 2005.

Schweppe, Ellen. "Legacy of a Landmark: ISTEA After 10 Years." *Public Roads Magazine*, November/December 2001.

Shoup, Donald. *The High Cost of Free Parking.* Chicago, IL: APA Planners Press, 2005.

Sloan, Eugene. *The Complete Book of Bicycling.* New York: Simon & Schuster, 1988.

"Sports Participation." Mount Prospect, IL: National Sporting Goods Association, 2006.

Statistical Yearbook 2008. Voorburg and Heerlen: Statistics Netherlands, 2008.

Statman, Pamela. *Raising Careful, Confident Kids in a Crazy World.* Oakland, CA: Piccolo Press, 1999.

Stutts, Jane et al. "Bicycle Accidents: An Examination of Hospital Emergency Room Reports and Comparison with Police Accident Data.". *Transportation Research Record* 1168.

U.S. Physical Activity Statistics. Centers for Disease Control and Prevention. Located at http://apps.nccd.cdc.gov/PASurveillance/StateSumV.asp.

Vesselinovitch, Andrew. "Pedal Politics." *The New York Times*, Aug. 20, 2006.

Transportation Statistics Annual Report. Washington, D.C.: Transportation Research Board. Multiple years.

Travel and Environmental Implications of School Siting. Washington, D.C.: U.S. Environmental Protection Agency, 2003.

Travel to School: The Distance Factor. NHTS Issue Brief. Washington, D.C.: Federal Highway Administration, 2008.

Urban Transportation Report Card 2007. San Francisco Bike Coalition, Cascade Bicycle Club; Chicagoland Bicycle Federation, Transportation Alternatives. 2007.

Van Houten, Ron, and Cara Seiderman. *How Pavement Markings Influence Bicycle and Motor Vehicle Positioning: A Case Study in Cambridge, MA.* Preprint Version for Transportation Research Board annual meeting, 2005.

Vuori, Ilkka. "Physical Inactivity as a disease risk and health benefits of increased physical activity." In: Oja P., and J. Borms (eds), *Perspectives—The multidisciplinary series of physical education and sport science: Health enhancing physical activity.* Vol 6, 2004.

Walker, Ian. "Drivers overtaking bicyclists: Objective data on the effects of riding position, helmet use, vehicle type and apparent gender." *Accident Analysis & Prevention*, March 2007.

Wang, Guijing, et al. Cost-Benefit Analysis of Physical Activity Using Bike/Pedestrian Trails. *Health Promotion Practice*, April 2005.

Wray, J. Harry. *Pedal Power.* Boulder, CO: Paradigm Publishers, 2008.

Wolfcale, Joe. "Novato girl molested while walking home in Pleasant Valley neighborhood." *Marin Independent Journal*, Sept. 28, 2006.

Yergin, Daniel. *The Prize.* New York: Simon & Schuster, 1991.

2005-2006 West Babcock Street Pedestrian and Bicycle Monitoring Project. Bozeman, MT: Bozeman Planning and Community Development.

Zegeer, Charles V., et al. *FHWA Study Tour for Pedestrian and Bicycle Safety in England, Germany and The Netherlands.* Washington, D.C.: Federal Highway Administration, 1994.

Index

8/09 796.6
MAPES